MANAGEMENT SCIENCE IN ACTION

MANAGEMENT SCIENCE IN ACTION

By

WILLIAM T. MORRIS

Professor of Industrial Engineering
The Ohio State University

1963

RICHARD D. IRWIN, INC.

HOMEWOOD, ILLINOIS

First Printing, April, 1963

Library of Congress Catalog Card No. 63–14219

To

M.L.M.

PREFACE

This book is addressed to those who share the excitement of studying management problems scientifically. It examines a problem which is of interest, I hope, to Industrial Engineers, Operations Researchers, and Management Scientists. I hope also that it will come to the attention of an occasional manager, to whom it is addressed as well.

It aims at taking a first step toward rationalizing the relations between scientifically trained advisers and managers. What can they expect of each other? Our studies of the management decision process have seldom included the staff advisers who seek a place in this process. The book attempts to discuss these problems without resort to specialists' jargon or impressive mathematical expressions. I have tried to write something which could be read.

A study such as this hopes to contribute insights and relationships by building on the work of others. My intellectual debts are far greater than I have been able to acknowledge in the references. Perhaps the greatest is to the work of James G. March and Herbert A. Simon. Their *Organizations* is a *vade mecum* for anyone working in management science.

My chairman, Paul N. Lehoczky, has provided stimulation and encouragement in many forms, as well as the scarcest of all academic resources, time to think. The typing was cheerfully done by Loretta Johnstone, Nancy Long, and Peggy Warrens.

WILLIAM T. MORRIS

Columbus, Ohio
November 16, 1962

ACKNOWLEDGMENTS

Appreciation is expressed to the following for permission to quote from copyrighted publications:

The Free Press of Glencoe for permission to quote from *Strategic Intelligence and National Decisions* by Roger Hilsman.

Harcourt, Brace, and World, Inc. for permission to quote from *Religion and the Rise of Capitalism* by R. H. Tawney.

Macmillan & Co., Ltd. for permission to quote from *The Life of Robert Owen* by G. D. H. Cole.

McGraw-Hill Book Co., Inc. for permission to quote from *Mirror for Man* by Clyde Kluckhohn.

Professor C. Northcote Parkinson for permission to quote from *Parkinson's Law*.

Penguin Books Ltd. for permission to quote from *The Social Psychology of Industry* by J. A. C. Brown.

Prentice-Hall Inc. for permission to quote from *Prediction and Optimal Decision* by C. West Churchman.

Time, Inc. for permission to quote from *The Executive Life* by the Editors of Fortune.

The University of Michigan Press for permission to quote from *The Image* by Kenneth Boulding.

The Yale University Press for permission to quote from *The Folklore of Capitalism* by Thurman Arnold.

TABLE OF CONTENTS

PART I. THE SETTING

PART II. SCIENCE IN ACTION

PART III. LINE AND STAFF DYNAMICS

INDEX

PART I The Setting

Chapter 1:

KNOWLEDGE AND POWER IN MANAGEMENT

"There are mountain piles of books on salesmanship, which is not disinterested advice, and a molehill of books on leadership, but nothing on the technique and difficulties of trying to put knowledge at the service of power. The right relation of knowledge and power is, however, one of the key problems of our age."

—LYMAN BRYSON[1]

One view of the classic manager in industry sees him as a man of subtlety, intuition, and confidence, who makes decisions and uses his power in complicated organizations with a skill born of years of unanalyzed experience. He may, in a single day, make policy choices on everything from basic research to high finance. His mind is that of a generalist, dealing in ways he himself can seldom explain, with a great variety of problems. He can, with little hesitation, commit the resources of his firm on the basis of what some circles would regard as knowledge so limited as to border on ignorance. He turns his decisions into actions by "knowing people," drawing on their knowledge, motivating them, and coordinating their actions in more or less subtle ways.

The scientist and engineer, pictured in their professional roles, often appear to be quite the opposite of the manager in their patterns of thinking and acting. Professional conservatism seems to restrain scientifically trained persons from drawing conclusions or taking actions in the face of limited knowledge and without careful study of the problem at hand. Increasingly a specialist, the engineer and scientist are committed to explicit statements of the evidence and reasoning processes on which their actions are based. Their cardinal principle is objectivity, which is to be guaranteed by drawing conclusions in such a way that they can be independently verified by others. These men are widely regarded as being insensitive to people and impatient with the art of "human relations."

[1] Lyman Bryson, "Notes on a Theory of Advice," *Political Science Quarterly,* Vol. 66, No. 3 (1951).

If these stereotypes are approximately correct, it is not hard to imagine that difficulties will arise when a scientist or engineer working in a staff position undertakes to provide a manager with scientifically based advice on how to make decisions. It is not hard to discover evidence that such difficulties do in fact exist. For a number of years I have had opportunities to talk with young engineers and scientists operating as professional advisers or staff men in industry. When they spoke of their triumphs, and more often of the frustrations, they seemed most frequently to speak of their relations with the managers to whom they submitted information and recommendations. These men saw their professional identification as being with industrial engineering or operations research, and their recommendations usually had to do with management problems. Recently, I have had conversations with a number of managers, many of whom had occasion to receive this sort of information and recommendation. These managers seemed to share some general misgivings about their advisers. They felt these engineers and scientists had a mistaken impression of the range of their professional competence, and they had trouble getting along with both management and men in the shop.

These symptoms are by no means new, nor is our lack of general knowledge concerning the diagnosis and treatment of the conditions which produce them. More precisely, some attention has been paid to the relationship between industrial engineers and workers when new policies are being implemented. Beginning with the Hawthorne studies, there has been scientific evidence that this was not altogether a problem which would yield to "brute-force" directness.[2] On the other hand, the relations between advisers who rationalize management problems and managers themselves seem to have provoked only generalizations of the following sort: (1) managers are often reluctant to "buy" the recommendations produced by their industrial engineering and operations research staffs, and thus a part of the staff man's natural function is to "sell" his results; (2) little can be said about how to "sell" since one learns this by experience and it is much a matter of "personalities." I recall my very first day as a staff engineer with a large corporation, and the sense of inadequacy which followed my initial "talking to." "All that theoretical stuff you got in college won't amount to a hill of beans around here unless you

---

[2] Elton Mayo, *The Human Problems of an Industrial Civilization* (Boston: Division of Research, Graduate School of Business Administration, Harvard University, 1946).

can sell it." This had been said often before, but in the months that followed my appreciation for its truth grew in direct proportion to my frustrations. It has been said many times since (a fair number of times in my own lectures) with the same lack of guidance as to how this "selling" is to be done. I am unaware also of any concerted attempt to probe the relationship between adviser and manager for clues as to how it might be made more effective. This is the task here begun, the first step of which is to provide a considerably sharper conception of the situations to be studied.

The general problem of the relation between advice and power has recently been examined from a number of viewpoints in the context of an assortment of institutions. Cast in the role of adviser have been such stereotypes as "the expert," "the intellectual," "the scientist," "the engineer," and "the professor." On the receiving end have been the men of affairs in the government, the military, and business. Examinations of how they ought to or actually do get along with each other have covered the gamut of the casual, the theoretical, and the empirical. Many of these will presently be examined; however, the instances of making knowledge available to those with the power of action on which we wish to focus are more limited.

Working in a particular context, this analysis deals primarily with:

1. Advice given in the context of industrial and business management rather than the government, military, or other organization.

2. Advice which claims to stem primarily from scientific knowledge rather than advice based upon intuition, particular experience, or unverifiable knowledge.

3. Advice which generally falls within the professional province of the industrial engineer, the operations researcher, and the management scientist.

These limitations require some explanation.

The first is a matter of the availability of experience and evidence, and a matter of beginning to fill what may be an important gap in the fabric of organizational knowledge. The second limitation arises out of the increasing availability and use of scientific knowledge as well as the special problems of scientifically based advice such as those stemming from the requirement for objectivity.

There is a good deal of historical confusion about scientific management, but much of the legitimate work of putting science to work on management problems has emerged in the profession of industrial engineering. Since 1946, "operations research" and "management science," together with a considerable number of related

terms, have appeared. Rather than constructing a system of definitions which would be hopelessly arbitrary if they succeeded in being
anything like exhaustive and exclusive, it appears more useful to
concentrate on the area of common interest and methodology many
of these emerging disciplines share. To some extent they all appear
interested in the problems of management and in approaching these
problems by means of science. For a central concept it is useful to
choose management decision making.

The classical idea of management functions consists of planning,
directing, and controlling. The same idea is suggested by the more
scientifically oriented terms: designing the system, programming,
monitoring, and controlling, where the system is the business enterprise. The sort of advice relevant here is that which supports the
decisions managers make in carrying out their planning and controlling functions. I have chosen to use the term *management science*
henceforth in this discussion.

The roles of science in connection with managerial decision
making vary from active to passive. In an active role the scientist
or engineer attempts to study the decision in much the same way
it appears to the manager himself. The scientist tries to examine the
courses of action open to the manager, predict their consequences,
and perhaps evaluate these consequences in terms of their desirability to the manager. If the two work well together, their conceptions
of a given decision situation may eventually become quite similar.
The scientist is thus actively involved in the study of the manager's
choice problem. A passive role for science is one in which the
scientist does not share to any appreciable degree the manager's
conception of the decision. Instead, the scientist is simply called on
to perform specific subtasks within the process of deciding. He may
be asked to answer particular questions out of context, to supply
certain facts, or to do some analysis, but he operates as a specialist
in some field other than that of the manager himself. The manager's
job includes putting together the passive contributions of scientists
and engineers speaking from the depths of their various specialties
into a conception of his own decision problem. The kind of situations
to be studied here, exhibiting the essential characteristic of management science, are those in which the role of science tends to be more
active than passive. The question of whether there is any use in
attempting to generalize what follows to other situations, I will
make no pretense of answering.

The motivation for all this stems from observing what may be some basic confusion on the part of scientists, engineers, students, managers, and various staff people as to what kind of advice can be given on the basis of scientific knowledge, how it is to be interpreted, and how it is to be used. To many this effort will doubtless seem a foolish academic speculation quite removed from the realities of practical affairs. This may be true, in the sense that the only people unclear about the nature of advice may be those who have devoted the most effort to the study of its nature. On the other hand, those involved in the business of giving and using advice have, in my experience, often recognized some difficulties not at all removed from the problem of getting on with the affairs of the organization. For example, some managers reject all attempts to provide them with any sort of scientific advice. Some advisers and, indeed, some other managers expect advice to go much further toward solving the problems of the organization than in fact it can. Some have suggested the possibility of technological unemployment within the ranks of management arising from making advice so scientific that it can be used by computing machines to fulfill completely the functions of the managers.

A large and prominent agency whose function was to provide advice to the military has recently experienced front-page difficulties.[3] One hears frequently of staff groups in industry being established with high hopes and others being abandoned with frustration and bitterness. While it would be presumptuous to pretend knowledge of the real reasons for these events, it might be useful to hypothesize some of the factors that might be present.

There is also the history of attempts to bring science into closer association with management. This history is complete with legitimate and illegitimate motives and capabilities, and with both satisfactory and unsatisfactory outcomes. I hope to shed some little light on these events.

The question of what is or is not science, what it can be used for, and what problems can be studied scientifically appear the subjects of considerable misunderstanding. To cite but one recent example, there has been on public view what one writer chose to call a civil war in the advertising business between those who favored a scientific approach to advertising and those who favored intuition.[4] In

---

[3] "Army Severing Tie with Johns Hopkins in Research Clash," *New York Times*, May 28, 1961.

[4] Robert Alden, "Advertising: A Formula or a Delicate Art?" *New York Times*, May 7, 1961.

this, as in many similar discussions, one often has the feeling that if only some light could be shed on the nature and uses of science everyone would come to agree that some things a trained scientist can contribute to advertising or to management and some things must be done by those with other skills.

Academically, one might say three very general questions are confronted.

What sort of advice can be given?
How can such advice be used by those in authority?
What sorts of relationships exist among those who have the knowledge to give advice and those who have the authority to use it?

If funds were suddenly available for the study of problems surrounding the relationship between management and their scientifically trained advisers, what would one do? One might hope eventually to examine the phenomenon in the flesh, to see advisers and managers at work together, and to search out generalizations about the process which seemed relevant to making it more effective. Before doing this in any large-scale manner, one might prudently wish to work with some laboratory situations in which the "group dynamics" of advising and decision making could be examined under controlled conditions for a first refinement of hypotheses. This is hardly likely to be less difficult or less expensive than looking at the "real thing" and thus great care would be necessary in selecting the hypotheses to be tested. The sort of advising in mind here takes place over an extended period of time, not during an encounter lasting an hour or two. Further, it would take a particularly clever experimenter to suggest laboratory studies which would allow one to penetrate very far into this complex social process. This sort of experimentation is not to be discounted, for as we go on insights will be suggested which are drawn from just such work.

Perhaps, however, the place to begin is with the development of some hypotheses about the production and consumption of scientifically based advice. This, at least, is the job here undertaken. The objectives, briefly stated, are:

1. To bring together from many sources hypotheses about the competence of management science and the relation of management scientists to managers. The assertions presented can hardly be interpreted as observations, inferences, laws, or conclusions, but only as hypotheses. They have been selected on the simple basis that they appear to be useful. To confirm or disprove them in specific instances would seem helpful in understanding the problem.

2. To marshal some of the data available on various aspects of advising

and managing. While this study makes no pretense of empiricism in the formal sense, it is hoped that most of the assertions do have some basis in experience. Where possible, data appear which are more or less supportive of, or at least in general agreement with, the hypotheses. It must be admitted that this is a casual kind of empiricism, but it is nevertheless an important beginning step. It is in the spirit of this attempt to suggest that it will take considerable re-sources to make an empirical beginning to the problems but that nobody is likely to make the resources available until existing hypotheses and evidence have been woven into something like a coherent and testable fabric.

3. One hopes, however, for more immediate benefits, in the form of active consideration on the part of both advisers and managers of these ideas in con-nection with the actual situations which alone provide the ultimate verification. Perhaps a start could then be made to match their experiences with a coherent theoretical foundation.

4. Perhaps the most idealistic aim is actually to remove some difficulties that may exist between scientifically trained staff people and the managers who consume their knowledge. I hope to do this not by writing an essay on sales-manship but by trying to promote understanding, by weaving together some ideas about management science which would be useful to managers, and some ideas about management which would be useful to management scientists, with the hope that knowledge is the most effective kind of persuasion to bring a more useful relationship between scientific staff and line management. We are going through a period during which these two groups are getting used to each other and learning what to expect from one another. This study would be more than successful if it makes some slight increase in the rate at which this process of acquaintance goes on. Certainly a part of the problem arises because each has unrealistic expectations about the other.

It is supposed from the very outset that improvements in the use of scientifically based advice by those who must make decisions of great consequence will result in part from an increase in two kinds of understanding. All concerned need a fuller understanding of how science operates and what it can be expected to accomplish in the particular case of management science. Further, a careful elaboration of hypotheses regarding the troubles advisers and man-agers have with each other will, it is hoped, ultimately have good effects. Such suppositions are hardly novel in themselves and it is not surprising that others have considered these questions in other contexts. There is a fair amount of work in other fields which, while addressed to quite different groups of advisers and decision makers, is more or less relevant to the case of management science. In one sense, much of this book is simply an attempt to draw together from previous work hypotheses which seemed applicable and to focus them on the industrial management situation.

It is not easy for the nonscientist to get a useful picture of the competence of science; nor, for that matter, is it any easier for the scientifically trained person to generalize about the possibilities of an emerging discipline like management science. Popularizations are often vulgarizations which serve to mislead and create unrealistic expectations. Most of the vast literature on the philosophy of science is not particularly inviting to the adviser or to the manager. The questions it examines sometimes are too fundamental, such as, "What can we know, and how can we know it?" Its answers are usually discouraging to the man of action, as when it says, "No scientific law can ever be completely verified." It concerns itself with a logical reconstruction of how scientists verify assertions. It has little to say about how these assertions are produced in the first place, what use can be made of them, or what kind of problem the manager might best pose to his scientifically trained staff. Most important, it is difficult for the manager to find a basis for integrating scientifically based advice with other kinds of advice and with the wealth of his own experience. It is sometimes remarked that there are two kinds of managers: those who have complete, unquestioning faith in scientific inputs to their decisions and those who have no use whatsoever for anything of the sort. This study will try to suggest some of the things management science actually does in management, and something of what it can and cannot do as well.

The not-altogether-happy relations between advisers and decision makers have attracted the attention of social scientists, although not to any great extent. They have been conscious of these relations for they themselves have sometimes taken advisory positions in government. Their work has been used extensively as a source of hypotheses translated into the particular context of management science. The sum total of their conclusions is quite pessimistic. With few exceptions, they have had little to offer in the way of constructive possibilities to improve these frustrations, either by means of persuasion or by education of the officials they have advised.

In the literature, the persons in advice-giving positions are spoken of as experts, scientists, engineers, professors, and intellectuals. A closer examination of some distinguishing features of various classes of advisers may help to locate management scientists within this larger population. One way of classifying advisers is to examine the resources from which their recommendations come. We might suggest, for example:

1. Factual experts, whose advice and usefulness derive from the considerable store of factual knowledge they possess.

2. Predictive experts, who can, in an implicit fashion, make more reliable predictions than the average person.

3. Scientifically trained experts, who have at their command the well-established laws of some science such as physics which they have been trained to apply in useful ways.

4. Scientifically trained experts, whose sciences have not yet produced an extensive body of well-established law but who are equipped with a variety of well-developed hypotheses and the means for testing them in particular situations.

Management scientists, whether working under the title of industrial engineer, operations research analyst, or whatever, fall in the last of these four groups, along with some other emerging scientists. This, as we shall see, presents special problems for the management scientist, as, for example, the virtual impossibility of making quick, unequivocal responses to questions from management.

In terms of functional roles, experts may sometimes be distinguished by asking whether their work is to supply facts, to analyze available facts, or to make recommendations for action. Management scientists, where their roles are fully developed, do all of these things. In some problems, however, they may be prevented by the state of their art or the resources available from doing more than the first or second of these tasks. Many other scientists have taken the view that they are willing to supply facts and do analyses, but have avoided entirely making any recommendations for action.

A tentative statement of the defining characteristics of the particular group of advisers in whom we are interested might say:

1. They hold staff positions.
2. They are scientifically trained.
3. They are interested in management problems and are working toward recommendations for management action.
4. They tend to apply scientific criteria to their output of advice and avoid statements which do not to some extent meet these criteria.
5. They identify themselves with a profession which may be called industrial engineering, management science, or operations research.

A few examples of related work will suffice to show what this discussion is building upon. In sociology, Robert K. Merton has gathered together the literature dealing with the frustrations of the intellectual who is lured away from the university into an advisory position in government.[5] His disillusionment includes the discovery

[5] Robert K. Merton, *Social Theory and Social Structure* (Glencoe, Ill.: The Free Press, 1957).

that his function may be simply to provide justification for decisions already made by those in power, and that he himself is quite powerless. The Kennedy administration has brought such problems into public prominence.[6] It is not difficult to find parallel situations involving management scientists in industry. Rensis Likert, attacking the difficulties of making social research a useful element in policy formulation, has offered some excellent suggestions for overcoming this impotence.[7] He cautions against creating unrealistic expectations as to what research can do. Better to give decision makers quite moderate expectations of the assistance which will be produced, especially during the early stages. The staff should not, he suggests, report to the decision maker whose functions will be directly influenced by the resulting recommendations, for this may result in threats to the scope and existence of staff activities. The staff should report to higher authority, but this authority is to be used sparingly. He also raises a point that needs much attention in the particular case of management science; the traditional distinction men of action have tried to make between "theory" and "practice." It is no easy task to show managers that there is truth in Kurt Lewin's remark, "Nothing is so practical as a good theory."

A rare and first-rank empirical study has been done by Wilensky on the role of intellectuals in labor unions.[8] Using unions as his laboratory, he set out to examine the question of whether experts are indispensable to the functioning of large organizations and are thus rising to power or whether they are simply powerless bystanders and passive tools. He found experts in unions could be classified as:

1. Facts and figures men, whose job it is to supply these things.
2. Contact men, who can "arrange" things because of their relationships with people of influence.
3. Internal communications specialists, whose job is to pass the word effectively down through the organization.

These experts are used to provide window dressing on the one hand, and to take the blame for mistakes and objectionable policies on the other. They often help those they serve to justify prior beliefs. But

---

6 See, for example, A. A. Berle, Jr., "The Case for the Professor in Washington," *New York Times*, February 5, 1961; "Kennedy's Brain Trust," *Science*, July 22, 1960; "Political Scientists and the Working Politician," *Science*, October 28, 1960.

7 Rensis Likert, *Some Applications of Behavioral Research* (ed. Rensis Likert and Samuel P. Hayes, Jr.) (Paris: UNESCO, 1957).

8 Harold L. Wilensky, *Intellectuals in Labor Unions* (Glencoe, Ill.: The Free Press, 1961).

they also appeared to perform some useful functions once one looked below the surface of things. They helped to sharpen and clarify definitions of the problems their organizations faced. When policy was vague they helped to refine it and make it explicit. In a general way, their contribution seemed to be that of creating a gradually improving climate for more rational and effective decision making. This they often did with considerable subtlety, for as one expert remarked, "The boss may not even realize he's being influenced."

From political science, from economics, and from psychology have come somewhat more limited studies of these problems.[9] All try to illuminate in one way or another the incompatibilities between those who have knowledge to offer and those who have decisions to make.

A study that emphasizes and attempts to clarify the difficulties which arise when advisers offer scientifically based advice to managers is bound to sound somewhat critical and negative. This discussion runs a heavy risk of creating the impression that everything is bad, that advisers in general are frustrated in their work and managers in general are mistaken in their evaluations of this work. It should be quickly pointed out, then, that there is a long and distinguished record of giving and using scientific advice in management. Industrial engineering has grown both academically and in industry to a profession of major importance. The demand for industrial engineers in industry continues to exceed the supply. Surely this is indicative of the effectiveness of industrial engineering as a prominent source of support in management decision making. Operations research, though far younger, has blossomed in company after company. Of 631 firms responding to a recent survey, 324 reported they were using operations research, and 144 indicated they were considering its use.[10] Here, too, the demand for trained people exceeds the supply. Operations research has now reached the stage where many of the groups involved can point to enviable records of success. Success is most simply and most dramatically measured

---

[9] See, for example, Roger Hilsman, *Strategic Intelligence and National Decisions* (Glencoe, Ill.: The Free Press, 1956); Vernon Van Dyke, *Political Science. A Philosophical Analysis* (Stanford, Calif.: Stanford University Press, 1960); W. A. Johr and H. W. Singer, *The Role of the Economist as Official Advisor* (London: George Allen and Unwin, 1955); Jaleel Ahmad, *The Expert and the Administrator* (Pittsburgh: The University of Pittsburgh Press, 1959); William A. Reitzel, *Background to Decision Making* (Newport, R.I.: The United States Naval War College, 1958).

[10] Clifford Craft, reported in *Systems and Procedures,* May–June, 1961.

by the frequency with which management acts upon the advice it is given. In both industry and the military there are already histories of scientific advisory groups with very high percentages of implementation of their recommendations. In fact, management science has grown to such an extent that there is no longer any possibility, as there seemed to be in its earliest years, of keeping track of its successes.

Some records of success of particular techniques are impressive. Charnes and Cooper, in their recent volume on linear programming, mention that they themselves have participated in some 60 actual studies involving the techniques.[11] An older device such as statistical quality control has been adopted by industry in uncountable situations.

One rough gauge of management science's success is the number of people who make a living either teaching or doing it. This can be very roughly estimated by examining the size of some relevant professional societies. For example, the approximate memberships in the four leading groups in 1962 were:

American Institute of Industrial Engineers 10,000
Operations Research Society of America 3,500
Institute of Management Sciences 2,700
American Society for Quality Control 15,000

Clearly some memberships overlap here and some group members could not be counted as directly involved in advising managers, but the orders of magnitude are perhaps sufficient to tell the story.

A certain amount of confusion about the competence of an emerging science must be expected.[12] Differences in the educational backgrounds of the members of the profession tend to be marked due to rapidly changing college curricula. Much work reported in the literature is of a pioneering nature and whether the competence of the profession is markedly increased by any given piece of work may be neither obvious nor decidable with any assurance. Likewise, the consumers, who tend to be further removed from evidences of

---

[11] Abraham Charnes and William W. Cooper, *Management Models and Industrial Applications of Linear Programming*, Vol. 1 (New York: John Wiley & Sons, Inc., 1961).

[12] See, for example, Robert C. Sampson, *The Staff Role in Managements—Its Creative Uses* (New York: Harper & Bros., 1955); Ernest H. Weinwurm, "Limitations of the Scientific Method in Management Science," *Management Science*, Vol. 3, No. 3 (1957); "The Myth of Magic Numbers," *Duns Review and Modern Industry*, March, 1961; Robert Alden, "Advertising: Is Pseudo Science a Crutch?" *New York Times*, February 5, 1961; Hanson W. Baldwin, "An Uneasy Military—I," *New York Times*, January 18, 1962.

emerging competence, must suffer the misinformation of hearsay and the promotional articles of the trade journals which are notoriously uninformative ("New Technique X can cut your costs up to 20%").

It is in no way prejudicial to suggest that management science is best characterized as on its way to becoming a science.[13] Its contributors in general are scientifically trained, understand the requirements for an activity to be a science, have made great progress in the proper direction, and have encountered no provably insurmountable obstacles. The sole reason for the "on-its-way" view is that management science's findings are as yet far from the generality of those of, say, physics. But it shares this emergence with many other sciences.

It shares with medical science the unenviable history of facing conditions which must be dealt with and will not wait, and of continually being reminded that what is scientifically possible, lags behind the unexplainable successes of practitioners. This book tries to deal with the situation as it is presently, rather than speculate on future possibilities, such as the displacement of middle managers by computing machines.

The essential feature of management science, then, is its attempt to study a decision situation which confronts a manager and to produce some kind of a recommendation as to the choice the manager might best make. It is important to make clear some basic difficulties in doing this, and in doing it in a fashion which can be regarded as scientific. For a management science study to come off, three things must be accomplished:

1. There must be a model, however simple or complex, which relates the evidence at hand with the recommendations offered.

2. There must be evidence, data, or facts on which the recommendation is based.

3. There must be an acceptance by management of the recommendations. This is by no means a slavish compliance with an adviser's recipe for action, but to claim success some relevance as a basis for choice must be recognized.

Several points may be noted immediately. For example, advice is not an indispensable factor of production, such as land, labor, and capital. Management can get along without it, and success in business is hardly universally dependent on having this sort of assistance. There is a difference between advice on how to do something

---

[13] Harold F. Smiddy, "The Present Status of the Work of Managing," *Management Science*, Vol. 2, No. 3 (1956).

which could not otherwise be done, and advice on how to do something better which is already done rather well. Knowing how to get
to the moon is essential knowledge, but knowing the cheapest or
safest way to get there is not essential however valuable it may
ultimately prove to be.

Management science is, by definition, action oriented. It must
be prepared to furnish advice under the pressures with which the
actors contend. The time, money, knowledge, and other resources
devoted to advice are usually strictly limited. As a scientific activity,
advice giving has something less than the leisure that investigations
for the sake of knowledge itself have traditionally enjoyed.

The scientist's criteria for good science are not necessarily the
same as the manager's criteria for good advice. This tends to produce troublesome basic conflicts which will occupy considerable
attention in the discussion that follows. It is clear, however, that the
adviser cannot ignore either set of criteria, and much of what he
does must be an attempt to find workable compromises between
them. This contributes to what may sometimes be a particularly
difficult relationship between the man whose mind is trained for
careful, explicit reasoning from factual data and the man whose way
of life is action in the face of implicit and fragmentary knowledge
of his world. Here we find the basis for a host of problems in communication and understanding.

It is clear too, that scientific advice, when properly stated and
understood, presents the manager with an element of indeterminacy.
The scientist's knowledge is always incomplete and imperfect, for
it always depends on some assumptions which cannot be tested and
on limited amounts of evidence. The scientist is trained to avoid
filling in the gaps in his knowledge with hasty speculations. He is
thus at a disadvantage when giving advice, for others construct vast
generalizations on the basis of their limited experience, draw firm
conclusions on the basis of their intuitions, and offer the manager
complete and unequivocal recommendations. To the manager, who
is a generalist himself and perhaps not scientifically trained, the
"if's," the conditions, and the reservations science insists upon may
be a considerable annoyance.

Science, by its insistence on observable evidence and by the use
of rather strict rules for drawing inferences from this evidence, is
quite limited in the predictions it can make about the future. Its
best use is in the repeatable situation. It is by no means clear to
what extent, if at all, the situations in which management decisions

must be made are repeatable. Many managers tend to focus on the differences between their own business and others and on the differences between one decision and the next.[14] "My business is different; you just can't predict" is a frequently heard conclusion. Scientists, on the other hand, have tended to look for aspects of situations which are repeated, working from an implicit faith that regularities exist which will be discovered by the clever and the diligent.

In management, science addresses itself to the task of saying what can be said about the results of future policies on the basis of past data. New factors and changes not revealed through these data must be anticipated by management and are not subject to rigorous analysis in the usual sense. The point of management science is, in a way, to form a workable division of labor with management, line, and staff, each carrying on that part of the task it can do most effectively. Such a division of labor is designed to relieve management of some of the pressure of affairs and permit it to concentrate on those aspects of anticipating the consequences of policy which science finds most difficult to treat.

---

[14] On the other hand, some managers have deep insight into the uses of management science. See, for example, the discussion by the president of North American Aviation, Inc., J. L. Atwood, "The Challenges We Face," *The News in Engineering*, Vol. 34, No. 3 (1962).

Chapter 2:

THE EMERGENCE
OF MANAGEMENT
SCIENCE

"A science which hesitates to forget its founders is lost."

—ALFRED NORTH WHITEHEAD

The elaboration of historical connections among people, events, and ideas is not the end of all research, but it has its uses. One can, perhaps, better appreciate the conditions which surround the giving of scientifically based advice to managers, with some knowledge of how things have gone in the past. One sort of historical exercise traces the origin and development of ideas. It often points out that what is regarded as new is really very old. This tends to temper the enthusiasm of those who oversell their ideas on the basis of originality and to mitigate the disappointment of others who discredit such ideas entirely when they discover nothing really very new is being proposed. Management science has been the center of such discussions, some feeling it was distinctly novel while others tended to minimize it as a barrage of new words for old ideas.

The history of the scientific study of management problems consists, as does that of many other fields, of episodes in which problems were raised but were eventually suppressed rather than solved. Attention was drawn away from the difficult problems to others that seemed more promising. Some knowledge of the past is often needed to make one aware that such problems have been noticed and that there is some background of effort to solve them which should be reviewed when they come under active consideration again. The problem of how to evaluate the consequences of management actions is roughly of this sort. That the importance of consequences could not be expressed simply in terms of cost and profit was noted very early in the engineering literature.[1] Little

---

[1] Henry R. Towne, "The Engineer as Economist," *ASME Transactions*, Vol. 7 (1886); Arthur M. Wellington, *The Economic Theory of Railway Location* (New York: John Wiley & Sons, Inc., 1887).

attention was given it by engineers, however, until rather recently. In fact, during the intervening years it was passed over rather quickly in most engineering discussions. Some basic suggestions on the problem made by Daniel Bernoulli in 1730 have since found active role in current analysis.[2]

Not the least of the benefits of historical research is its suggestion of the extensive time lag which has sometimes occurred between the first statement of an idea and its eventual general application to management problems. This may not only stimulate efforts to reduce such lags in the future but also may give the adviser some tolerance for the frustration which results when his suggestions are not instantly carried out by managers.

The basic hypotheses with which this study briefly examines the past have to do with the emergence of industrial firms that needed, could afford, and would accept scientifically based advice; the development of science to the point where it was not only able but willing to give advice; and the coming together of these two lines of evolution. We begin with science.

It will be useful, not only for sketching the development of science itself but for later attempts to explain what it can do, to define a few philosopher's terms.[3] The most useful products of science for decision makers are predictions. Predictions are stated in the form of sentences such as: "The number of employees is an exponential function of the age of the company." If this statement is true for all companies then it is very useful, for it can be applied to particular companies in which the decision maker might, for example, wish to invest. Such a prediction is called a *synthetic* statement. To the philosopher this means it does two things:

1. It informs him about matters of fact and adds something to his knowledge.

2. It is subject to doubt, and thus something must be done to demonstrate its truth or falsity.

Consider, however, another kind of sentence: "All company presidents are members of management," or another example: "A corporation is a legal entity having limited liability for its owners."

---

[2] J. A. Schumpeter, *History of Economic Analysis* (New York: Oxford University Press, 1954); George J. Stigler, "The Development of Utility Theory," *The Journal of Political Economy*, Vol. 58 (1950).

[3] In what follows I have depended heavily on two very excellent books: John G. Kemeny, *A Philosopher Looks at Science* (Princeton, N.J.: Von Nostrand and Co., 1959); Hans Reichenbach, *The Rise of Scientific Philosophy* (Berkeley: University of California Press, 1959).

These statements are *analytic* because they simply analyze the terms they contain. The fact that company presidents are members of management is something we already know if we know a definition of the term "management." The truth or falsity of the sentence is only a question of whether or not it is consistent with our definition of the word. Similarly, the truth or falsity of the remark about corporations is only a matter of the definitions of the words used. Thus analytic statements do not add to one's knowledge, they simply explain and define terms, or analyze the meaning of words. Their truth or falsity is a matter of definition alone and is not subject to doubt or uncertainty. Analytic statements are obviously of quite a different sort than synthetic statements.

Next, two more useful terms: an *a priori* statement is one which can be shown to be true or false by pure reason alone, and thus its truth is known *before* any observations or experiments are conducted. An *a posteriori* statement is one which requires observation, experiment, and empirical testing to demonstrate its truth or falsity. A posteriori statements include all those whose truth cannot be known a priori.

Reason and observation or experiment are the two ways of deciding truth we have at our command in scientific work; and of course reasoning and observing are the main business of science. We can now put together these two methods of deciding truth with the two kinds of statements we have to deal with, to form four combinations.

	a posteriori	a priori
analytic	1	2
synthetic	3	4

Each combination is worth examining; they are keys to both the development of science since its earliest times and its competence as an aid to management decision making.

1. There are no statements which are both analytic and yet require experimentation to demonstrate their truth. The analytic, a posteriori is an empty category.

2. The truth of analytic statements is to be demonstrated a priori, by appeal to reason, and not by observation and experiment. Logic is the tool by which one argues for their truth or falsity. This seems harmless enough until we examine such statements as: "Businessmen ought to choose the program of action which will maximize their expected profit." Is this an analytic statement? Is it a logical consequence of an acceptable definition of a businessman? We

shall see later on that it is sometimes meant this way and that some difficulties in management science follow directly from misunderstanding the nature of statements such as this. More important, it turns out that many conclusions in management science have been arrived at by logical deduction from definitions of abstract and highly simplified management situations. Such conclusions are analytic statements whose truth is based upon their relation to the management problem originally defined. When one wishes to apply these conclusions to a particular decision in a particular company they must be transformed from analytic to synthetic statements. They must tell us something, not simply about the definitions of words but about the company under consideration.

3. The position of modern science is that any meaningful statement makes a prediction, and predictions must be verified by observation and experiment. Producing synthetic statements which add to our knowledge and verifying these statements is the main business of science.

4. The category of the synthetic, a priori is last since it is here that the history of scientific thought centers. Can the truth of synthetic statements be established on the basis of logic or pure reason, without the necessity for appeal to the data of experiment and observation? Plato thought the answer was "yes." He even urged the astronomers of his time to stop gazing at the stars if they wished to find the laws which would predict their motion. Instead, he felt that knowledge of nature could be obtained by thinking and reasoning alone.

The notion that useful predictions could be made without collecting data has come to be called rationalism. The way in which this was to be done was patterned after the view of geometry learned men held in Plato's time. One began with a few axioms which were viewed as so obviously and so necessarily true that no sensible person could fail to agree with them. From these axioms, deductive reasoning led to a rich variety of other statements which, of course, possessed the same unquestionable truthfulness. No other view of geometry seemed possible at the time and it was not until mathematicians developed alternate geometries, very different from Euclid's, that the idea of the synthetic a priori statement began to waver. Then it became clear there was a choice between alternate sets of axioms. If a decision maker was interested in obtaining true predictions he had first to decide which set of axioms was in fact in agreement with his experience. Thus it became a matter of making some observations to see which geometry was most consistent with events, and the notion of geometric axioms as synthetic, a priori statements was shattered.

This denial of empirical science has a plausible explanation. It persisted all the way down to Kant (1724–1804) who believed that Newton's physics could be developed by deductions from synthetic, a priori statements. Newton's Laws, he thought, could be shown to be derived from reason alone and thus necessarily true. What lay behind this wishful thinking?

Experience and observation, especially when turned into predictions and used in making decisions, is none too satisfactory. In fact, experience always leaves the careful observer with a residue of uncertainty. A few simple generalizations can be made from experience which seem to be without exceptions, but most are quite unreliable. Experience indeed leaves the decision maker with considerable doubt as to what confidence he may place in the statements he can spin out from what he has observed. Now, if predictions could be based on reason alone this residue of doubt and uncertainty would disappear. The predictions would be quite reliable because they would be necessarily true. If knowledge could be established on the basis of rationalism, then science would be the perfect tool for the production of decision-making advice. It would be an indispensable source of assistance for the man of affairs. Reason would then point the way to decisions which could be made without doubt or uncertainty as to the outcomes.

Thus we might guess that one motive of the philosophers of rationalism stemmed from the need for certainty, the need to free themselves from doubt as to the truth of their predictions. This basic human desire for dependable knowledge will be met again when we examine the needs of the manager who seeks advice for decision making. The eventual discovery that rationalism could not produce certainty and that predictions must necessarily be uncertain was reluctantly acknowledged by scientists and philosophers. This fact is indeed a part of the manager's disappointment when he turns to science in his own search for certainty.

To Francis Bacon (1561–1626) goes the credit for elaborating the importance of observation and experiment.[4] With Bacon begins the modern development of empirical science which holds that observation is the source of all knowledge that can be used in making predictions. He saw clearly, however, that logic plays a vital role, although its role is not that of judging the truth of synthetic statements. Logic was necessary to make sense and order out of observations, and from this order further predictions could be deduced. The test of the truth of these further predictions was in more observation and experiment. Galileo (1564–1642) and Sir Isaac New-

---

[4] See A. R. Hall, *The Scientific Revolution* (Boston: The Beacon Press, 1956); Morris Kline, *Mathematics in Western Culture* (New York: Oxford University Press, 1953).

ton (1642–1727) are the towering figures who began modern physical science, the most successful of all the sciences. Their decision to express the relations among their observations in mathematical form brought together the immense power of mathematical logic and the experimental method to produce the basic aspects of science as it is today. We now call this combination—mathematical reasoning along with the appeal to experiment as the judge of truth—the hypothetico-deductive method. It is the method by which one constructs explanations in mathematical form from which observable facts are deducible. If the observations tend to agree with the mathematical explanation, now called a model, then further deductions from it form the predictive statements used in making decisions. This method accounts largely for the success of modern science.

One problem arose which was the source of particular difficulty and remains the cause of considerable concern even in present-day applications of science to business affairs. Deductive reasoning, the sort of reasoning which goes on within the framework of mathematics, does not introduce any synthetic knowledge into its conclusions. Deduced conclusions are neither more nor less true than the axioms or assumptions from which the reasoning is begun. Thus deductive reasoning does not increase nor decrease the doubt and uncertainty attached to the premises. Inductive reasoning is something else again. If someone points out that simply because the sun has always risen on every morning which we have observed the statement that it will continue to do so in the future cannot be accepted without some risk of being wrong, we regard him as logically correct but perhaps given to overcaution. On the other hand, if a manufacturer has seen the sales of his firm grow in a linear fashion over the past few years the assertion they will continue to do so is one we are more willing to doubt. These statements are inductive inferences which take one from events which have been observed to events which have not been observed. Such inductive statements, which include all the predictions we wish to make for decisions which confront us, are subject to varying degrees of doubt. The theory of probability turned out to be the device that made some sense out of the doubts and uncertainties attached to predictions.

The development of statistical inference proceeded slowly through the nineteenth century but made great advances in the first quarter of the twentieth century. During this latter period, the statistical hypothesis tests which provide the logic for all inferences in scientific work were developed. The names of the developers include "Student" (W. S. Gossett), Pearson, and Neyman. Much more recently the late Abraham Wald seized upon the very important idea that an inference cannot reasonably be divorced from the decision situation within which it arises. Modern statistical decision theory thus incorporates inductive inferences into the structure of the choice problem which confronts the decision maker.[5]

Jacob Bernoulli (1654–1705) in his *Ars Conjectandi* put forth the famous law of large numbers. This became the basis for many misinterpretations by decision makers who based their actions on various notions of the "law of averages."

The problem of inductive inferences is of course the central problem of decision making so long as one is interested in the possible consequences of one's action. Probability theory and inferential statistics put induction on a quantitative logical basis. Cardan (1501–1576) and Pascal (1623–1662) began the study of probability, and it was applied to many areas of decision making by Laplace (1749–1827). An early attempt to deal with induction was made by Thomas Bayes (d. 1761) whose famous theorem has very recently come into renewed use as central to the study of decisions.[6]

After prediction, the second major problem in the analysis of decisions is evaluating the consequences of one's actions. From the very beginning of the industrial revolution there was no question in the minds of managers but that the values placed on the outcomes of their actions were to be calculated in terms of profits. All the notorious evils of the early factory system can be thought of as the result of a single-minded devotion to profit as a measure of the effectiveness of one's action. The factories of the early nineteenth century employed many children, some as young as six or seven. Wages were pitifully low, the working day as long as sixteen hours, and working conditions were of no concern whatsoever to management. If a woman or child grew tired and production slowed, a beating might result; if production went up, a beating might make it climb further. Work not acceptable could result in a fine deducted from one's pay.[7] The insights such managers attained into their

---

[5] Much more will be said on this. For an introduction to statistical decision theory see Herman Chernoff and Lincoln E. Moses, *Elementary Decision Theory* (New York: John Wiley & Sons, Inc., 1959).

[6] See Chapter 16.

[7] See Schumpeter, *op. cit.*; Eric Roll, *A History of Economic Thought* (Englewood Cliffs, N.J.: Prentice-Hall, Inc., 1956); Robert L. Heilbroner, *The Worldly Philosophers* (New York: Simon and Schuster, 1953); J. A. C. Brown, *The Social Psychology of Industry* (Baltimore: Penguin Books, 1954).

decisions were not sufficiently subtle to suggest that the minimization of costs might not result in the maximization of profits.

These decisions makers began their work with profit as their objective. They probably had little inclination to seek advice on the matter and there were no established customs of advice giving. If they did, however, consult the sources of knowledge and advice of their day they found nothing but the strongest justifications for their profit seeking. More precisely, they found the ideas of their time could be interpreted in this way.

If the nineteenth-century manager had consulted the best-known economist of his time, an absent-minded professor at the University of Glasgow, he might have been rewarded with the following astonishing advice: The manager should conduct his affairs so as to maximize his own personal profit with the assurance that, although "he intends only his own gain, he is in this as in many other cases, led by an invisible hand to promote an end which is no part of his intention. . . . By pursuing his own interests he frequently promotes that of society more effectually than when he really intends to promote it." This famous idea was set down by Adam Smith in 1776, and seems often to be regarded as the second most important event of that year.[8] The usefulness of this argument as a defense of profits was so great that it continues to persist. Adam Smith also advised that if God's plan for progress were to be worked out by self-seeking, free competition and a free market must prevail. No interference from governments could be tolerated.

If Dr. Smith had actually been employed as an adviser to the managers of his time he might have suffered the same frustration advisers do today. They choose to take those parts of his famous *Wealth of Nations* which suited their purposes and to ignore those that did not. Actually, the invisible hand of which he spoke was the mechanism of the free market under conditions of perfect competition. This was the force to keep the self-interest of men channeled in the direction of social benefit. He was not against the government taking actions to promote the general welfare even though he felt the market should be left alone. He clearly saw that the tendency of businessmen to combine in order to raise profits and the tendency to seek monopolistic advantages would upset the workings of the

---

[8] Adam Smith, *The Wealth of Nations* (Chicago: Henry Regnery Co., 1953). The quotation is taken from George Soule, *Ideas of the Great Economists* (New York: Mentor Books, 1952), p. 42. An excellent interpretation of Adam Smith's ideas is given in Heilbroner, *op. cit.*, pp. 28–57.

system he felt would be so beneficial. He specifically declared himself against "the mean rapacity, the monopolizing spirit of the merchants and manufacturers,"[9] but this of course was ignored.

Managers found no opposition, in the advice the Protestant religion gave them, to the abuses of the early factory system. As R. H. Tawney has shown, Protestantism not only removed the earlier moral restrictions on the gaining of wealth but gave a tremendous positive impetus to it. Calvinism provided an ethic which held that salvation was the free gift of God and that no earthly action could change a man's position among the chosen or among the doomed. Wealth, however, was a sign a man was among the elect. "For, since conduct and action though availing nothing to attain the free gift of salvation, are a proof that the gift has been accorded, what is rejected as a means is resumed as a consequence, and the Puritan flings himself into practical affairs with the daemonic energy of one who, all doubts allayed, is conscious that he is a sealed and chosen vessel."[10]

Parenthetically, it is useful to note that Protestantism encouraged a no-nonsense attitude toward business decision making. Managers were to employ all their intelligence in the conduct of their affairs and make every effort to improve their operations. Max Weber in "The Protestant Ethic and the Spirit of Capitalism" sees rational decision making as a fundamental aspect of the capitalism which arose with the industrial revolution: ". . . It is one of the fundamental characteristics of an individual capitalistic economy that it is rationalized on the basis of rigorous calculation, directed with foresight and caution toward the economic success which is sought in sharp contrast to the hand to mouth existence of the peasant, and to the privileged traditionalism of the guild craftsmen and of the adventurers' capitalism, oriented toward the exploitation of political opportunities and irrational speculation."[11] The rational and systematic seeking of profit is the attitude Weber calls the spirit of modern capitalism.

While modern capitalism was getting under way, the thinkers of the day were giving some attention to the explicit study of decisions as such. The idea that decisions could become matters for logical

---

9 Heilbroner, *op. cit.*, p. 52.

10 R. H. Tawney, *Religion and the Rise of Capitalism* (New York: Harcourt, Brace & Co., Inc., 1926), p. 191.

11 From the selection appearing in V. F. Calverton, *The Making of Society* (New York: The Modern Library, Random House, Inc., 1937), p. 529.

analysis and experimentation was developed and many of the difficulties such a program would encounter were recognized.

In 1730, Daniel Bernoulli worked on a problem which has an
important place in the basic analysis of business decisions.[12] Like
most people interested in probability theory at the time, Bernoulli
worked with games of chance and studied suggestions for successful
gambling decisions. One particular game, called the St. Petersburg
game, raised some interesting difficulties. Suppose that, on payment
of an entrance fee, you are given the opportunity to enjoy the
following seemingly harmless pastime. You flip a coin until a head
appears for the first time. If the first head appears on the first flip
you are paid $2, on the second flip, $4, and on the nth flip, 2^n. It is
commonly supposed that if the entrance fee is equal to or less than
the average payoff, one would be willing to participate. In this game,
however, the expected payoff is *infinite*, yet people are just not
willing to pay very large entrance fees to play it. Part of the problem
lies in the limited resources available for making payoffs. Leaving
these considerations aside, the commonly observed decision-making
behavior might be explained by taking one of the following ways
out:

1. Some principle other than maximizing average dollar return lies at
the root of decision-making behavior.
2. People try to maximize average return well enough, but they are using
probabilities other than those commonly associated with repeated flips of a
fair coin.
3. Again the principle is right, but people attach some other value to the
payoffs than simply the number of dollars involved.
4. Some combination of the above three explanations.

How explanations of decision-making behavior are formulated
tends, even today, to be a question of which one of these explanations is to be used. Bernoulli tried to save the principle of maximizing average gain by saying it was the "moral expectation" and
not the dollar expectation that a reasonable decision maker used.
To make sense of the problem one had to distinguish the "utility" of
a man's wealth from the dollar amount of it, and utility had to
increase at a decreasing rate as wealth increased. This is simply to
say that the richer we get the less importance we attach to an
additional dollar. Rich people take taxis when it rains; poor people
walk. The moral expectation was then calculated using utility rather
than dollars, and the result was indeed a finite number.

---

[12] Schumpeter, *op. cit.*, p. 1053.

This particular way out led Bernoulli to a logical explanation for many modern business policies. He could explain the wisdom of diversifying investments, of insuring, and of such useful ideas as a merchant putting his cargo in several ships rather than all in one. Indeed, his ideas form the basis for the great variety of diversification policies managers use in making decisions in the face of risk.

Jeremy Bentham (1748–1832) is noted for his astonishing proposal that the consequences of one's actions could be quantitatively evaluated and the resulting numbers used in calculations which would guide behavior.[13] His formula was based on the axiom that men sought pleasure and avoided pain. Pleasure, he thought, had properties such as intensity, duration, uncertainty, and immediacy in time. Somehow the value of each pleasure was to be computed, considering these properties, for the person most affected by the consequences of an action. From the sum of the values of the pleasures one then subtracted the sum of the values of the pains. This was to be repeated for all persons for whom the action was of some consequence and the resulting numbers summed to produce a quantity called the utility of the action. Governments might then be advised as to how they should act to maximize society's utility. Bentham supposed the result of applying his calculus would be "the greatest good for the greatest number."

Some such scheme for the quantitative expression of the value of actions is necessary if explicit statements are to be produced by scientific advisers concerning how decisions are to be made. Unfortunately, Bentham did not produce a satisfactory scheme, but this is not surprising for even today one of the basic barriers to the advance of management science is just this lack of means for evaluating actions. Bentham's calculus did raise many questions one must still face in developing utility measures or measures of effectiveness. Bentham has little to say about the empirical problems of actually getting the numbers or making the basic measurements which were to go into his formula. Who was to judge the values of the pleasures and pains, and on what sort of a numerical scale they were to be expressed, were hardly matters of consequence in his rationalistic view. Reliability and validity were questions which did not occur to him.

Bentham's ethical calculus is worth remembering only because it was indeed an attempt at the mathematical formulation of an

---

[13] Jeremy Bentham, *Introduction to the Principles of Morals and Legislation* (New York: Hafner Publishing Co., 1948).

important aspect of the decision-making problem. It led eventually to welfare economics which still struggles with the problem of trying to identify actions "optimal" for a society as a whole. Attempts to evaluate actions optimal for a business firm in some sense other than the simple maximization of profit encounter what are, in principle, exactly the same problems.

Bentham's scheme was roundly criticized from every side. It seemed to reduce men to the stature of animals, unless pleasure and pain were interpreted in some larger sense than "beefstake morality." It could be used to justify majority cannibalism and the redistribution of the wealth from the rich to the poor. If, in a public health immunization program more children lived than died, the program could be shown to be a social success. Surely Bentham did not expect his calculus to be strictly applied in every decision, but unfortunately he did not show how it could be applied in any decision, except in a completely arbitrary fashion.

Still another and even more basic difficulty confronting the scientific study of management decisions had been noted much earlier. In Mantua in 1711, a man named Giovanni Ceva foresaw the way which lay ahead in the scientific approach to practical affairs. Real phenomena, he noticed, are always complex and obscure. To understand them we must simplify them, and this is done by constructing logical models of decision situations based on simplifying assumptions. These models should be in mathematical terms so that mathematical reasoning could be used to make deductions from the axioms. Otherwise, he said, "we must always move in the darkest of nights" in the conduct of practical affairs.[14] The art of simplifying situations and describing them mathematically turned out to be extremely valuable in sciences like economics and has come to be the main activity of the management scientist. This process of simplification is necessary and useful but, as we shall see, it is also dangerous.

Let us turn from the development of science to that of management, so that we will eventually see how the two came together to form management science.

The problems of industrial management in something like the form we now understand them must have been on the minds of managers at least by the middle of the eighteenth century. Coal, iron, and the steam engine set the conditions for large-scale manu-

---

[14] Schumpeter, *op. cit.*, p. 301.

facturing. The manager who could bring together the necessary capital and the labor force could find himself master of a plant which employed several hundred people. It is likely, however, that these men viewed their problems and worries with greatly different emphasis than is now the case. After all, as the factory system began first things had to be dealt with first. To keep the machines running and get the product out the door was the central problem. Machines were probably better cared for than the the people who ran them. People, especially children and women, were easier to replace than machines and were far less expensive. The manager owned the machine and was thus responsible for its care and maintenance, but he bought only the labor of his employees and thus their maintenance and conditions of their existence were no concern of his. Labor unions were not yet there to trouble him, and, as we have seen, he found in the wisdom of his time every justification for his attitudes. As long as wages were sufficiently low he need not trouble about the niceties of management. If motivation and efficiency needed his attention, it was the stick and not the carrot which seemed most useful. But there were exceptions—exceptional plants run by exceptional managers. The year 1800 marked the retirement of one of these men and the assumption of major managerial responsibility by another.

The man who retired from active management of his firm in that year was a mechanical engineer who is usually remembered for his inventiveness in improving Newcomen's steam engine. Mr. James Watt, partner in Boulton, Watt and Company, operators of the famous Soho foundry, was also a dabbler in some theoryless experiments in industrial management which led to techniques far ahead of his time.[15]

There is no reason to suppose Watt was any more given to getting his knowledge from books than managers before or since, but it is useful to see what he would have had to work with if this had been the case. Accounting, the most fundamental of all management tools and surely the device which marked the beginning of the importance of staff advisers to management, was ancient by 1800.[16] In twelfth-century Venice, sophisticated accounting devices

---

[15] Eric Roll, *An Early Experiment in Industrial Organisation* (London: Longmans Green & Co., 1930).

[16] For the history of accounting see Schumpeter, *op. cit.*, p. 156; Heilbroner, *op. cit.*, p. 27.

were already at the service of merchants. By 1494, Pacioli had written a treatise called *Summa de Arithmetica* which marked the literary beginning of the history of modern accounting. In Germany in 1549, the first book in that language explaining double-entry bookkeeping appeared. *Zweifach Buchhalten* by a certain Herr Schweicker was the first of many such accounting texts which came out in the sixteenth and seventeenth centuries. The great Goethe himself was impressed by the subtlety and effectiveness of this management device and called it "one of the finest inventions of the human mind." By 1800, double-entry books were common practice for merchants and manufacturers alike. Characteristically, Watt developed for his firm the improvement which made the device vastly more useful to managers. Boulton, Watt and Company had a cost accounting system.

Books on management up to this time had concerned themselves with recipes for success in commerce. Little had been written about industrial management. One of the great classics of the business literature was *Le Parfait Negociant,* written by Jacques Savary in 1675. Classical is the proper term for this work because it reappeared in the last of many editions in the very year of James Watt's retirement. Education for success in business management appeared in the form of Thomas Watt's work of 1716 which he titled *An Essay on the Proper Method of Forming the Man of Business.* A number of handbooks for managers appeared in the eighteenth century which claimed to reveal all the knowledge of commercial operations then known. Typical of these is the *Universal Dictionary of Trade and Commerce,* the work of Malachy Postlewayt in 1755.

Watt may have been acquainted with Adam Smith's great passage describing the division of labor in the pin factory, but it is interesting to note that it was some time before the Soho foundry evolved to an organization in which extensive division of labor was practiced. Certainly Watt, who had visited many plants as a consulting engineer on steam engines, was aware of the extent job specialization in manufacturing had developed at the time. He was, however, basically an experimentalist who worked things out for himself in his own plant.

Division of labor did, however, reach a high degree of development in Watt's factory and the catalog of management techniques which went with it reads much like an outline of the ideas that were to occupy industrial engineers a hundred years later. To begin with, the plant was not arranged just by whim or expedient. Careful attention was given to plant layout, and a sensible scheme of departmentalization was the result. The product and the methods of production were standardized through management planning. A scheme we would now call a routing system controlled the flow of material through the shop. Most of the workers eventually were put on piece rates, which again was the result of management attention. Records of production were kept in elaborate fashion and these forerunners of time study were even used to develop mathematical formulas relating various aspects of the task to the performance time. All the problems of piece rates based on time standards were evidently a part of Watt's experience for in 1791 some of his men had gone on strike in a dispute over rates.

Delegation of authority was worked out in a well-organized plan and, as already noted, a cost accounting system was devised as a means of controlling the resulting management hierarchy. Watt already knew that cost accounting could be the basis for pricing the product and even more useful for detecting "waste and inefficiency." When new policies or reforms seemed called for, elaborate statistical reports were prepared, which must surely have some claim to marking the earliest utilization of the staff industrial engineer.

The Soho foundry was, of course, an exception. But the important things to note about it are these:

1. It marks an early discovery of the immense importance of separating the planning of production from the work of production itself. Here was the key to modern staff organization.

2. The twin problems of motivation and control of the manufacturing organization were put on a rational basis.

3. There was no theory on which Watt could draw. He was a typical cut-and-try empiricist, but it does not seem to have occurred to him that these experiments could be conducted in anything except the most expensive possible way. He experimented with the plant itself. This is not suprising, for the idea that staff advisers could reduce the need for and enhance the success of such costly tests is a very modern one indeed.

Also in the year 1800, another bright young man bought himself a cotton mill employing roughly 2,000 people in the little town of New Lanark in Scotland. This man was hardly likely to be admired by managers of his time, or by those who have prospered under free enterprise since, for he was given to forming utopian socialist communities and was eventually to have a major part in the rise of the British trade union movement. He was, however, like Watt, an experimenter with the courage to try his ideas in practice at the risk of his own capital. His name was Robert Owen.[17]

When Owen took charge of the New Lanark mills the working and living conditions were as bad as anywhere else. Of his work force, some 400 to 500 were children between the ages of five and ten. They worked a thirteen-hour day, after which they slept through what passed for their education. The adults who worked at New Lanark did so as a last resort. One went to work in the mills only when all other means of livelihood seemed to fail. Drunkenness was a common occurrence in the mill. Owen, like Watt, made some changes in the machines and their arrangement, but his great experiments ran in another direction. He set out on a great program of social reform which centered around his mills but extended into the community to include education, religion, and public health. He wanted to change not only the material existence of his employees but their habits and character as well. And of course they systematically opposed him. It was not until the company continued to pay wages through a long period of unemployment that Owen began to have their confidence.

Owen clearly understood his program of reform in the mills could not be a sudden revolution. Over a period of twenty-five years he got the children out of the mills and into schools, shortened the work day, and made extensive improvements in working and living conditions. His biographer, Cole, says, "He meant to make New Lanark not merely a success as a factory, but the laboratory for a great series of social experiments in education and moral and physical reform."[18] Owen saw himself as an experimenter too, for he remarked on taking over the mills, "I had now, by a course of events not under my control, the groundwork on which to try an experiment long wished for, but little expected to be in my power to carry into execution."[19]

Owen saw, perhaps for the first time, that after certain minimum material needs had been taken care of other incentives began to emerge alongside the financial one. His system of "silent monitors" was a marvel of simplicity and directness. Over each machine hung a piece of wood painted a different color on each of four sides. The shop foremen rated the conduct of each employee and his block of

---

[17] G. D. H. Cole, *The Life of Robert Owen* (London: Macmillan & Co., Ltd., 1933); Robert Owen, *The Life of Robert Owen* (New York: Alfred A. Knopf, Inc., 1920).

[18] Cole, *op. cit.*, p. 78.

[19] *Ibid.*, p. 81.

wood revealed for all to see his deportment on the previous day.
The black side signified bad behavior; the white side, excellent
behavior; blue and yellow fell in between. Owen could tell much
about how things were going in the mills by a glance at the colors
which met his eye.

What was the result of this great experiment in industrial relations? Owen's mills prospered and provided him with a substantial
fortune. Indeed they might have continued to enrich him for a life-
time if he had not eventually taken his wealth and lost it in his far
less successful experiments in socialist communities. Interestingly
enough, the experiments at New Lanark were widely known and his
fellow industrialists came to see the secret of his prosperity. He had
no imitators among them, however. Facts alone do not change
people's minds.

Robert Owen, then, made the first industrial experiment in
human relations. He demonstrated two astounding facts which were
perhaps unbelievable to the managers of his day.

1. Men are not machines.
2. The simple, brute-force minimization of costs does not necessarily result
in the maximization of profits.

Like others of his time, Owen experienced the difficulties which
played a part in the rise of the modern corporation. He could not
himself raise the capital to buy the New Lanark mills so he had
partners. His partners were few in number and of course did not
take at first to his novel schemes for management. In 1812 he had
to form a new partnership which included Jeremy Bentham. The
larger and the more mechanized industry became, the greater grew
its need for capital. Eventually the corporation as a mechanism for
capitalization evolved. One of its most important aspects, for our
purposes, was the separation of ownership from management. The
division of labor in production was the first great specialization
which began the industrial revolution, and the division of ownership
and management was the second. Thus began the rise of the professional manager, a vital prerequisite to the emergence of advisory
staffs.

Many commentaries on modern management have noted the
important differences between the professional manager and the
entrepreneur.[20] The latter was a founder, a pioneer, a man of great

---

[20] One good example is Robert A. Gordon, *Business Leadership in the Large
Corporation* (Washington, D.C.: Brookings Institution, 1945).

confidence and self-reliance, and—above all perhaps—a great and fearless risk taker. Many of these men failed and many fail today, chiefly, it is thought, because of what we now call managerial ability. The firm that begins with a competitive advantage based on the particular skills of its founder arrives, if it grows, very quickly at a critical period. Soon the founder must cease playing the central role in all the activities of the firm and hire others to work for him. He then becomes a manager in the modern sense, and there is a great possibility that the skills which brought the firm its initial success will not give way to those which can now keep it growing. The entrepreneur must become a manager of other people. He may well find that it is time to hire a professional to do this. And so it is that many of the firms which survived came sooner or later to have professional managers who continued on even though the shares of ownership changed hands often.

The professional manager, who may own very little stock in the firm he manages, sees his decisions quite differently than did the entrepreneur. He would be glad if he could to dignify his profession by calling it scientific, and thus he tends to be generally receptive to movements in this direction. His decisions are made with conservatism, for he is not the fearless risk taker. R. A. Gordon in one of the classic studies of professional managers concludes, "Among professional executives scientific caution may degenerate into a tendency to play safe. They do not receive the profits which may result from taking a chance, while their positions in the firm may be jeopardized in the event of serious loss."[21] This attitude toward decisions—which has more recently been verified empirically by the Meyer and Kuh study of the capital investment decisions professionals make[22]—opened the way for advisers who could reduce the uncertainty in business decisions and base their results on methods at least partly scientific.

Two other fundamental movements in the direction of specialization contributed to the emergence of advice as a factor in management. The first has already been seen in embryonic form in the Soho foundry. Separating the task of planning production from the work of production itself gave management much more to do. This, as has been said, is the central idea in modern enterprise. This propensity to plan, which continues to grow even now, was the result

---

[21] *Ibid.*, p. 167.
[22] John R. Meyer and Edwin Kuh, *The Investment Decision; An Empirical Study* (Cambridge, Mass.: Harvard University Press, 1957).

perhaps of three other factors. First, if a manager is to take time out from the pressures of keeping the business going from day to day in order to plan for the future, he must have fairly good control over his current affairs. A certain amount of stability was necessary in industry before the propensity to plan could flourish. Second, to plan for the future is to assume there will be a future. The basic philosophy of the modern corporation is that of indefinite existence, independent of the mortality or whims of any particular owner. Third, the propensity to plan arises out of the need for caution and the reduction of risk and uncertainty the professional manager feels.

The growth of planning brought the last great movement toward specialization, which is manifested by the presence of the formally constituted advisory staffs in management[23] that appeared in force from the beginning of the present century. This move was the specialization of function within management itself. It mirrored the specialization in production of the previous two centuries. Management produced decisions, and these could be more efficiently produced if there were advisers among management who specialized in marketing decisions, or production decisions, or finance decisions. No manager could be expected to find the time or the mental capacity to produce the highly specialized inputs to the increasingly complex decisions which confronted him. Staff specialists were the answer. It was clear, however, that if these specialists, each with depth in his own area but limited consequently in breadth, were themselves allowed to make the decisions, things would not go well at all. The manager became increasingly concerned with coordination and reserved for himself the final act of choice. This produced the convention that advisers advise but managers have the authority to decide.

The growth of the firm is such an important determinant of the way these four tendencies toward specialization develop that the following chapter is devoted to an examination of such facts as are available to supplement the folklore.

It is hard to know what effect the experiments of Watt and Owen had on the managers who participated in the great industrial changes of the nineteenth century. There were no journals, no meetings, and no professional groups to communicate and develop re-

---

[23] For a definitive study see Leland H. Jenks, "Early Phases of the Management Movement," *Administrative Science Quarterly*, Vol. 5 (1960). See also Harold F. Smiddy and Lionel Naum, "Evolution of a Science of Managing in America," *Management Science*, Vol. 1, No. 1 (1954).

sults. Indeed, these things were not to come for almost 100 years. The managers of the time most likely found their attention absorbed by the events which provided the basic sources of success for industrialization. Technology began to proliferate the number of commercially practical products and processes. The twin developments of mass production and mass markets began to indicate the possibilities open to managers. There were basic problems to think about and large profits to be made by those who could find rough and ready solutions. The time had still not come to think about refinements and niceties in the art of management.

The first scientifically trained person to interest himself in management problems seems to have been Charles Babbage (1792–1871), professor of mathematics at Cambridge University.[24] Babbage devoted thirty-seven years to an idea which was finally realized a century later: the automatic computing machine. Babbage, having only mechanical components to draw upon, wanted to build a machine that would perform any mathematical operation, store numbers in a memory device, and do the other tasks we now expect from computers. He worked hard and brilliantly at the project, but success had to wait for the development of electronics.

For Babbage and many other scientists who followed, management problems were a secondary interest. He brought to them his mind and powers of observation, but not his mathematics. While working on his computing machine, Babbage visited a large number of plants in England and Europe. This experience moved him to publish in 1832 an essay, *On the Economy of Machinery and Manufactures*. The book was widely read and admired for many years and was still receiving complimentary notices in 1910. It was no mere description of management as he had seen it but was filled with his recommendations as to how things ought to be done. He saw the importance of collecting data in an orderly fashion as a basis for making decisions. He tackled problems of work methods, performance times, cost reporting, cost reduction, and incentives. He proposed profit-sharing plans to demonstrate to employees that they shared a community of interest with management and he pointed out many of the problems which would attend such plans. He dealt with such a current thorn as technological unemployment, and much of what he said was rediscovered many years later.

During the nineteenth century, and for the early part of the

---

[24] See Raymond Villers, *Dynamic Management in Industry* (Englewood Cliffs, N.J.: Prentice-Hall, Inc., 1960), pp. 15–25.

twentieth, science was occupied with other things. The physical sciences were building an astonishing record of success, both in fundamental knowledge and in technological end products. Physical scientists were too busy to take much interest in policy problems. Nor had they any particular motivation to do so. The social sciences, which made their beginnings by direct concern with problems of social policy, turned away from any concern with decision and action in the nineteenth century. Social scientists, as E. A. Shils sees it, tried to emulate the natural sciences in many ways, including a complete divorce from policy problems.[25] They wanted nothing to do with real choices which involved values. Business was an activity unworthy of the attention of a social scientist and the possibility that a concern with "practical problems" might advance sociology or economics was unimaginable. Indeed, this view was not to change until World War I forcefully revised it. One fundamental consequence of this is that management science in the twentieth century had no great store of basic scientific knowledge on which to draw—a consequence which will be with us for some time to come.

The next step was thus to be taken by a man who was not primarily a scientist. He was a man with all the talents of a great innovator who could question custom and routine and propose startling revisions. He was also a man given to the relentless imposition of his ideas on others. His story begins in college where he played baseball. The game could surely stand improvement over its traditional form, he thought, and he soon concluded that the underhand pitch, used exclusively at that time, needed attention. He simply began to pitch overhand. Some other players immediately objected that the rules did not allow this. They were told that if this were so, the rules should certainly be changed because the overhand method "got results." In this fashion Frederick W. Taylor began a pattern which eventually established for him the role of "father" of scientific management and earned him the name "Speedy," along with the sincere hatred of many workmen who fell within his schemes.[26]

The story of Speedy Taylor is well known and even those who have not heard of him often hold a vague but uncomplimentary

[25] See E. A. Shils, "Social Science and Social Policy," *Philosophy of Science,* Vol. 16, No. 3 (1949).

[26] See F. B. Copley, *Life of Frederick W. Taylor* (Taylor Society, 1923); H. B. Drury, *Scientific Management—A History and Criticism* (New York: Columbia University Press, 1922); F. W. Taylor, *Scientific Management* (New York: Harper & Bros., 1947). For an excellent survey see Villers, *op. cit.*

image of a mechanistic world which would result if the "efficiency experts" had their way. Taylor is also the center of a whole constellation of men, some legitimate contributors to improving the art of management, others ready to profit from whatever expectations are created by the label "scientific management."

While there is certainly much room for discussion about what meaning Taylor attached to his term "scientific management," and just how scientific it was in terms of present-day definitions, certain clearly scientific tendencies took form in his writings. He appears today as a massive and courageous innovator who may well have been subjected since his death to a good deal of trivial criticism. The outstanding features of his thought are:

1. Traditions and rules of thumb are to be abandoned.
2. Those things formerly left to accident will now become the subject of planning.
3. Work methods are no longer to be left up to the workers but brought as closely as possible within the control of management. Along with this goes the control of output through the wage-payment plan.
4. Work methods are to be designed on the basis of empirical observation.

All this represented quite a change from the prevailing ad hoc improvisation that characterized management at the turn of the century. Taylor suffered from lack of scientific training, and more seriously from the lack of existing basic science from which to draw. He was too ready to advocate his own hypotheses as scientific laws, a reflection perhaps of his general excess of enthusiasm and confidence. He was some years ahead of the general discovery that there are important differences between workers and machines. It seems clear, however, that Taylor laid two essential foundation stones for management science in a decade of innovation between 1895 and 1904. He successfully gave root to the idea that planning and doing ought to be separated. The propensity to plan, as has been suggested, is a necessary condition for the emergence of staff specialists whose work is essentially that of planning alone and who are not involved in the doing. Taylor also got the idea well on its way that these staff specialists were to be scientific in their outlook. While Taylor and those who followed him busied themselves for the most part with planning at levels of management below that of the plant superintendent, they saw at least in principle the possibilities at higher levels of management. By 1910, Harrington Emerson was advocating the line-and-staff principle of organization and planning was well on its way toward an established place in industrial management.[27]

Not the least important activity of any science is the public communication and cumulation of its results. Here Taylor laid the second of his foundation stones, the beginnings of a growing literature. Along with this development went the trappings of a profession tending to give coherence and prestige to those who dealt with the knowledge which accumulated and restricting to some extent the numbers of those who were to profit from it. Publication of material dealing with scientific management grew rapidly in the early years of the century. In 1911, Taylor's first attempt to institutionalize his movement produced "The Society for the Promotion of the Science of Management." The tenor of the group is suggested by some references to it as "the almighty and his disciples." Later came the Taylor Society and, in 1934, the Society for the Advancement of Management.

Some years after Taylor's movement got under way, a few scientists began to take an interest in management problems. These men were to a large extent dissociated from the followers of Taylor and the scientific management group. Three names stand out among these men: Hugo Munsterberg, Elton Mayo, and Walter Shewhart.

In 1879, Wilhelm Wundt took a major step in transforming psychology from a branch of speculative philosophy to an experimental science by establishing at Leipzig the first laboratory for the study of human behavior.[28] An eventual consequence was that one of his pupils, Professor Munsterberg of Harvard, published in 1913 *Psychology and Industrial Efficiency.* Munsterberg and the industrial psychologists who became important during World War I devoted their attention largely to fatigue, working conditions, and tests for job assignment. These early studies have been criticized for emphasizing too directly the problem of arranging the conditions of work so as to increase output. J. A. C. Brown comments, "But the mind of the worker was not the concern of the employer—nor, to all appearances, was it a matter of any serious concern to the early industrial psychologist. The latter's idea of a good factory was one which produced the goods with maximum efficiency and minimum effort, although with the passage of time, when the worker's bodily health came to be tied up with the concept of efficiency, his ideal factory came to bear a close resemblance to a model cow-house.

---

[27] Jenks, *op. cit.*
[28] Brown, *op. cit.*

When lighting, heating, ventilation, humidity and every other con- ceivable factor in the physical environment was so perfect, what right had the worker to grumble?"[29] This attitude was soon corrected, thanks to experimental science, although it reappears from time to time even now. The point is that experimental scientists were at work, doing experiments bearing directly upon management prob- lems, and the effects of science in its best sense were soon to be felt.

The Hawthorne experiments are universally regarded as the great landmark in the scientific understanding of what goes on in industrial plants. Elton Mayo, again a scientist and again doing con- trolled experiments, dramatically demonstrated that the behavior of workers was in part a social phenomenon and that a man's produc- tivity, morale, and job satisfaction depended upon his attitudes toward his supervisor and his associates.[30] These experiments in the late 1920's were remarkable for the fact that the management of the Western Electric Company was willing to carry them on in the plant at no sacrifice of realism.

Walter Shewhart of the famous Bell Telephone Laboratories took the step in 1924 which seems to have begun the great modern movement toward the use of probability theory and statistics, not only in the study of management problems but as the foundation for many methods of managerial decision making and control. This introduced the modern use of inferential statistics in experimental design and analysis and suggested probability theory as a source of the language to express the uncertainties and risks managers con- tinually face. Shewhart's concept of statistical quality control was an idea so fundamental, so useful, and so important, that it opened up new possibilities for the use of science in many phases of manage- ment decision making.

These men mark the beginning of the trained scientist's interest in management problems. World War II was to draw scientists from many fields into operations research and set the stage for the great postwar advances in management science.[31] This gave impetus to a renewed attention on the part of managers toward the possibilities for scientific support in decision making. It brought forth a host of

---

[29] *Ibid.*, p. 16.

[30] Elton Mayo, *The Human Problems of an Industrial Civilization* (Boston: Divi- sion of Research, Graduate School of Business Administration, Harvard University, 1946).

[31] See, for example, Martin L. Leibowitz (ed.), "Symposium on Military Opera- tions Research," *Operations Research*, Vol. 9, No. 2 (1961); A. Boldyriff (ed.), "A Decade of Military Operations Research," *Operations Research*, Vol. 8, No. 6 (1960).

mathematical techniques with a clear and demonstrable application to management problems, filling the need for formal mathematical structure on which to base hypotheses. Thus management science emerged with the logical and experimental aspects which typify our notion of a science today.

Following World War II came as well the turning of attention to decisions in all areas of management functioning. No longer was work concentrated largely on production decisions, but decisions at the higher levels of management and decisions which crossed traditional lines of responsibility received attention. Marketing, finance, organization, communication, and the problem of decision making itself attracted the attention of scientifically trained people.

When "scientific management" is inverted into "management science," it is an attempt to suggest the change that took place between the work which was begun by Taylor and that which has resulted from the application of science in the modern sense.

Chapter 3:

BIGNESS

AND

STAFF

ADVICE

*"In any public administrative depart-
ment not actually at war, the staff
increase may be expected to follow
this formula—*

$$x = \frac{2k^m + L}{n}$$

k *is the number of staff seeking promotion through the appointment of
subordinates;* L *represents the difference between the ages of appointment and retirement;* m *is the
number of man-hours devoted to
answering minutes within the department; and* n *is the number of
effective units being administered.* x
*will be the number of new staff re-
quired each year."*

—C. Northcote Parkinson

Big organizations have, quite naturally, been the object of the
attentions of those interested in the development and application
of management science. In fact many discussions of scientific assistance for managers are introduced with a standard and seemingly
harmless phrase something like, "Because of the increasing size and
complexity of industrial firms, management must have the assistance
of . . . (this or that technique)." While such remarks may be true
enough, their meaning and the evidence in favor of them are seldom
examined very carefully. Here we will take a somewhat closer look
at the implications of size for advice giving and the nature of the
assistance managers "must" have.

Along with the endless discussions of whether or not big business
represents a threat to our economic system, a number of impressions
of the nature of large firms have gained currency. Terms like
"organization man" and "corporate image" have entered our vocabulary with a variety of meanings attached. Professor Parkinson has
suggested that as an organization grows the number of clerks in it
will grow at an alarmingly faster rate until, if the organization

depends on profit for existence, it must collapse under the weight of its own overhead.[1] This is consistent with the supposition that as organizations grow the number of managers must grow faster than the number of employees in order to keep things under control. This, in turn, generates paper work at an accelerating rate. Overhead mounts, delays in decision making increase, one department no longer knows what the others are doing, and so on.

Even some gross statistics for manufacturing in the United States as a whole give one pause.[2] In 1935, industry had about fourteen nonproduction employees for every one hundred production and related employees. By 1947, this had grown to twenty per one hundred, and in 1958 there were more than thirty-six nonproduction employees for every one hundred production and related workers. Such numbers are to be understood in terms of a complex of causes, but it is clear that something is happening.

Still another impression is that every large organization must be run by someone close in touch with the details of its operations who "knows what's going on." In 1935, Justice Brandeis suggested to Henry L. Stimson that the corporate system had outgrown the capacity of the human brain to manage it. The only solution, he thought, was to return to the small business unit, thus cutting power down to fit the capacity of men.[3] We do not really understand, in the sense of science, what happens when a corporation grows very large. Yet men have demonstrated competence in managing large organizations and in leading them to grow still larger. This is but another instance of the fundamental idea that scientific understanding is not a necessary condition for action. It will always be true that we can do far more things than we can understand. There remain, however, the questions of the reliability with which we can do things we do not understand, and the cost of the failures with which success is bought.

We do understand, though, that large organizations can be managed not by a single brain but through the coordinated decisions made by many. Just how decisions are to be thus delegated and the resulting actions coordinated is a central question for management science. It seems clear that since the information-handling and

---

[1] C. Northcote Parkinson, *Parkinson's Law* (Boston: Houghton Mifflin Co., 1957).

[2] *Statistical Abstract of the United States*, 1960 (Washington, D.C.: U.S. Government Printing Office), p. 780.

[3] Arthur M. Schlesinger, Jr., *The Politics of Upheaval* (Boston: Houghton Mifflin Co., 1960), p. 220.

decision-making capacities of the chief executive are finite the organization must eventually grow beyond the point where he alone can manage it. If he does not delegate, his capacity becomes a limiting factor bringing about diminishing returns. Things begin to get out of hand and the organization is regarded as too big.[4]

Thus, as organizations grow their forms and structures must change. Mason Haire, whose quantitative analyses of this process we shall examine shortly, suggests an analogy to the biological model called the square-cube law.[5] D'Arcy Thompson pointed out that giants ten times as big as men but with the same proportions would be quite harmless, contrary to all fairy tales. The giant's weight would be 10^3 or 1,000 times that of a man, but the cross-sectional area of his leg bones would increase by 10^2 or 100 times. Thus his legs would have to support ten times the load, and if they were of the same material as human bones they would immediately collapse. If the giant is to survive he must change his shape and structure from that of a man.

The square-cube law suggests simply that if things grow without changing their shape, their volume or mass increases by a cubic function while the surface enclosing them increases by a square. Haire was able to draw an analogy between volume and those employees who worked internally in the firm, and between surface and those whose work had to do with things primarily outside the firm. In four companies which he studied, the cube root of the number of internal employees and the square root of the number of external employees were indeed related in a way very nearly linear, as the law would suggest. Inside the firms, however, important changes in structure accompanied growth.

As a firm grows, one might imagine the transformation of its

---

4 Useful references on organizational growth and size include: E. P. Adler, "Relationships Between Organization Size and Efficiency," *Management Science*, Vol. 7, No. 1 (1960); Reihard Bendix, *Work and Authority in Industry* (New York: John Wiley & Sons, Inc., 1956), pp. 211–26; Kenneth Boulding, "The Jungle of Hugeness," *Saturday Review*, March 1, 1958; Sune Carlson, *Executive Behavior* (Stockholm: C. A. Stromberg, 1959); Alfred D. Chandler, Jr., *Strategy and Structure* (Cambridge, Mass.: The MIT Press, 1962); Sidney Hook, "Bureaucrats Are Human," *Saturday Review*, May 17, 1958; James G. March and Herbert A. Simon, *Organizations* (New York: John Wiley & Sons, Inc., 1958), chap. 2; E. T. Penrose, *The Theory of the Growth of the Firm* (Oxford: Blackwells, 1959); N. S. Ross, "Management and the Size of the Firm," *Review of Economic Studies*, Vol. 19 (1951); Francis W. Terrien and Donald L. Mills, "The Effect of Changing Size upon the Internal Structure of Organization," *American Sociological Review*, Vol. 20, No. 1 (1951).

5 Mason Haire, "Biological Models and Empirical Histories of the Growth of Organizations," in *Modern Organization Theory*, Mason Haire (ed.) (New York: John Wiley & Sons, Inc., 1959).

internal structure taking place along the following general lines. When the chief executive finds his information-processing and decision-making capacities taxed toward their limit, he delegates some work to subordinates. Thus begins the emergence of an elaborate hierarchy of line managers who come into existence through delegation of the work of managing. This raises immediately the problem of coordination. How are the actions and decisions of these managers made compatible, each with the other and with the objectives of the firm as a whole? As the lines of communication multiply and lengthen the possibilities for delays in decision making, uncertainty as to what is going on in the firm and incompatible decisions increase.

As these processes are taking place through delegation, another kind of change emerges. The volume of decisions grows to the point where specialized information and advice to support various classes of decisions is not only required but can easily be justified economically. Thus begins the evolution of staff services within the company to fill these two needs. Some staff services, such as accounting, function chiefly to provide information for coordination and control, helping to assure the compatibility of decisions made by various managers within the firm. Other staff services give specialized advice, as in the case of the legal, marketing, or personnel staffs. Management science is, of course, intended to provide specialized advice in a variety of functional areas of management decision making.

Some have been concerned lest the process of delegation lead eventually to such a large and complex hierarchy of line managers that increasing costs of administration per worker and increasing delays in making decisions would result in a firm uneconomic to manage. When the chief executive finds the number of subordinates who report to him has grown beyond some vaguely defined point of effectiveness, another level in the organizational hierarchy is instituted. This process goes on, increasing the number of levels of management as the size of the organization grows. The number of subordinates reporting to a superior is called the span of control. Both experience and evidence tend to indicate that, contrary to such fears, the growth of line management will not itself create an excessive burden on the organization. If the span of control is kept constant, the number of line managers tends to grow exponentially with the number of levels in the hierarchy, but so also does the number of workers. Thus the ratio of managers to workers tends to remain nearly constant. In the companies studied by Haire, it also appeared that as they grew the span of control tended in fact to increase. In firms having between 20 and 50 employees, the average span of control was 11.5 subordinates per superior. When, however, these firms grew to a size of more than 200 employees, the span of control had increased to 21. Haire also discovered that the percentage of employees in top and middle management dropped over the same growth span from 13.6 per cent to 4.1 per cent. It may well be that in the long run the capacities of top management are not the limiting factor in the growth of the firm.

As the line functions grow, they must, however, be supported by the addition of staff services. How does the staff emerge and grow? Again, the four companies whose history Haire examined in detail give us the first clues. He defined staff as all those who provide specialized support, advice, and help for line personnel. Line in turn, includes all those directly concerned with the making and selling of the product. The companies he examined began with nearly everyone falling into the category of line positions. During the first six to ten years in the lives of these companies the proportion of staff increased very rapidly indeed. At the end of this period, however, the per cent of staff people tends to stabilize, in two of the firms at around 50 per cent, and in the other two at about 25 per cent. If one were to generalize from this it might be suggested that in the early years the staff will grow geometrically while the line grows linearly, but later this relation relaxes into one of parallel growth. It is interesting to note that staff employment appears more stable than line employment, remaining quite insensitive to reductions in the work force.

Another study, somewhat differently conceived from that of Haire, has been done by Baker and Davis.[6] They also were interested in the emergence and growth of the staff, but chose to study some 211 companies of various sizes at a single point in time rather than examine the life histories of individual firms. Out of such data came a number of interesting statements. They suggest that every time a firm adds 100 direct workers, the number of indirect workers increases by 75, regardless of the size of the firm before the addition. This agrees in general with the pattern of parallel growth which emerged in the later years of the companies Haire examined.

---

[6] A. W. Baker and R. C. Davis, *Ratios of Staff to Line Employees and Stages of Differentiation of Staff Functions* (Columbus, Ohio: Ohio State University Bureau of Business Research, 1954).

Accounting tends to grow at the fastest rate, adding about 4.6 people with every addition of 100 direct workers. Personnel grows at a rate of 1.46 staff people added for each 100 new direct workers. Industrial engineering, which Baker and Davis conceive rather narrowly as time and motion study, grows at the rate of 1.10 staff members per 100 direct workers. Some groups of indirect workers such as inspection, cafeteria, maintenance, and engineering tend to grow at an increasing rate as the number of direct workers grows. As Haire noticed, Baker and Davis show that the number of top-management executives tends to grow at a decreasing rate.

The emergence of various staff functions as differentiated groups in the organization proceeds at varying rates. By the time a firm has from 75 to 99 workers the functions of accounting, purchasing, and engineering are completely differentiated. Yet production control, time and motion study, personnel, and inspection do not emerge until the company has grown into the range of from 100 to 499 employees. In the case of time and motion study in particular, 78 per cent of the firms employing less than 300 direct workers either did not have this function or allowed it to remain completely integrated with other functions. Among companies with more than 300 direct employees, time and motion study had emerged and was completely differentiated as an organization entity in 69 per cent of the firms studied.

These studies suggest some useful hypotheses. Apparently the emergence and early growth of the staff is rather dramatic while the firm is small and young. The staff groups quickly achieve an institutional existence and come to constitute an important portion of the organization. As time passes and the firm grows, the expansion of the staff settles down to a pattern which parallels that of the line or direct employees. At the same time, the number of middle and top managers increases at a decreasing rate, so that this group comes eventually to constitute a smaller portion of the organization.

Haire has suggested that the sorts of changes in form and structure which take place as an organization grows are those necessary to meet and overcome the forces tending to destroy the organization. This principle, drawn from studies of the growth of organisms, suggests that the emergence and growth of the organization's staff functions, in association with and in response to delegation, shore up the organization where the need arises. The functions of the staff groups include the gathering and processing of information for decision making, coordination, and control, and furnishing specialized advice in particular fields. Thus the staff is the chief bulwark against lack of communication, conflicting and incompatible decisions, and general disorganization—the potential destructive forces threatening the large firm.

From the negatively accelerated growth of top and middle management one might also draw the conclusion that the staff is an effective means of increasing the abilities and capacities of management. It appears that the staff groups make possible the management of larger firms with relatively fewer managers but without a runaway increase in the size of the staff itself. Clearly, it does not appear that the staff-management hierarchy is going to become a limiting factor in the growth of the firm.

In the particular case of management science, emerging in staff departments under titles such as "operations research," or in industrial engineering departments of greatly expanded scope, we have as yet little evidence on patterns of emergence and growth. In this instance it is likely that not only will the size and age of the firm be important but also the relatively short time during which management science has been available together with the high rate at which its competence is increasing. It will, however, be some time before anything like stable patterns of institutionalization are clear for management science.

Let us next take a closer look at the role of the staff groups in the growth of the enterprise. We have seen that the basic internal transformation involves the processes of delegation and the formation of staff groups. In these ways management can effectively increase its own capacities so as to control large organizations without excessively multiplying its own numbers. The role of the staff in the process of the firm's expansion begins with a key event, reaching a size at which the institutionalization of a specialized staff function appears justified to management. This implies the firm has grown to a point where there is sufficient demand for the services of a staff group so that the functions it will perform can no longer remain integrated in the other elements of the organization. Once this emergence takes place the important benefits of specialization become available. In a sense, once a firm finds itself large enough to afford the services of staff specialists it may be in a position to grow faster and more effectively than before. The staff group, particularly a management science group, may itself be instrumental in the further expansion of the firm.

Growth implies a transformation from owner management to

professional management. Professional managers, as distinct from the owners of the firm, are less willing to take large risks in their decisions. Professional managers find it not only in their own interests but in the interests of their firms to be increasingly conservative in accepting the risk and uncertainty in decisions involving capital investment and expansion. Since one major role of a management science group is the reduction of risk and uncertainty, the role of the staff in planning for the firm's future tends to be emphasized. Thus planning for growth tends to become a specialized function and presumably is carried on more effectively as a result.

It appears also that the daily tasks of coordination and control together with the pressure of immediate decisions tend to take priority over problems of planning for the future in competing for the time and attention of management. Although the staff attempts to relieve management of routine problems so as to make time available to consider plans for growth and expansion, this is only partially possible at present. Thus innovation, planning, growth, and the functions of entrepreneurship tend to become institutionalized in the staff.

This tendency is reinforced by another which is suggested by the hypothesis, "Pressure favors intuition against analysis." This implies that in the decisions which must be made more or less immediately under some pressure, management tends to rely on its own intuitions rather than on the support of the analytical efforts of the staff. Analysis takes time and is not always possible in the face of the pressure of deadlines. As a result, the staff tends to be more concerned with the long-run problems for which time to do adequate scientific study is available.

The decision to expand is, like any other management decision, based ultimately on management's conception of the alternatives and future possibilities involved. The considerations which prevail in this decision are well suited to discovery and analysis by staff groups. The primary consideration is often management's conception of the demand for its products. Here, staff analysis can and usually does contribute both to the prediction of future demands and to the design of management and production systems which effectively respond to increased demand. Among the important correlates of growth are two sorts of effects, one called economies of specialization and the other, economies of indivisibility. The staff itself is a typical example of an economy of specialization which accompanies growth. As we have seen, once the size is reached which permits a specialized staff function to exist, the work of such a group is presumably performed more effectively than when done by nonspecialists. Obvious and well-known economies of specialization occur in production, in marketing, in research, and, of course, in management itself. Economies of indivisibilities arise because often it is not possible to match one's resources perfectly with the demands for these resources. An obvious example is the basic steel industry where there is a minimum output below which one cannot justify a blast furnace and thus cannot go into the business at all. Once, however, one owns a blast furnace, increases in the volume of production tend for a while to be accompanied by lower production cost per unit, as the fixed charges are "spread" over a larger number of units. The analysis of such relations is a traditional and effective area of operation for the staff, giving them a central role in the rate at which the firm expands.

One correlate of growth especially important in understanding the relationships between management and their staff advisers is the change in risk and uncertainty management experiences as the firm expands. One sort of uncertainty, internal uncertainty, has already been considered in introducing the emergence of the staff as an organizational entity. As the firm grows and delegation is necessary, it tends to become increasingly difficult for each decision maker in management to know what the others are going to decide on matters in which they must operate interdependently. Thus uncertainty as to what is going on within the firm tends to increase. This is countered by systems for coordination and control which tend to reduce internal uncertainty and in which the staff plays an important part. We shall return to the staff contributions to countering internal uncertainty very shortly.

External uncertainty, or uncertainty due to management's lack of information about future events which will have an influence on the progress of the firm, tends in some senses to increase and in others to decrease as the firm grows. As a firm grows larger, both its size and the associated inertia require its predictions to be extended further and further into the future. The familiar principle that the further in the future a predicted event lies the greater the uncertainty associated with it, thus exposes the firm to increasing uncertainty as it grows. Not only longer-range predictions but a greater number of predictions of the future are required by the large firm. Its decisions involve broader and more complex actions, thus increasing in some rough way the amount of risk and uncertainty associated with them.

Perhaps more important than the relative increase in uncertainty as a function of size is the decrease in the amount of risk and uncertainty a firm (or really, its management) is willing to tolerate. It is even supposed that the decreasing tolerance for uncertainty may be one of the factors which does ultimately limit the expansion of the firm. This declining willingness to expose oneself to uncertainty can be understood from several viewpoints.

It has already been suggested that the firm's tolerance for risk is decreased as the firm makes the transformation from owners and founders as managers to the use of professional managers. This is evidenced, for example, by the investment behavior of professional managers. The traditional entrepreneur is willing to borrow money from any source to take advantage of a seemingly profitable investment opportunity. Professional managers, as is well documented, tend to limit their investment programs to the amount of funds available from sources within the firm, such as retained earnings and depreciation, rather than make use of outside sources. This has the effect of reducing the risk of serious difficulties arising out of indebtedness when investments fail as well as reducing the risk of losing their positions. It also means management tends to concentrate on investment opportunities which appear to have satisfactory return and relatively little risk and uncertainty for them. As a firm grows larger one would also suppose it has more to lose than when it was smaller and is thus less willing to take risks. This may be coupled directly with a diminishing marginal-utility hypothesis which suggests that the larger a firm grows the less important each additional increment of expansion becomes, and thus the less the tolerance for risk and uncertainty associated with expansion.

It is clear that the desire of management for staff services that could have the effect of reducing risk and uncertainty might well be expected to increase as the firm grows. This indeed one supposes to be a basic function of management science.

However, in some senses the large firm is able to reduce risk and uncertainty because of its size, in addition to its employment of staff groups for this purpose.[7] The principal mechanism is diversification or the pooling of risks so as to take advantage of long-run effects. The classic example is the large firm which offers a diversified

---

[7] Frank H. Knight, *Risk, Uncertainty, and Profit* (London School of Economics and Political Science Series of Reprints of Scarce Tracts No. 16, 1933).

line of products thus smoothing out the variance of its profit and greatly reducing the risk of serious difficulties. A similar strategy applies to decisions of many other sorts made throughout the firm. In any situation in which a large number of independent decisions can be considered together the firm has the opportunity to turn uncertainty into risk. Here again the staff may play an important part in the discovery and development of diversification strategies of all kinds.

The effectiveness of large firms in the reduction of risk is well known. The failure of a firm large in its own industry is an event so rare as to escape recent memory. While there is considerable argument as to whether large firms are more profitable than small ones, it is well known that size brings stability of earnings. This low variance of income is, of course, the symptom of a low general level of risk to which the large firm is exposed.[8]

As the firm expands and accommodates itself to the capacities of management through delegation the need for coordination increases. Studies of how executives use their time reveal large portions of it spent in giving and receiving information. Some have supposed the difficulties and costs associated with coordinating widely delegated decisions would eventually operate so as to limit the growth of the firm. Admittedly this is a difficult problem for large management hierarchies but experience confirms it is by no means an insoluble problem. Ways have been discovered of dealing with it, and in many of these ways management science plays an important part.

When decision-making responsibilities are delegated, responsibilities for coordination of decisions at lower levels are delegated as well. Thus the demands of coordination placed upon different members of management may be varied by altering the structure of the organization itself. A critical variable in understanding the problems of coordination in any organization is the degree of self-containment of the organization's various subunits.[9] When two or more units compete for a share of some common resources, such as the capital budget of the firm, or when the output of one subunit forms the input of another, they cannot be considered highly self-contained. The less the degree of self-containment the greater the need for detailed coordination and control. One outstanding trend in management in recent years has been the movement toward de-

---

[8] Penrose, *op. cit.*, p. 226.
[9] March and Simon, *op. cit.*, pp. 28–29.

centralization of various large divisions of a firm. This is an effort toward making these divisions self-contained to a greater extent and thus reducing the burden of coordination. The ultimate extension of this line of development, which is often discussed but seldom truly approached in practice, is to permit the divisions to operate as virtually independent business units so that coordination will be reduced to a minimum. The trick, of course, is to do this and yet assure that the divisions operate so as to advance the objectives of the firm as a whole.

The evolutionary changes in the design of the subunits of the organization are often thought to proceed along the following lines. When the organization is small the subunits tend to be formed by grouping similar processes together, as for example in the typical departmentalized manufacturing plant. As the organization grows, however, the advantages obtained from process-organized subunits tend to be outweighed by the increasing costs of coordination. The advantage shifts eventually to the organization of subunits according to purpose or end product, thus substantially reducing the need for coordination.

One very important aspect of the problem of coordination is seldom mentioned in analytic studies. An organization in existence for some time which has achieved some measure of stability finds itself staffed and managed by people who require progressively less guidance and control. As these people grow used to the organization, grow used to each other, and share the experience of having worked together for a long period of time, the need for coordination declines. Such groups can often achieve a level of consistency, efficiency, and compatibility in broad areas of operation which reduces the need for detailed and constant coordination. This growing ability to work together, while important, is seldom sufficient by itself. It cannot be relied upon in organizations where there are appreciable changes in personnel, rapid shifts in the functions and the environment of the organization, or where decision makers do not share a common operational set of objectives.

Management scientists and their predecessors have played a central role in developing effective schemes for coordination and control. Many studies have set out quite deliberately to cut across organizational lines in an attempt to identify and resolve specific ways in which decision makers act in conflict with one another. Efforts are made to coordinate such decisions through appeal to a common understanding of the objectives of the firm as a whole and the avoidance of behavior aimed at subunit goals alone. The classic example is the firm in which financial management, production management, and sales management find their perceived goals in conflict. The sales department demands large inventories of a wide variety of products in order to satisfy its customers. Production wants to make long runs of a few products and avoid special orders and rush orders. This, coupled with ample in-process inventories, makes for easy production scheduling, high machine utilization, and low unit cost of production. Those concerned with finance aim for low inventories that turn over rapidly and are thus a modest drain on the firm's working capital. Management science has had some success in bringing cooperation out of conflict by substituting objective analysis of these decisions in terms of their consequences for the firm for heated arguments over the pursuit of conflicting departmental ends.

Much of the most useful work of management science has been in the development of management control systems. Rationally constructed routines involving data collection, information flow, decision, and action lie at the center of many advances in the art of managerial control being made today. The whole realm of standard procedures, budgets, standards for accomplishment and utilization, and exception reporting has vastly facilitated the task of coordination. The remarkable developments in the techniques of information handling have contributed as well. The capacity of management to maintain control of large organizations continues to increase as this work goes on.

One interesting hypothesis emerging from the study of management decisions is that although managers make very good decisions when considered on a long-run average basis the variations about this average may need attention. This is to say, it may be the lack of reliability, the lack of consistency, or the variability from one decision to the next which holds the potential for improvements to be realized by bringing management science to the aid of experienced managers. Much of the work may thus be viewed as making decisions more reliable and consistent and less subject to the momentary variations of the human as decision maker. In some cases, minor decisions can be programmed to be made routinely by a computer, thus removing human variability to a large extent. It is too soon to suppose a large number of management decisions can be made objective to this extent, but every contribution of management science helps, to some extent, to make decisions more reliable and predictable. This, in turn, eases the burden of coordination and control.

In summary, then, as an organization grows, delegation of decisions and the emergence of staff services seem the internal structural changes which must be made if it is to survive. Fortunately, it seems reasonable to begin with the hypothesis that neither the number of managers nor the size of the staff will grow at such a rate as to make the organization top heavy. In fact, there is some evidence that as the size of the firm increases managers become more effective and thus their number may grow at a decreasing rate. The staff, and management science in particular, appear to play an important part in maintaining the effectiveness of the organization and in increasing the capacity of management. Management science provides specialized planning for growth, helps reduce the risk and uncertainty in decision making, and attacks directly the problem of systems for managerial coordination and control.

The next task is to examine the particular virtues one may expect to find in management science as a staff function which produces *scientifically* based advice. It is widely agreed that what science is after is to make predictions of interesting events in the future and have these predictions turn out to be right rather more often than not. To the manager, looking for advice on the questions "What policy should we adopt in this situation?" and "What will happen if we elect this particular policy?", such predictions are naturally attractive. There are, however, a number of different kinds of producers from which the manager might buy his predictions. We wish to single out management science from the various "prediction-mongers" and to inquire into the methods by which its predictions are produced.

PART II   Science in Action

Chapter 4:

WHAT REALLY

HAPPENS?

"I discovered it by accident."
—True confessions
of a scientist.

What does one expect from a science? Such a question seems to bring to many minds the more dramatic technological end products which result from the application of the discoveries of science. It will serve our purposes better to look into the hard work of the production of knowledge and inquire into the attributes this work must have in order to qualify as science. A rough consensus of expressions on this subject indicates the attributes an activity must have (or must aim for) in order to qualify should include *verifiability, generality,* and *system.*

Verifiability means here that the results of one investigator are stated in such a way that other investigators can check them by repeating the original work. By explicitly exhibiting the reasoning and observations that tend to confirm a result, scientists try to get away from purely personal opinion and experiences which cannot be shared with others. The words *intersubjective testability* and *objectivity* express the desired goal. This is usually difficult to achieve and the necessity of insisting on it creates the impression the pace of science is plodding when compared to the leaps made by hasty speculation.

Generality simply means the statements a science produces try to say things about the largest possible class of events. The more situations to which knowledge is believed to apply, the better. Psychology would like to say things about people in general and management science would like to say things about management in general. The generality of a statement can be crudely gauged by the number of "if's" or conditions associated with it. Newton's Laws are presented without many conditional reservations but if one wishes to assert, "Managers limit investment to that which can be financed from internally available capital," then a great number of conditions are probably necessary to indicate those situations in which the statement will be confirmed. The work of science often consists of trying to remove the conditions, assumptions, or limitations that confine the class of events to which a statement refers. Generalization means increasing the size of the reference class of a statement.

A mere collection of facts is not admissible as science since it does not exhibit system. The facts must be connected with one another by relations; the relations, in turn, must be connected with one another; and so on. The statements with which science works must be connected with reason. One may think of science as working toward a deductive system in which a rich variety of useful conclusions can be shown to be the consequences of reasoning from a few basic postulates. The telephone book is the well-worn example of a collection of facts which are verifiable but lack system. Presumably, systematization would require a few basic assumptions from which one could deduce the telephone number desired.

There is no use in asking whether or not management meets these qualifications. Everybody knows the answer. Nor does it help very much to raise the question of whether or not certain traditional techniques in time study and methods study are scientific, even though they have been loosely referred to as parts of "scientific management." These techniques received their impetus from people with a scientific turn of mind, but fell often into the hands of others inadequately trained in science. As we have seen, "scientific management" simply failed to attract the attention of a sufficient number of scientists.

The right question is whether science can produce a body of ideas which can develop toward these attributes and at the same time relieve the manager of some of his decision-making tasks so he may concentrate his own particular talents on others. The activity making notable headway in these directions is what we have chosen to call management science. In terms of the expectations set out above, it is an emerging science in the sense of demonstrating it can work toward the targets of verifiability, generality, and systematization. In this regard it is like political science, but unlike physics. Management science has indeed committed itself to the hard and painfully slow grubbing for knowledge which is required. It seems willing to resist the impatience which leads one to complete the work of science with overgeneralization.

The point of looking at the attributes of science is to suggest that nearly all of what is written and taught about how science does its work deals with verification. This is because much more is known about the process of verification than about the other things that must be done to produce a science. To know how to verify a statement is quite different from knowing how to produce an interesting and potentially verifiable statement in the first place. The work of verification is again quite different from the work of generalization and systematization.

It is easy for the student of science to satisfy himself prematurely that what goes on in science is something like the following:

1. A hypothesis is proposed.
2. The hypothesis is translated into mathematics and the manipulations of this mathematics produce an idea for an experiment or series of observations.
3. Recourse is made to the microscope, the stop watch, or the telescope to get "the data."
4. If the data confirm the hypothesis, it is named, published, and eventually finds its way into handbooks for application.

Another version of this recipe starts with a great mass of facts from which laws are somehow extracted.

This view of scientific proceedings is fostered by many introductions to the scientific method and by many scientists who present their work to their colleagues and their consumers (managers, in our case) as though this is the way it all happened. To those who may feel this "straw man" is somewhat overdrawn, the evidence of the graduate student trying to get started on his own work is submitted. Even after making some progress, one can almost sense that the young investigator, to whom it did not happen this way, has some doubts as to whether or not he has really done a scientific piece of work. The important insight here is that the scientific method is a method of verification and not of discovery.

Perhaps the most basic clue to what goes on in scientific work and thus to the short-run limitations of science is this distinction between verification, which is a logical process, and discovery, which is a psychological process. Einstein said, "There is no logical way to the discovery of these elemental laws. There is only the way of intuition, which is helped by a feeling of order lying behind their appearance."[1] We know enough about the logic of verification to make it a dominant part of a scientific education. Indeed, the formal part of what a scientific education tries to do is to report what has already been discovered so that the student will not trouble to dis-

---

[1] Quoted in W. I. B. Beveridge, *The Art of Scientific Investigation* (New York: Random House, 1957), p. 77.

cover it again, and provide training in the design, conduct, and analysis of experiments just in case anything else should be discovered and require verification. Thinking creatively can be exemplified, encouraged, and rewarded, but, however important, it remains largely outside the formal process of education.

The ways in which important discoveries have been made as described by the discoverers themselves have been examined for clues to the nature of the process. The role of chance has been emphasized by Beveridge in his very useful discussion of *The Art of Scientific Investigation*.[2] The discovery of penicillin is a familiar story of this sort. Fleming, working it seems in an old building with considerable dust in the air, was troubled by the accidental contamination of some of his bacteria cultures. This much indeed was chance, but taking notice of such an event and going on to find penicillin is something else again.

Jacques Hadamard has explored the reports of some of the great mathematical discoveries, looking for patterns of behavior. One such tentative generalization may be turned into the following advice.[3] Work very hard on a problem until no further progress appears possible. Then drop the problem and work on something else. After an extended interval, perhaps several months, return to the original problem. The solution may be then found in a relatively short time. Clearly, we are dealing here with what must surely be among the highest of "the higher mental processes." Explanations seem necessarily to ascribe a significant role to the subconscious. One theme, however, is common to most of the anecdotes of discovery and can be called a necessary but not a sufficient condition for achieving insight. This is the prepared mind and the intelligent opportunism which can make the most of an "accidental" observation or a chance association of ideas.

Dr. Otto Loewi, a Nobel Prize winner in 1936, has described how he demonstrated the chemical theory of the transmission of nervous impulse.[4] The original hypothesis occurred to him during a conversation in 1903. Seventeen years later he awoke one night and scribbled some notes on a piece of paper. The bedside pad and pencil are not uncommon among men deeply committed to creative work. The following night the ideas returned to him again. This

---

[2] *Ibid.*, chap. 3.

[3] Jacques Hadamard, *The Psychology of Invention in the Mathematical Field* (Princeton: Princeton University Press, 1945).

[4] "The Night Prowler of Nobel's Laurels," *Saturday Review*, Oct. 15, 1959.

time he realized he had discovered a simple experiment that could test his original hunch. He went immediately to his laboratory and did the experiment which became the foundation of the chemical theory of what, to that time, had been taken to be an electrical phenomenon. Years later he realized that apparently he unconsciously associated his original idea with an experimental technique he had used on other work some two years before the nights in question.

Incidents of this kind are intended to reveal how little one could be taught about how to discover knowledge.[5] Management presents much the same picture if one inquires how much of the skill of the really successful top manager could be taught to anyone else. It is perfectly true that progress in any science does not consist exclusively of important insights like that above. It is essential that a huge amount of hard work go on, without "flashy" results, to fill gaps and provide the groundwork for major advances. So important is this kind of work that it has been realized in recent years that one possible strategy for speeding up progress in a science is to put teams of men to work on problems. This has had its impact on management science and in the years immediately after World War II there was considerable emphasis on the interdisciplinary research team.

The arguments for and against such group research have been more suppressed than resolved. However, two hypotheses may find some support in this connection. Groups of people do not have a collective mind which can achieve insights. Thinking is done in individual minds and individual minds may or may not be stimulated by their interaction in groups. The "team" notion is somehow related to a method of operation in which a quarterback calls a play and every lineman fulfills his blocking assignment while some backfield hero carries the ball. It would seem that for at least some members of a research group the work can be little more than a job; the depth of commitment which seems to characterize really great discoverers is unlikely.

All this points to the basic fact that it is difficult to produce scientific discoveries on a schedule. This is of some consequence in management science since the manager who wishes scientific advice on policy matters yields often to the pressure of affairs. If advice is

---

[5] See also Brewster Ghiselin (ed.), *The Creative Process* (Berkeley: University of California Press, 1952).

available it may be used when the decision is made, but if the advice is not available the decision will in all likelihood be made without it. Verification, carried on according to a rigid set of rules, can often be conducted according to a rather precise time schedule. The discovery of fruitful hypotheses is much more difficult to plan.

Some will argue that these kinds of conclusions refer only to "basic" research carried on outside of the context of an actual management decision problem. Indeed, one involved in a real problem is dealing in "engineering" and not research. This study hopes to show that the present situation in management science makes the work which must be done a great deal more like research in the ordinary sense than engineering in its more routine phases. It will be argued as well that actual management problems can be usefully worked on without the need for great, fundamental discoveries. Indeed, much of the highly successful work has been of a fairly routine nature. First, one should be cautious in labeling routine work as such, for most difficult things, after they are done and done well, have a routine appearance. Secondly, this involves choices on the part of the scientist. Should he make do with a hypothesis already in hand or should he hold out for the discovery of a better one? In action-oriented research such as management science the context of affairs in which the work is done may be a dominant consideration in such choices, while in research not immediately action oriented the scientist himself may consider personal values more heavily. Here is a source of difficulties which requires a closer examination.

Chapter 5:

TOUGHMINDEDNESS

"In general, what we mean by any concept is nothing more than a set of operations; the concept is synonymous with the corresponding set of operations."

—P. W. BRIDGMAN in
The Logic of Modern Physics

A prominent manager with a considerable gift for scholarship chose to pass on some of his experience in the following terms: "The fine art of executive decision consists in not deciding questions that are not now pertinent, in not deciding prematurely, in not making decisions that cannot be made effective, and in not making decisions that others should make." This is from Chester I. Barnard's classic, *The Functions of the Executive.*[1] However much we may appreciate this man's attainments as an executive (which included the presidencies of the New Jersy Bell Telephone Company and the Rockefeller Foundation), and however much we may respect his intentions in writing of his reflections, we are entitled to ask what use can be made of this statement. That is, how can it be pressed into service as a guide for other executives?

One sort of answer is that such statements are inspirational and subjective. They are to be interpreted by each reader in his own way and applied to his own problems as he sees fit. This admits the possibility of assigning an endless collection of different meanings to the remark. It also means that in any particular instance of executive decision the question of whether or not the decision was, say, made prematurely may be answered differently by different observers. More basically, little can be said to the executive who asserts the statement is false since it is not clear what is promised to those who practice the "fine art." It is difficult to think of the circumstances in which it could be put to the test of use in practical affairs to yield some results which would attest to its truth or falsity. The possibili-

---

[1] Chester I. Barnard, *The Functions of the Executive* (Cambridge, Mass.: Harvard University Press, 1958), p. 194.

ties of teaching men to become executives using a curriculum of such statements are similarly limited, although this should not be taken to imply any better sorts of statements are necessarily currently available for this express purpose. In short, we could make many meanings for this statement but there is no way we can tell which of them, if any, was the author's meaning.

This unprovoked attack on Mr. Barnard must be conditioned in two important ways. First, the statement is intended only as a sample from a rather extensive body of literature on management, much of it written by people with considerably less impressive credentials as managers. Second, these are the sorts of questions likely to be raised by people attempting to go at management scientifically, and there is no reason to expect managers, men of great accomplishment in action, suddenly to produce scientific statements when they write about their work. Theirs is not the task of building management science.

A philosopher of science might regard the statement somewhat as follows. (Scientists to whom these things are largely taken for granted would be unlikely to verbalize in this particular way.) Perhaps the statement is intended to be a definition of the concept "the fine art of executive decision." It is an analytic statement. Science, however, must insist that definitions relate concepts to experience and in an objective fashion. The way this is done is to specify (or at least imply) the operations to be performed in order to bring the concept within the range of one's experience. Furthermore, the operations indicated must be intersubjective, meaning competent observers can all carry them out with approximately the same results. The classic example is the concept of length. To define length science begins by putting the term in a context such as the sentence, "The length of this table is 60 inches." The definition specifies the operations of placing a measuring tape along the table so that one of its ends rests on an end of the table and so on. If the other end of the table is observed to be next to the 60-inch mark of the tape, then we can assert the truth of the sentence. Admittedly, to specify this measuring process completely so that there would be no chance of a different observation would be a dull and probably impossibly long task. This notion of definition, like most other ideas, can be pressed to the ridiculous. Specifying the conditions under which the operations would have to be carried out should not be regarded as entirely trivial, though, since this sort of thinking was set in motion by Bridgman under the stimulus of Einstein's theories of relativity.[2] Einstein, after all, showed that the length of the table depended upon its velocity.

The point is, however, that one can make important strides in associating concepts with experience in an objective fashion by using Bridgman's scheme to produce what are called *operational definitions*. This tendency to look for operational definitions is what we might call toughmindedness. The toughminded person is likely to experience considerable difficulty in constructing useful and widely acceptable operational definitions of the terms "pertinent," "premature," and "effective," to say nothing of the concept of who should make what decision.[3]

A second but related view a philosopher of science might take of Barnard's remark is that it seems to imply that if one does the things indicated something good will happen or things will turn out "fine." Looked at in this way, the statement is a prediction of the form: "If an executive does A, then the result will be B." This views it as a synthetic statement. We have already examined the difficulties associated with the meaning of A, and clearly if some B is implied it is so vague that we could never objectively do the experiment (carry out the operations) which would permit us to assert the truth or falsity of the prediction. Since the main business of science is indeed to predict, this cannot be a very important statement in science. Another classical statement which exhibits this difficulty is the "law" which says: "No person should supervise more than five, or at the most six, direct subordinates whose work interlocks." Aside from the difficulties of obtaining operational definitions for the terms, the law does not predict what will happen if it is not "obeyed" and thus we can hardly tell in application whether it is true or false.

Now suppose one looks at a simple policy statement from a scientific point of view. "The best inventory position to maintain in commodity X is ninety days' sales." This sentence may be viewed as a prediction that if a certain inventory position is maintained things will turn out to be better, in some sense, than they would with any other inventory position. The question of interest is whether

---

[2] P. W. Bridgman, *The Logic of Modern Physics* (New York: Macmillan Co., 1928).

[3] See also Philipp G. Frank (ed.), *The Validation of Scientific Theories* (Boston: The Beacon Press, 1954); James G. March and Herbert A. Simon, *Organizations* (New York: John Wiley & Sons, Inc., 1958), p. 30; Henry K. Mehlberg, *The Reach of Science* (Toronto, Ont.: University of Toronto Press, 1958); and Anatol Rapoport, *Operational Philosophy* (New York: Harper & Bros., 1953).

or not the sentence can be interpreted in a set of operations (an experiment) which would cast some light on the truth or falsity of the prediction.

First would come the necessity of making the terms in the sentence operational. Perhaps we might define inventory position in commodity X as the number of units of this commodity in the warehouse less the number for which orders have already been received. It seems clear that the operations of counting units in the warehouse (a physical operation) and adding up the number of units indicated on the orders received (a mental operation) could be specified to a degree sufficient to lead to interpersonal agreement as to the result. Likewise, operations could be worked out for the concept "ninety days' sales" which would involve, among other things, specifying whether one was to take the sales over the last ninety business days, over the last three calendar months, or averaged over some representative period. Greater difficulty may arise when we tackle the concept "best." Typically this might mean the events predicted are represented by the costs associated with them. In particular, we might be interested in predicting the cost per unit time of being unable to fill orders as they are received. Usually the first of these costs is considerably easier to make operational than the second. The cost of not filling an order as it is received may involve loss of customer good will or damage to a reputation for good service. These concepts present exceedingly difficult problems of definition in terms of clear and objective operations. Such is the importance of precisely this kind of definition that it forms a major limitation on the work of management science. This question will be taken up at some length in Chapter 10.

Suppose one agreed that the orders not filled upon receipt are withdrawn by the customers and placed with a competitor. The business is thus lost and the cost of this may be made operational by computing the profit thus foregone. If one limits the definition to this aspect alone the original prediction presumably has been brought to the point where it can be confronted with the facts and its truth confirmed or denied. It should be emphasized that this confrontation is conceivable, but whether or not it will actually take place is quite another question. Much of what is interesting in management science consists of finding economical ways in which to make such a confrontation. At the moment it is only suggested that the original prediction seems to have some chance of surviving the ordeal of toughmindedness.

In what appears, perhaps, to be an unseemly haste to show the inventory policy statement might be made operational, at least two fundamental points have slipped by. First, it may well be that in making the concept of cost operational a part of the phenomenon has been left out of the prediction. Suppose the management of the firm hypothesizes that the consequences of being unable to fill an order on receipt include both the immediate loss of the order and the future loss of some orders from present and potential customers. It has been suggested that the latter consequence might present insurmountable difficulties of cost measurement and thus may simply have been left out of the prediction. (Admittedly, one could conceive of situations in which this could be made operational.) Thus there turns out to be a difference between what can be made operational and what we or management may take to be the nature of the phenomenon. This is hardly surprising, but more will be said about how management science attempts to contend with so fundamental a limitation.

The second point is that if one actually goes on to confront the prediction with facts, one hardly expects it will be confirmed under any and all conceivable circumstances (assuming it is confirmed at all). Indeed we might have in mind all sorts of happenings we would expect to upset the prediction. One custom is to string along with the prediction, a proviso known in the trade as the *ceteris paribus* assumption: all other things being equal, if everything else remains constant, or as long as nothing happens except those events implied in the "if" of the "If . . . , then . . . ." prediction statement. Now this is not too helpful when we go on to test the prediction against the facts. Clearly, not *everything* has to be equal, for neither could we make this condition operational nor do we really expect that there are consequences for our prediction in every other event. What we really mean is that we suspect certain things could upset our prediction and we want to learn the truth or falsity of the prediction given these particular things do not happen. It follows that objectivity will require operational definitions of these conditions to be controlled. Without this precaution there will be no end of arguments to the effect that the prediction was "really true" but failed because of some uncontrolled condition. Now all this is simple enough to call for but uncommonly difficult to attain in many cases. This is another point which will be examined later.

Toughmindedness, then, is the tendency to turn all statements into predictions and to look for the operations to be carried out and the results to be experienced in order to confirm or disaffirm the prediction. It is sometimes insisted the operations must be manipulative, that is, deliberately carried out by the observer. This is not at all the case. All that matters is that the required events occur; the observer is not responsible for their occurrence. Management science shares with astronomy and economics something less than the laboratory scientist's opportunity to manipulate the materials of his discipline.

Nothing about operationism or about science generally requires *all* concepts be operationally definable. Indeed, quite the opposite is true, for many concepts not operationally defined are employed because they lead, in various ways, to the discovery of fruitful hypotheses which can be made operational. In much of the thinking done by scientists considerable vagueness of ideas and freedom from anything like strict operationality are present. This thinking is, however, carried on because it is a useful way to arrive at operational hypotheses. Thus, for a concept to be interesting it may itself be operational or it may be a possible source of operational concepts.

In looking at the conventional management literature, one may be tempted to soften one's opinion of it on the supposition that, while it lacks operationality, it is suggestive of useful hypotheses which could be made operational. The criticism is, however, that in most cases no particular effort was made in the literature to move in the direction of operationality. Thus, the assertions can have no objective, verifiable basis in fact and many people remained undisturbed by this.

All this has been verified by the puzzlement of students who read this literature, the supposition that when they became managers it would all have meaning, and the general neglect of it by managers who usually referred to it as "theory." Theory in this sense means abstract and meaningless.

Given a basic understanding of the implications, managers might find these ideas (operationism) to a considerable extent compatible with their general view of the conduct of affairs. They imply:

1. Action.
2. Precise meaning to "getting the facts."
3. Elimination of vague, untried, irrelevant, "theory" in the sense managers often use the term.
4. No-nonsense views of the discussion of policies and management problems.

One can hardly fail to notice that the prediction of the inventory-policy statement is somehow at a lower level of importance in the purview of the manager than the Barnard quotation on the fine art of executive decision. This difference is not entirely accidental and lies at the root of the idea that the "grand questions" of management cannot (yet, at least) be examined scientifically. Certainly the two statements differ in generality; one referred to a single decision and the other (presumably) to all executive decisions. They differ also in complexity in the important sense of the complications involved in the task of making the concepts operational. Clearly, this task is somewhat simpler for the concept of "inventory position" than it is for, say, the pertinence of a decision. In this way, toughmindedness limits, often severely, the level of generality and the level of complexity at which the phenomenon may be examined. While saying nothing at present about future possibilities for management science, it is clear there will often be a difference between the amount of reality which can be brought within the domain of science and that part of reality with which a manager must deal in the conduct of business affairs.

All this might be suffered if the ideas, however vague, we have about management showed some kind of agreement. Often they do not. To mention but one example, it appears rather widely accepted that when responsibilities are delegated in an organization considerable care must be taken to assure the assignment of these duties is clearly defined and is not violated, either through infringement or neglect. Most writers on the subject say something like this. On the other hand, William B. Given, another prominent and thoughtful executive, has written a book the essence of which is contained in the remark: "Success for you and the company requires your gambling with the dangers inherent both in pushing your own boss for more freedom and in reaching out into other bosses' departments."[4] Reportedly President Franklin Roosevelt deliberately failed to define clearly the apportionment of responsibilities among the agencies of his administration. This had the useful effect of causing conflicts which could only be resolved by the President himself, thus assuring he remained rather well informed as to what was going on.[5]

The notion of making concepts operational plays another role

---

[4] William B. Given, Jr., *Reaching Out in Management* (New York: Harper & Bros., 1953), p. 16.

[5] This and other aspects of Roosevelt's methods of administration and decision making are described in Arthur M. Schlesinger, *The Coming of the New Deal* (Boston: Houghton Mifflin Co., 1959), p. 528.

in management which is suggested by the greater influence goals, objectives, or performance criteria that can be made operational have over those that cannot. It is generally agreed that a desirable feature of an incentive system is that the relation between performance and reward be as objective as possible in this sense. On the other hand, if some goals are operational and some are not, the operational ones tend to become most influential in the processes of decision making. One example is the division manager who was judged in part by return on investment. The operations associated with this concept were clear to him and it was immediately obvious that the ratio could be increased by decreasing investment as well as by increasing return. As a result he sold some equipment not immediately useful and thus reduced the investment in a situation where the future need for this equipment indicated it might better have been held. This concept appears in the work of Selznick and Haberstroh.[6]

Now, the notion of operationalizing a concept requires some instructions for connecting the concept with experience and, secondly, that all competent observers give approximately the same report of this experience. Now it must also seem reasonable that the greater the clarity and explicitness of the operations the more nearly alike the reports of observers will be. In other words, operationality and thus objectivity are a matter of degree. Any effort to define a sharp line separating objective from nonobjective concepts is likely to prove somewhat fruitless. Unfortunately, however, just such questions have at times plagued attempts to bring more objectivity into management. Many of these difficulties have arisen in the struggle to make operational the concept of a "fair day's work" in the well-known and universally professed dictum, "A fair day's pay for a fair day's work." The time-study approach to this concept encountered the difficulty of operationalizing the concept of "normal effort" or "normal pace" in the performance of a task. Subsequently, the term "fatigue" also entered the problem. These ideas may help to illustrate something of the problem which arises here.

Let us begin with a concept widely considered safely in the operational camp—length, in the particular instance of the diameter of a metal cylinder. Assuming the cylinder in question is of the

---

[6] Philip Selznick, *Leadership in Administration* (Evanston, Ill.: Row, Peterson & Co., 1957); Chadwick J. Haberstroh, "Control as an Administrative Process," *Management Science*, Vol. 6, No. 2 (1960); and Chadwick J. Haberstroh, "Administration of Safety in the Steel Industry," *Management Science*, Vol. 7, No. 4 (1961).

order of three quarters of an inch in diameter, the operation understood to relate this concept to experience would be the reading of a
micrometer. Experienced machinists will have no trouble with either
the operation or the result. The "tendency" of the machine operator
to assert the diameter lies within tolerance limits and the "tendency"
of the inspector to assert that it does not can be quickly resolved to
everyone's satisfaction, that is, objectively. (We assume a great deal
about agreement in calibration of micrometers, measurements taken
at the same position on the cylinder, and so on.) It is instructive to
reflect on a familiar and highly revealing experiment which has been
repeated often. A group of students, largely lacking in machine-shop
experience, are given verbal instructions and an accompanying
demonstration in the use of the micrometer. When the students then
independently measure the diameter of a given cylinder their results
usually show rather considerable variation. The variation is almost
certain to be of such magnitude that the usual machine-shop practice would not regard the situation as one of "substantial agreement
among observers." The response to this experiment is to say, in part,
that the operation in question cannot be made entirely explicit and
the student must practice on a gauge block of known dimensions
until his readings consistently confirm these dimensions. The student must thus learn the feel of the instrument since, among other
things, the reading varies with the amount of torque exerted by the
fingers on the thimble. Admittedly this can be obviated by equipping
the micrometer with a ratchet device which standardizes the torque,
by bringing into play instruments to measure the torque, or by using
measuring instruments other than the micrometer. The point is that
the need and, indeed, the use of these other means arise out of
difficulties with making the concept operational. The fact is that
soon the student does get the feel of the micrometer and there is
no further need to worry about it. The concept can be taken as
operational in that it provides an objective basis for action in the
shop. It remains true that if some itinerant philosopher wants to
make something of it we would have to admit the notion of diameter
was not "completely" objectified. We would also point out to him
it was sufficiently objective so that we could make the necessary
decisions which follow from this measurement with interpersonal
agreement as to the diameter of any particular cylinder.

To spin this tale out but a little more, we might consider a
further experiment to get at the nature of this "variability" the

beginning students exhibit. Suppose we got each student to make several independent measurements of the diameter. Appropriate experimental methods must be used to keep the student from the realization that he is making a series of measurements on the same cylinder, thus roughly producing independence among the readings. We would normally find a given student exhibits considerable variation among his own readings. This might be given the name "intrapersonal reliability." It might be measured by computing some function of the variation of the student's observations around the average of his observations.

If data from this experiment are collected over several students, the fact that students differ among themselves will give variability in the results additional to that produced by lack of intrapersonal reliability. The first would be referred to statistically as variation among students, while the second is spoken of as variation within students. Statistical techniques make it possible to conduct an experiment involving several cylinders and to separate the variability which can reasonably be called within students from that which might be attributed to differences among students.

The question of whether all this variability could be eliminated is not especially important here, because it is well understood that enough of it could be gotten rid of so that the observations can be viewed as objective in terms of the use to be made of them. That is, enough interpersonal agreement can be obtained on the concept of diameter so as to regard it as objective from the viewpoint of the decisions which must be based upon it. These decisions often have to do with the acceptability of the cylinder relative to some tolerance limits, which in turn depend on the functional application of the item.

To draw a contrast, consider the concept of rating the effort or pace of an operator in performing a production task. The rating process is supposed to produce a relation between the observed performance and some concept of normal performance. The specification of operations generally suggest the observer should make a judgment as to what percentage of normal pace he is observing. Problems arise both in making the concept of "normal" operational and in specifying further the operations by which this comparison is to be made. One scheme sometimes used is to show the observers a film which is stipulated as portraying normal pace on some particular task, say task A. This occupies the position of the gauge block in the micrometer problem. The observers then make judgments, without further explicit instructions, of the level of effort for other films of task *A* and for films of other tasks. They practice, with knowledge of results, until a satisfactory amount of intrapersonal reliability and interpersonal objectivity are obtained.

Now the parallels between these two processes are clear. The first is widely accepted as objective, while the second has been the subject of extensive disagreement as to "whether or not it is scientific." We wish to argue that the differences are in degree and not in principle. In particular, it is suggested that:

1. Objectivity is not a matter of trivial agreement in either case since factors which might lead to bias may be present. Relations between operator and inspector, or producer and consumer in the first case and labor and management in the second, are illustrative.

2. The initial lack of objectivity is attacked in each case by the process of "calibrating" observers. In the second case, the complexity and the diversity of the phenomena upon which the operations are to be performed are vastly greater. This is a feature often encountered in management science and again confronts one with a difference in degree but not in principle.

3. In each case we can get some idea of the degree to which the concepts are imperfectly operational by using statistical measures of variability. Just where along this continuum "science" stops is pointless speculation. Toughmindedness is the attitude of working for a reduction of this variability by explaining phenomena in terms of concepts increasingly operational. The extent to which this program ought to be pressed in the short run can only be discussed in terms of the decision-making uses of the observations. This will shortly be explored.

4. As a practical matter, eventually both concepts can be made sufficiently operational so that in most cases the decisions as to what action is to be based upon the observations can be made with interested observers stipulating as to the observations. The observations are thus removed from the areas of concern or doubt arising out of possible bias. Admittedly, disagreements are more frequent in the rating of a performance than in the measurement of a diameter. (It is interesting to note in passing that people's interests are not always good predictors of their observational biases. Union observers sometimes rate performance lower than company observers.)

Questions of the general nature of the time-study rating come up in various contexts, such as job evaluation, merit rating, and credit rating, where judgments must be made which stem from the inability to make concepts sufficiently operational. However, the presence of such judgments is well known in literally all management decisions and the only question is one of degree. The toughmindedness of management science denotes not so much where it is but the direction in which it is moving. Its program may be characterized as the progressive operationalizing or rationalizing of management decisions.

An interesting and obvious solution to the problems suggested here will be mentioned briefly now (we will return later for a more detailed look). Suppose, to pick up the time-study example again, we define "the level of effort being exerted in the performance of a particular operator on a given task" to be "the answer you get when you ask observer x." We would want to make all sorts of provisions as to the qualifications of observer x, such as: he must be an engineer trained in time study and employed under a contract clause calling for an independent arbitrator to settle certain disputes. This definition is operational to a degree which gets around many of the problems we have noted. To a scientist, this sounds a little like side-stepping the issue. He would feel an urge to study observer x and make explicit the process x uses. He would also want to think up experiments to test the reliability of x and look around for other observers to compare with x. Managers prevented by the pressure of affairs from pursuing such inclinations often find the sort of objectivity they require in this scheme. The philosophical case for observer x has been made by Helmer and Rescher.[7]

Lord Kelvin's famous remark that if it can't be measured it isn't science may perhaps evoke too narrow an idea of the possibilities for measurement among those not familiar with the social sciences.[8] This idea is expressed in the notion of exactness. Exactness is the result of progressive refinements in measuring instruments so as to permit increasingly fine distinctions between events. The implication, of course, is that these distinctions are operational. Students of science are impressed with the exactness of a balance which can detect the difference in weight of a scrap of paper before and after a name has been written on it. This exactness has been vital to modern physics because many effects studied could not be discerned without it. To take but one example, the famous Michelson-Morley experiment performed in 1881 was able to demolish the concept of "the ether" by measuring the velocity of light with great exactness.

---

[7] Olaf Helmer and Nicholas Rescher, "On the Epistemology of the Inexact Sciences," *Management Science*, Vol. 6, No. 1 (1959).

[8] In this connection, see Poul Anderson, "How Social is Science?" *Saturday Review*, April 27, 1957; R. J. Chambers, "Measurement and Misrepresentation," *Management Science*, Vol. 6, No. 2 (1960); Russell Kirk, "Is Social Science Scientific?" *New York Times*, June 25, 1961; Vernon Van Dyke, *Political Science: A Philosophical Analysis* (Stanford, Calif.: Stanford University Press, 1960); and Ernest H. Weinwurm, "Limitations of the Scientific Method in Management Science," *Management Science*, Vol. 3, No. 3 (1957).

They required an apparatus which would detect differences of the order of 40 miles a second in a velocity which had been measured at 186,284 miles a second. (They found no such difference.)

The point at issue was neatly put in the remark that other sciences should try to do *what* physics does rather than *as* physics does. That is, objectivity but not necessarily exactness are worth working for, and certainly not exactness if the price is too great a sacrifice in scope. A slavish devotion to exact measurement may not be the key to scientific progress. The level of observation at which interesting differences appear in modern physics requires exactness of measurement. Interesting events can often be discerned in management science, as in psychology or economics, without comparable exactness.

A broader view of measurement suggests a hierarchy of measuring scales.[9] A scale is a device which provides the language in which observations are reported, as for example, the centigrade and Fahrenheit scales for reporting temperature observations. Sciences begin with taxonomy, the classification of events. Such a scheme for classification is sometimes called a nominal scale since it associates a name with an object or event. The establishment of categories is based at first on qualities or attributes which can be objectively discerned and which may indeed form concepts in interesting predictive statements. For example, we may classify people as union members or not union members, as line or staff, as policy makers or not policy makers, and these concepts may be sufficiently exact to enter into useful predictions. The chief shortcoming of such a rudimentary measuring scale is that it does not make available the well-developed reasoning processes of the familiar branches of mathematics.

Moving one step upward toward greater exactness one encounters ordinal measuring scales, or rankings. In making decisions we often wish to rank the alternative courses of action in terms of their desirability. Perhaps this can be done by measurements exact enough to allow the conclusion: "Action *A* will be more costly than action *B*." Now, a good deal of logical structure is available to per-

[9] Morris R. Cohen and Ernest Nagel, *An Introduction to Logic and the Scientific Method* (New York: Harcourt, Brace & Co., 1934); Norman Campbell, *What is Science?* (New York: Dover Publications Inc., 1952); and C. H. Coombs, H. Raiffa, and R. M. Thrall, "Mathematical Models and Measurement Theory" in R. M. Thrall, C. H. Coombs, and R. L. Davis (eds.), *Decision Processes* (New York: John Wiley & Sons, Inc., 1954).

mit reasoning with concepts so measured. For example, we may argue:

> If A is more costly than B, and
> if B is more costly than C, then
> it must be that A is more costly than C.

This sort of reasoning has turned out to be of considerable importance in the study of the preferences of decision makers. However, if we assign the number 1 to be the rank of A, the number 2 to B, and the number 3 to C, we cannot do anything useful in the way of deduction by adding or multiplying these numbers.

Next in exactness might be interval scales in which one is free to establish the zero point on the scale wherever he pleases and to adopt any unit of measurement he pleases. The only proviso is that the unit of measurement be constant everywhere along the scale. Again, the centigrade and Fahrenheit temperature scales provide the classical physical examples. Suppose, for example, we wish to use the concept of marginal cost of producing an additional 1,000 units of product. The unit of measurement chosen may be dollars and the zero point on the scale may be the level of expenditure at the current level of production, say, 10,000 units. Now, if some visitor wishes to know the total cost of 11,000 units of production in pounds sterling, we can convert the measurement to his scale by changing the zero point (adding a constant) and changing the unit of measurement (multiplying by a constant). Notice that some care must be taken in the way one reasons with the resulting numbers. If the marginal cost of 2,000 units is 2.4 times the marginal cost of 1,000 units, it does not follow that the total cost of 12,000 units is 2.4 times the total cost of 11,000 units. Less obviously, if the marginal cost of 1,000 units is x, it is not necessarily true that the marginal cost of 2,000 units is $2x$. Although it is obvious that if the marginal cost of 2,000 units is y, we can say that $x + (y - x) = y$. We may summarize the reasoning possibilities open to us by saying that all arithmetic operations are possible on differences between pairs of numbers on an interval scale.

Finally, we come to what is called a ratio scale. It is not in principle more exact than an interval scale, but it has a constant although arbitrary unit of measurement and an absolute zero point. This happens when the concept involved suggests a natural and well-defined point which can be taken as a zero point. Weight, length, absolute temperature, and profit are examples of such scales.

All arithmetic operations may be performed on the resulting numbers.

Exactness certainly has its advantages in terms of identifying refined differences between experiences and in making available to one the well-developed logical structures of mathematics. If, however, one confines attention to exactly measurable concepts, many things of interest may be passed over. The classic Hawthorne studies may be partially interpreted in this light. As long as one focused on concepts such as "level of illumination" and "production rate," one had considerable difficulty in explaining why production went up if the level of illumination was increased and also went up if it decreased. Another concept, perhaps called "employee attitudes," had to be brought into play. Attitudes cannot be measured exactly in any broadly objective fashion, although great progress has been made. We might, however, make some progress with a crude prediction such as, "The greater the sense of responsibility, of belonging to a group, and of job importance, the greater the production." Still another result of this study was that the exact rate of pay was far less a determiner of employee satisfaction than the (ordinal) relation among rates of pay. Again a less exact but objective measure proved the more useful.

An important frontier in management science lies just beyond the traditional use of profit as a representation of managerial objectives in the scientific study of decision making. The current efforts to go beyond this concept into the consideration of other objectives which cannot presently be measured with anything like the exactness of profit would appear to promise considerably more useful insights than any insistence on exactness would have permitted.

A large number of the predictive statements of interest in the everyday work of management science contain the term "probability." For example, "If an inventory level of x units is provided at the beginning of the month, the probability of a stockout during a month is y." One view of this statement is that here the work of science is unfinished. At best it can only be accepted as an interim remark until knowledge can be brought to the point of asserting, "If an inventory level of x units is provided, there will (or will not) be a stockout in January." This view, related to a deterministic notion of the physical world, has been widely discarded since physics has come to accept the notion that the term probability can never be eliminated from some of its predictions. In management science the question of whether the probabilistic nature of the statement is ultimately unavoidable is suppressed. Practical considerations such as the cost both in resources and in time make it necessary to proceed with such statements as a basis for action since they must be regarded as the best evidence obtainable.

The word probability holds such vagueness in its conversational use that it cannot be said to be operational in any obvious sense. One often hears such remarks as, "The board does not try to pin down the future to certainties. We work out our decisions in terms of probabilities—then we adjust the details as they develop." This remark is attributed to Harmon Whittington of Anderson, Clayton, and the following one to Edward Willkie, president of Pacific American Fisheries, Inc. "Very few things are black and white; mostly they are grey. I don't consider decisions certainties ever. But certainly I consider them good probabilities."[10] Indeed, there is considerable discussion among all sorts of decision makers of "running the calculated risk," without any real intention of *calculating* the risk.

The task of producing useful operational definitions of probability is by no means simple, as Chapter 16 will show at some length. However, as a practical matter it can in many contexts be made suitably operational. To anticipate the kind of trouble ahead, suppose we define the probability of heads when a coin is flipped as the limit approached by the ratio of heads observed to total flips as the total number of flips is increased indefinitely. If we assert the probability of heads is one half for a certain coin, we cannot actually carry out the operations which will confirm or deny this statement. None of us will be around long enough to carry out the required indefinite repetition of the coin flipping. Practically, we content ourselves with a tentative confirmation based on something less than an infinite number of replications. This particular operational definition is, however, something less than universally applauded as useful. If one's life depended on predicting the outcome of a single flip of a coin, probability thus defined does not appear relevant to the decision.

The attitude of toughmindedness has been much analyzed by philosophers of science in their search for understanding of truth, meaning, and knowledge. While we can suppress many of their studies of the most fundamental questions of all in favor of our interest in action, the growing self-consciousness of management

---

[10] These quotations are from the editors of *Fortune, The Executive Life* (Garden City, N.Y.: Dolphin Books, 1956).

science calls for a brief pause. Under various names, such as logical positivism or logical empiricism, philosophical positions have been developed which converge upon a principle of verifiability or the verifiability theory of meaning.

Very roughly, the principle is based on the notion statements can have two kinds of meaning. Some statements are logically meaningful—analytic truths they have been called—but these do not add to our knowledge. The more interesting kinds of statements are synthetic statements which can, at least in principle, be verified by observation. These statements provide us with the facts, and there are no facts that do not originate in experience. The toughest form of toughmindedness asserted statements not immediately verifiable in experience were meaningless. This proved far too restrictive because it did away with concepts which were not in themselves verifiable but were productive of reasoning which led to verifiable statements.

Eventually a more liberal position emerged which freed theorizing in science of all restrictions save only that it must ultimately produce statements which may be verified through experiment. Scientific concepts must ultimately be rooted in experience but the conceptual freedom necessary for the production of really fruitful ideas is assured. This kind of utilization of what some have called the "metaphysical impurities of science" plays an important role in the lengthening grasp of management science. The vital obligation, however, to link concept with experience so as to make possible the verification of predictions bears some repeating. It seems to have a way of succumbing to a series of well-intentioned postponements.

There is, after all, a perfectly reasonable tendency for a division of labor in the work of science. Those who are skilled theory builders should by all means build the theories. The fact they are incensed when accused of producing sterile speculations which lack operationality is an indication of their tendency to postpone this step or leave it to the experimentalists. These latter specialists are skilled in the design and analysis of experiments, and they should indeed test the theories. Their occasional tendency to amass data which have no theoretical structure waiting is another postponement. After all, one must get some facts before constructing one's theories of them. This may, however, provoke a charge of "blind empiricism."

This toughminded attitude of science, this insistence on making concepts operational, is the means by which it tries to safeguard its objectivity. It is precisely this objectivity, the independence of its

finding from the judgment of one particular person, that distinguishes science from intuition. Some have felt that science, if it
limits itself to the operational and the measurable aspects of management, can never become a really significant influence in management. These limitations it places on itself are thought to relegate
science forever to the trivial, the unimportant, the "puzzles," and
the set-piece decisions in management.[11] The big, important, and
complicated decisions will always remain in the realm of intuition.
Few people suppose science will replace managers, but on the other
hand it is well known to be highly dangerous to assert that science
will never make progress in some particular direction. Time will
reveal how far management science can go and there is little reason
to suppose toughmindedness will raise an ultimate barrier.

---

[11] Some problems can best be treated quantitatively, but others may indeed
be more hindered than helped through quantification. See W. C. Krumbein, "The
Computer in Geology," *Science,* Vol. 136 (1962), pp. 1087–92; and Weinwurm,
op. cit.

Chapter 6:

MODELS

". . . To educe and form axioms from experience . . . to deduce and derive new experiments from axioms. . . . For our road does not lie on a level, but ascends and descends; first ascending to axioms, then descending to works."

—Francis Bacon

The preceding logical reconstruction of scientific work might suggest that, having made operational definitions of concepts, the next step is to hypothesize some relations between these concepts from which some verifiable predictions might be deduced. Insistence on operationality tends to insure the possibility that predictions can be examined experimentally and confirmed or denied by observation. Such a logical reconstruction reflects little of the way in which the work proceeds, but it does serve to show the position of relations between concepts. The statements of these relations will be called *models*.

By the broadest possible definition of the notion, a model is an attempt to impose a conceptual order on the perceptual confusion in which experience first comes to us. This book is particularly interested in models that can be and are communicated. Everybody works with schemes for organizing the data of experience, but these schemes must be made explicit, their vagueness reduced to the point where they can be written down and expressed in a language that allows one to talk about them and teach them. As has been suggested, it is not entirely necessary that all the concepts in a model be operational in a strict sense. It is necessary, however, that the model produce some predictions both verifiable and interesting in the context of a management decision.

It has also been noted that from a science we expect a systematizing of knowledge.[1] The role of models is to express the links of reason

---

[1] "System is no mere adornment of science, it is its very heart. To say this is not merely to assert that it is not the business of science to heap up unrelated, haphazard, disconnected bits of information, but to point out that it is an ideal of science to give an *organized* account of the universe—to fit together in logical relations the concepts and statements embodying whatever knowledge has been acquired. Such organiza-

which bind concepts into a system. For, as Sir James Jeans insisted, a heap of facts is no more science than a heap of bricks is a house. How are concepts related? What statements can be produced by means of deductive reasoning from other statements? Are two statements consistent with one another? Can both be logically true? These questions require a fabric of reasoning to bind together our operational concepts. Ultimately, one hopes a large part of our experience could be predicted by deduction from a relatively small number of basic postulates or assumptions. This is the "unity" and the systematization which define "knowing" and "understanding," as these words are used in relation to the goals of scientific study. The desire is to predict more by assuming less.

Various sorts of distinctions are made between models. One such classification identifies models as laws, theories, or hypotheses. This is sometimes taken to mean that they differ according to their degree or confirmation and acceptance. A new model, with little or no evidence to confirm it, is classed as a hypothesis. When some work has been done toward confirmation, the results seem promising, and people are actively engaged in the study of a model, it may be classed as a theory. When sufficient evidence toward confirmation has accumulated so that workers in the field are no longer actively interested in testing and developing a model, it is called a law. Such a set of distinctions is of limited use, largely because it is exceedingly vague and overburdened with contradictions.

Distinction making is further confused by the fact that how well confirmed and accepted a model apears to be is bound up with its generality or the extent of the reference class to which the model refers. This is especially the case in an emerging science. In management science one may ultimately hope for models general in the sense they hold not only for a particular management decision in a particular company but for large classes of decisions involving numbers of managers and companies.

Generality, in turn, is bound up with the exactness of the predictions made by the model. Keeping in mind that we are concerned with empirical or synthetic truth (analytic truth is taken for granted) and leaving aside the question of confirmation, consider the following example. Suppose a model predicts, "If policy A is adopted, sales will go up by x dollars next year." If we insert a number for x,

---

tion is, in fact, a necessary condition for the accomplishment of two of science's chief functions; explanation and prediction." Richard S. Rudner, "An Introduction to Simplicity," *Philosophy of Science*, Vol. 28, No. 2 (1961), p. 112.

then it is an exact prediction but would be expected to hold only for a given company. If the model is modified so that it predicts, "If policy A is adopted, sales will go up next year," then we might reasonably expect it to apply to a large class of companies. It has become less exact but more general. It is sometimes hoped this trade-off between exactness and generality is a temporary situation in the progress of management science. Whether or not this is the case will be clear only in the rather distant future.

Still another dimension might be associated with models: the level of observation or analysis at which the phenomenon is examined. For instance, if we are interested in human beings the levels of observation lead, say, from electrons, atoms, molecules, up to cells, tissues, and organs, and eventually to persons, groups of persons, and finally the human race. In management decision making the level of observation at which one must ultimately make predictions is governed to a large extent by the kinds of actions management feels it is able to take. If, for example, one is concerned with granting credit to customers, the firm with a relatively small number of customers can treat them as individuals in the matter of credit risk but the firm with a large number of customers must set down policies based on the characteristics of large groups of people. Again, the salesman has to make decisions about individual accounts but the sales manager may have to act with respect to whole classes of accounts. Thus, to some extent the management scientist is not free to choose his level of observation or units of ultimate analysis. These tend to be fixed for him by the nature of the action management contemplates. Although the ultimate level of observation or analysis is fixed, one has the opportunity of reaching this level by starting at lower levels of observation. For example, if we need a prediction of total annual sales for a company, we could start by predicting sales by product, or by customer, or by industry, or by month.

Level of observation aside, a number of hypotheses seem to characterize the situation in management science today. (Hypothesis here means a statement formally unconfirmed but advanced as plausible to the extent of being worth testing.) Suppose we take as a standard of comparison the elementary laws of motion in physics. Let us agree these models are exact, general, and widely confirmed and accepted (in other words, let's stick to situations in which we can claim exactness without getting involved in Einstein's theories.) Nothing comparable appears in management science at present.

First of all, nothing in management science is remotely comparable with the number of physical situations which have been studied. Most models in management science have been confined to one or a small number of instances.[2]

Further, no models appear likely candidates for wide confirmation without considerable sacrifice in terms of exactness and generality. If this should turn out to be true then it has at least two important consequences:

1. In any given management decision models will have to be developed and tested on the spot.

2. Work in management science is a great deal more like research than like engineering.

A note of interest here, which is related to lack of wide confirmation of exact and general models, is the absence (at least to the present time) of constants in management science. When one studies physics one learns numbers such as the acceleration due to gravity, the charge on an electron, and the speed of light. These numbers are really widely confirmed and accepted predictions which are extremely general and highly exact. Nothing yet in management science corresponds to this.[3]

One way to approach an understanding of this is to arrange a hierarchy of ways in which the question, "What will be the sales of this company next year?" might be answered.

1. Looking into the body of knowledge which constitutes the science we might find a model which predicted, "Sales of this company will be $5,000,000 next year." This is the type of prediction called a constant, such as the speed of light.

2. At the next level, a model might say, "Measure two variables, x_1 and x_2. Substitute them in the relation

$$y = a + bx_1 + cx_2$$

The value of y is the desired sales prediction." This corresponds to a model such as

$$\text{force} = (\text{mass})(\text{acceleration})$$

To predict acceleration, just measure force and mass and use the relationship given.

3. At the next level, a model might suggest, "Sales depends on two quantities x_1 and x_2. First you must establish the relationship between sales and these quantities, then measure the two variables and substitute into the relation you have found." This kind of model is widely employed in management science.

---

[2] William H. Starbuck, "Testing Case Descriptive Models," *Behavioral Science*, Vol. 6, No. 1 (1961).

[3] Beginnings are being made, however. See, for example, Robert G. Brown, *Statistical Forecasting for Inventory Control* (New York: McGraw-Hill Book Co., 1959), pp. 213–16.

Nothing, however, would be more foolish than to relegate management science permanently to some sort of second-class citizenship under the assumption it will never produce "laws" which are usefully general, exact, and supported by wide confirmation. What counts here, as Isaac Newton demonstrated, is not the way things are but the remarkable, ingenious ways people discover for looking at things.[4]

Another sort of distinction between models divides those which are material from those which are symbolic. Examples of material or hardware models include the pilot plants used in the chemical industries, the wind-tunnel model of an aircraft, or the three-dimensional models of plants used in layout planning. An analog computer is also used as a model, in this sense, although it no longer looks like what it represents. Our chief concern will be with symbolic models.

Words strung together in sentences make perfectly good symbolic models. Indeed, some insist the literary mode of expression has been and always will be unsurpassed as a means of expressing and systematizing knowledge. Management science has come to rely heavily on more abstract symbolism in the manner of many other sciences. What one is after is not symbols alone, such as one finds on a circuit diagram, but symbols together with the presumption the symbols can be used in some well-developed logical structure. That is, if the symbol x is defined as a number, then the logical structure of algebra is open to us together with all is possibilities for reasoning. Likewise, if x is defined as a continuous variable, then the well-developed structure of the calculus becomes available. What turns out to be useful are, indeed, mathematical models.

There has been a tendency to identify management science with the terms "linear programming," "queuing theory," or "inventory theory." Now, these terms refer to large classes of models which have occupied a central position in the literature of management science in recent years. This is, however, quite different from the notion that management science is equivalent to any one or all of these classes of models. A great deal of potentially useful work has

---

[4] For an excellent summary of the situation in the social sciences, see M. G. Kendall, "Natural Law in the Social Sciences," *Journal of the Royal Statistical Society*, Series A, Vol. 124, Part 1 (1961). An example of an attempt to set out some general propositions is Edward H. Litchfield, "Notes on a General Theory of Administration," *Administrative Science Quarterly*, Vol. 1, No. 1 (1956). Morse has remarked on the possibilities for studying operations in a unitary way because of their similarities. See R. L. Ackoff (ed.), *Progress in Operations Research* (New York: John Wiley & Sons, Inc., 1961), Vol. I.

been done in elaborating the deductive properties of models in these classes. In addition, there is evidence of wide and fruitful application of models of these sorts to actual management problems. The focus of attention on these large classes of models appears, however, related to three tendencies which have provoked considerable concern.

1. There is, during a period in which the formal deductive structure of a class of models is being explored, a tendency to underemphasize the operationality of concepts. This is perhaps a consequence of specialization in research and the supposition that making a concept operational is a relatively minor problem. We run up against the difference between a concept operational in the sense that the operations are conceivable, and one for which the operations are not only conceivable but practically attainable. A fair amount of work in model development appears to contain concepts such as probabilities and costs which leave considerable room for doubt as to what operational definition is intended or possible.

2. Specialists in one class of models have appeared who gave the impression of looking for problems which would provide opportunities for the use of models in their particular class or of perhaps attempting to look at all problems in the light of their class of models. One man, who will be called X, was a specialist in linear programming models and had been personally responsible for much of their development. The saying was current at one time that, "If the world were linear, X would be king."

This is analogous to the situation in the plastics industry in the years after World War II. People who produced a particular material rushed around trying to find applications for it. Things improved to some extent when enough materials were on the market so that one could start from the application and look for the best material.

This, however, is not a simple question since the person who specializes in model development needs to hunt out applications. Again we have the phenomenon of specialization in research.

3. In the development of a large class of models it is often useful to demonstrate certain fundamental logical properties with a version of a model which has been shorn of all details and complications except those essential to the demonstration. Indeed, a good many such results appear in the literature. Some criticism has been leveled at these demonstration pieces for failing to capture the complexity of real situations, when unfortunately they were never intended to do this. A good general rule to follow is that models are never to be used "as is" or in "off-the-shelf" condition. As this book develops at some length, they are intended to be tailored to fit each situation.

These imbalances of viewpoint are momentary. They tend to emphasize again that models begin as analytic truths, but until they are tested against experience they predict nothing.

People are fond of saying about logical systems, whether in symbolic form like models or in hardware form like computing machines, that, "You get nothing out that you don't put in." This is true in the sense that the operations which go on in such systems are deductive and can produce only analytical truth and not synthetic truth. This, however, should not lead one to assume the work of logic is either easy or unimportant. The process of extracting the truths which are analytically contained in the original statements of the logical system, creates wealth in the same sense that all extractive industries do. Simply to know it's there is far from equivalent to getting it out so it can be used.

Our extractive efficiency is regarded by many as highest in the case of mathematical models. Mathematical reasoning is quick and concise. It can be taught, even to machines. It forces one to work out a complete statement of the assumptions to be made in a model and to assure that these assumptions do not contradict one another. It forces one to state what interpretation is to be made of the symbols. Mathematical symbols have no a priori meaning other than that one gives them by definition. Nothing, however, in the mathematics itself forces these definitions to be operational.

The central role of models in management science is not different in principle from the role they play in many other sciences.[5] The self-consciousness of management science, necessitated in part by various misunderstandings of the use of models, has led to a close examination of this role. The basic key is to understand that models allow one to progress, by means of deductive reasoning, from simple events well within our experience to complex events not a part of our experience. If, for example, one is willing to agree that the probability of heads when a fair coin is flipped is one half, what can be said about a more complex experiment such as flipping the coin twenty times? If one is further willing to grant that the flips are independent of each other—that is, what happens on one flip in no way influences what happens on any other—then

---

[5] See Kenneth J. Arrow, "Mathematical Models in the Social Sciences," in Daniel Lerner and Harold Lasswell (eds.), *The Policy Sciences* (Stanford, Calif.: Stanford University Press, 1951); Henry Margenau, "The Competence and Limitations of the Scientific Method," *Operations Research*, Vol. 3, No. 2 (1955); Paul Meadows, "Models, System, and Science," *American Sociological Review*, Vol. 22, No. 1 (1957); Arturo Rosenbluth and Norbert Weiner, "The Role of Models in Science," *Philosophy of Science*, Vol. 12 (1945); Herbert A. Simon, "Some Strategic Considerations in the Construction of Social Science Models," in Paul Lazarsfeld (ed.), *Mathematical Thinking in the Social Sciences* (Glencoe, Ill.: The Free Press, 1954); K. D. Tocher, "The Role of Models in Operations Research," *Journal of the Royal Statistical Society*, Series A, Vol. 124, Part 2 (1961); and May Brodbeck, "Models, Meaning, and Theories," in Dorothy Wilner (ed.), *Decisions, Values, and Groups* (New York: Pergammon Press, 1960).

reasoning with the aid of probability theory can help. It can produce statements about the results of the twenty-flip experiment which are *consistent* with one's belief about the one-flip experiment. The result is, of course, the familiar binomial probability distribution. An exceedingly important instance of this in management science involves the discovery of policies consistent with objectives. That is, if a manager states his objective is to carry out a certain operation at minimum cost, then, with some limitations we shall soon examine, it may be possible to use a mathematical model to show what policies are consistent with this objective. Indeed, much of the work of management science is of exactly this sort. If you wish to accomplish this, here is a course of action logically consistent with your objective. This is often what an adviser means when he suggests a policy a manager "ought" to adopt. "Ought" means consistent with some stated objectives.

Being able to proceed in a consistent fashion from beliefs about simple events to beliefs about complex events has some obvious and some not-so-obvious benefits.

First, as has been mentioned, this is the language by which we can systematize our knowledge. Mathematical reasoning makes it possible to show how, if at all, the results of one line of work relate to another. It helps to overcome the limited capacities of the human mind in the face of the huge volumes of knowledge being produced. This is the practical advantage of unity and system in a science. Instead of learning a great number of separate results, one can learn a few basic postulates and know that all the results can be produced from these by deduction. Being able to deduce more by assuming less is progress in science.

Again the example of the telephone book will illustrate. To admit this as a scientific document the knowledge it contains would have to be systematized. Suppose, for example, it were possible to produce a model with which one could, by simply knowing a subscriber's name, deduce his telephone number. Telephone books would no longer be needed since all the knowledge they contain would be a deductive consequence of the model, which everyone would presumably memorize. The next step, of course, would be to build the model into the telephone equipment so that instead of dialing a number we could dial a name.

While management science has a long way to go before it can claim much systematization, some notable attempts are being made. Work on the theory of the firm, the theory of organizations, and the theory of decisions may be viewed as one sort of systematization. Work in a functional area of management, such as inventory policy, or with a class of management science models represent other moves toward systematization.

Second, being able to connect the obvious with the nonobvious is a skill which allows one to connect assumptions which are practically testable with predictions which are of interest in policy decisions. It holds the possibility of discovering there are more economical ways of testing or verifying a model than might be obvious at first. One might think of a well-developed model as a source of a variety of deductive statements, each offering some opportunity for partial confirmation of the model. Ideally, the model can produce alternate sets of statements, each of which is a set of necessary and sufficient conditions for the validity of the model. Thus, one has several ways of testing from which to choose.

In the development of a waiting-line model, for example, one may picture the sequence of reasoning roughly in three stages.

1. Some statements are made, in the form of assumptions, about the behavior of the individual arrivals and the individual departures from the waiting line.

2. From these may be deduced statements about the pattern of arrivals, say the probability distribution of the number of arrivals in a given time interval, and some statement about the pattern of "servicing times," say the probability distribution of the service time.

3. From these can be deduced some statements about the behavior of the system as a whole, say the probability distribution of the number of customers waiting.

Now, the testing of any of these sets of statements would tend to confirm or disaffirm the validity of the model. The analyst has some freedom to choose which set he finds most expedient to test.

Third, mathematical models extend the grasp of the mind in ways of almost inestimable importance. They make reasoning in long and complicated fashion almost easy. So easy, in fact, that it sometimes comes to be called "crank turning." The extension of the mind might be roughly visualized as taking place in two dimensions. Extension in depth occurs when deduction begins with a few relatively simple assumptions and spins out, through a long chain of steps, the deductive consequences. Often one can begin with a few statements which seem plausible in experience and end with some quite unforeseen consequences which are interesting and useful in formulating policy.

Extension in breadth allows the mind to deal with a large number of initial postulates or assumptions. For example, in one application of linear programming to production planning the chief difficulty was a very large number of conditions and restrictions which had to be satisfied by a feasible production program. Experienced planners could set down these restrictions one at a time, but as the list grew longer they were less and less able to deal with them explicitly as a combination. The model simply permitted one to express these restrictions one at a time, to "tell it to the computer," and then to go on to the next one. The model presumably did not "forget" any of the restrictions, nor did it neglect to consider them in the development of a production program.

Fourth, models serve the useful purpose of purging our beliefs of inconsistencies. This is the general normative function of logic. It does not always tell one in what ways beliefs should be modified if inconsistencies are found nor does it insist that beliefs must be changed. It provides a standard which says, "If you wish to be logical in the sense, say that mathematics is logical, then the statements you make must agree with one another in certain ways." A man who wishes to be logical according to the standards of arithmetic will not want to operate one part of his business on the premise that two plus two are four and another part of his business on the premise that four and four are nine.

Most logic used as a basis for action is well correlated in experience. This is to be understood in the sense that Euclidean geometry predicts our ordinary experience but non-Euclidean geometries do not. Thus we have come to think of good prediction as being acceptable by the standards of logic. It is possible to run into difficulty here in a particularly disconcerting fashion.

Suppose, for example, a decision maker is confronted with various courses of action and we observe his behavior in a series of actual decision-making situations. Labeling three actions as *A, B,* and *C,* suppose we observe that:

1. When confronted with A and B, he chooses A.
2. When confronted with B and C, he chooses B.

Now we decide to get up a model to explain and predict his behavior. The model introduces the relation "is preferred to" as a relation which is to hold between actions. The data then are expressed in the form

A is preferred to B.
B is preferred to C.

Now we are almost bound to view the relation "is preferred to" as a good deal similar in its behavior to the relation "is greater than." Thus we predict that when confronted with A and C, our decision maker will choose A. This is equivalent to asserting that the relation is transitive. Now, if our prediction is confirmed in experience we say his behavior is logical in the sense that our model demands. If he chooses C in preference to A, then we can say:

1. If you want to be logical in the sense of our model, then something is wrong with the beliefs on which your choices are based.

2. We cannot say what is wrong—you must determine that for yourself—unless we have the opportunity to look further into the reasoning that led to your choices.

3. If you do not wish to be logical in this sense, we are hard put to know what to make of it. We would probably conclude we have not yet found a way of looking at the situation which makes it appear logical. We have a certain faith such a way exists.

This example has the air of nonsense when set out explicitly in stark abstraction; however, exactly this sort of thing seems to go on in some management situations. In fact, one might even hypothesize that a significant portion of the payoff from management science can be usefully viewed as simply resulting from the discovery of illogical beliefs leading to illogical behavior.

Fifth, medical statistics sometimes suggest an increase in the incidence of a disease over the years. Two effects are often hypothesized to explain this observation. It may be that the disease is, in fact, more prevalent, or it may be that doctors have come increasingly to look for the symptoms and to diagnose cases that would otherwise have been given other names. This often happens as the result of the discovery and distribution of a drug or treatment for the management of the disease. Apparently the same effect is operating in management science. When a model is developed it has the important result of sensitizing people to the sort of management problem which the model is useful in studying. "Little did we realize the extent of our problems in this area until we got onto technique X for solving them." This is particularly noticeable in the educational process where problems of management tend to get short shrift until an "academically respectable" model is produced for discussing them. This is part of the reason quality control has a longer academic history than, say, inventory control.

Medical students sometimes report they detect in themselves the symptoms of the diseases they are studying. Although this is illusory it happens often enough to managers who start reading the literature of management science. Models identify problems and serve as guides to the overall conduct of management science work. They become the basis of what one tends to notice in casual experience as well as for the data-collection programs which are undertaken to make experience more formal. They play a major role in conditioning one's perception. The apparently logical progression from problem to solution does not prejudice the psychological progression from solution to problem. Indeed, one might venture to suggest that at least some of the advances in management science will come not so much as the result of discovering solutions to what we now actively consider problems as from the discovery of new model classes or logical structures which focus attention on problems we now tend to suppress from active consideration.[6]

Models are simplifications of reality.[7] They are produced by, or at least have the effect of, abstracting from the rich complexity of experience a small number of concepts and relations to be studied.[8] It is a practical necessity that at any stage of scientific work there must be a temporary selection of a limited number of concepts for attention. One must decide what to include in a model and also what not to include.[9] Any logical structure must have a beginning and an end, covering a finite number of events which can be effectively handled by the analyst.

In fact, one of the skills most needed by the management scientist is that of creating a simplified model of a highly complex and confusing management situation. He does this in two general ways:

1. By considering only, say, k variables in what is perhaps an N-variable problem and studying their behavior with the remaining $N-k$ variables held constant.

---

[6] This important idea will be developed further in Chapter 8. It has been discussed in the case of political science by J. David Singer. "The point which needs to be stressed here is that political science in general, and international relations in particular, suffer from a serious paucity of concepts and models by which we might seek to describe, explain, or predict with fullness and clarity. Our conceptual poverty strikes this writer as perhaps the greatest single handicap in developing everything from low-level empirical generalizations to a full-blown theoretical scheme." *Behavioral Science*, Vol. 6, No. 4 (1961). For a very impressive discussion, see the report of the Behavioral Sciences Subpanel of the President's Science Advisory Committee, "Strengthening the Behavioral Sciences," *Science*, Vol. 136, No. 3512 (1962).

[7] See "A Panel Discussion of Simplicity of Scientific Theories," *Philosophy of Science*, Vol. 28, No. 2 (1961).

[8] C. West Churchman and others, "Realism in Management Science," *Management Technology*, Vol. 1, No. 3 (1961); Herman Chernoff and Lincoln E. Moses, *Elementary Decision Theory* (New York: John Wiley & Sons, Inc., 1959), pp. 228–44.

[9] What we are really seeking are *robust* models which give useful results in the face of deviations from their underlying assumptions—models, that is, not too sensitive to the relaxation of some of these assumptions.

2. By aggregating many variables into a few. For example, a plant producing many products using a variety of skill classifications may be studied by
considering aggregate production and aggregate work force.[10]

It is often extremely difficult for the management scientist to find
the courage to make this sort of simplification of reality. It requires
not only experience but a fair amount of "guts" to make a stab at
representing a highly complex business problem in terms of a half
dozen variables.[11]

The idea that a scientist works with a vastly simplified view of
reality is well established in the physical sciences. The ability to
make useful simplifications has been to some extent responsible for
the success of these sciences.[12] Kemeny suggests the whole tradition
of science indicates that important discoveries come from working
with simple hypotheses rather than complex ones.[13] It is natural to
expect difficulties to arise when conclusions arrived at in a simplified
world are put to work as the basis for actions in the unsimplified
world. The proximity to action which is characteristic of management science has magnified and dramatized this problem, but it is
not a new one. Engineering applications of the physical sciences have
long faced the same issues. Precious few perfect gases, incompressible
fluids, one-dimensional beams, or frictionless bearings are found in
the engineering structures that come off the drawing boards. Often
the difference between the world of the model and the world of
action is small and unimportant. However, the struggles of physical
principles with problems like weather forecasting indicate this is not

---

[10] Glen D. Camp has discussed types of approximations in similar terms. He considers (1) ignoring actual constraints or imposing artificial ones; (2) interchanging
discrete and continuous variables; (3) neglecting fluctuations, assuming random
variables have no variance; (4) aggregation of variables. J. Banbury and J. Maitland
(eds.), "Models as Approximations," *Proceedings of the Second International Conference on Operations Research* (New York: John Wiley & Sons, Inc., 1961).

[11] This has been called "The principle of guts." There are many examples of the
successful use of seemingly very simple models. Only the following examples are
noted: Edward H. Bowman, "Scale of Operations—An Empirical Study," *Operations
Research*, Vol. 6, No. 3 (1958); Robert S. Weinberg, "Multiple Factor Break Even
Analysis," *Operations Research*, Vol. 4, No. 2 (1956); and Charles C. Holt, Franco
Modigliani, John F. Muth, and Herbert A. Simon, *Planning Production, Inventories,
and Work Force* (Englewood Cliffs, N.J.: Prentice-Hall, Inc., 1960).

[12] This raises the question of whether the phenomena studied by management
science can be cut out of the real world and considered in simplified versions, or
whether the only useful approach is the wholistic or "systems" approach. One essential tactic of the physical sciences has been to abstract or cut out a small part of a
larger system for study. As a result, physical phenomena can often be studied using
relatively simple models. The same thing is much more difficult in management
science.

[13] John G. Kemeny, *A Philosopher Looks at Science* (Princeton, N.J.: Van
Nostrand and Co., 1959).

always the case.[14] Here again we encounter one meaning of the distinction between theory and practice which practical men like to draw. Those who point out or object to the difference between the model (theory) and the actual business situation (practice) are, of course, perfectly correct that an abstraction has been made from reality. The difficult question is, "If the model misses reality to some extent, of what use is it?"

In management science, as we are looking at it, the day of reckoning—the confrontation between the scientist with his model and the manager burdened with the complexity of affairs—cannot long be postponed. It cannot be argued that the complexity with which the manager views his problems is more or less realistic than the simplicity with which the scientist's model may portray them. Admittedly, managers are often critical of the oversimplification and omissions which characterize all models. It is interesting, however, that managers who actually participate in the work of model development are far less critical of simplicity, and perhaps even tend to oversimplify. Nor does the simplicity of models seem to have any particular bearing on the argument as to whether or not scientists make good managers. The issue is simply whether or not the model becomes a basis for improvements in the management of affairs.

The argument over this question must necessarily take place before it is answered experimentally. After all, a manager must have some conviction that the trouble and expense of actually trying the recommendations based on the model will be justified. These arguments are exceedingly difficult to resolve, aside even from the purely speculative nature of many of them. Let us attempt to suggest some of the underlying considerations.

1. There is evidence of instances in which a model could not improve or even equal the performance of an experienced manager—and this in situations where a management scientist might have felt there was a reasonable hope for useful work. This has been true in cases where the manager was using a policy too complex or too little understood by anyone to be written down, and also turned out to be true in cases where the manager was using a rather simply stated "rule of thumb" in making decisions. This is related to the problem of building a computing machine which can consistently beat a good human chess player.

2. Arguments based on what can be called the merits of the model tend to get mixed up with arguments related to the entire context of the adviser-

---

14 Another classic example is that of a piece of paper dropped from a man's hand. In spite of the highly developed body of physical theory it would be a formidable task to predict where the paper would land.

manager situation. The questions of merit relate simply to whether or not the model can ultimately assist in bringing about an improvement in the management of affairs. This question can, in the view of science, be answered only by experimental verification of the predictions of the model. The second kind of argument is the subject of the final section of this study.

If some answer to the question of usefulness could be given in advance of actual verification then one would know when to stop working to increase the complexity of the model. An important tactical approach to the development of models is to begin with a very simple structure and then enrich it toward a fuller picture of the real decision situation. After certain obvious first steps have been taken, this process often becomes difficult and expensive. It would be very useful then to be able to give some answer to the question, "Will additional effort devoted to the development of the model be repaid by greater usefulness in application?"

One way to look at this problem is in terms of the marginal cost-marginal revenue analysis which is traditionally applied to the inputs to a production process. Go on putting more and more effort into the development of the model as long as the rewards from doing so exceed the cost. This "reasonable" approach to model development fails because:

1. One can seldom predict in advance how much effort will be required to produce a specified enrichment of the model, nor can one tell in advance the gain to be realized in application as a result of a specified enrichment.

2. The process of model development is not a smooth and gradual application of resources. It is subject to discontinuities that make it quite different from the traditional application of increasing quantities of fertilizer to a plot of land.

As a result of the failure of this more or less reasonable criterion, the model builder usually stops in response to some far less explicit determination. One might hypothesize that an analyst has a level of aspiration with respect to the complexity of the model he is working on in a given situation and that he stops development when his aspirations are satisfied. His level of aspiration may depend upon such things as

1. How much can be done before it becomes no longer possible to postpone action.

2. How much complexity it will take to make a desired impression on the members of his profession.

3. The level of complexity of other studies to some extent similar to the one in hand.

4. The extent of his mathematical ability and ambitions.

5. Who points out, and how strongly, variables not included in the current version of the model.

A useful test to be applied at the completion of a management science study is to ask whether the actual management decision can now be completely surrendered to the recommendations produced by the model.[15] If the answer is affirmative there is in principle no reason why the model cannot be programmed on a computing machine and the decision made automatically. This would relieve the manager of further concern if his answer were both serious and right. Now it will happen in the vast majority of cases, one would think, that the recommendations of the model will not be accepted as a complete and sufficient basis for action. Indeed, to do so would be the height of foolishness in many cases. The point is that in actuality the role of the model, or the amount of influence it exerts, varies from a rather complete basis for action through a supplement to managerial action to a position in the file which has some indirect and untraceable bearing on the conduct of affairs. It becomes exceedingly difficult in this view to say anything about the relationship between the incompleteness of the model and the effectiveness of the action. Often one works in the middle ground where managerial judgment supplies in implicit or explicit fashion some of the knowledge missing from the model. This is the normal situation perhaps, and success is in part a demonstration of the manager's ability to *use* the model.

At this point three questions should be distinguished about models:

1. How can a manager be convinced of the usefulness of a model, at least to the point of putting it to a test?
2. What kind of scientific demonstrations can be given of the usefulness of a model?
3. What explanations might be advanced for the mounting evidence that, in spite of their admitted simplifying character, models are indeed useful in management decision-making situations?

The first of these we take up in the last section of the study; the second in the next chapter; and the third immediately. In formulating explanations for the success of models in management, the attempt is for the moment to focus on the a priori possibilities for reconciling simplification in conception with effectiveness in action.

First, and most obviously, one does not take too seriously the

---

[15] For an interesting parallel case in which some comparisons have been made see note 19 of Chapter 16.

attempt to find "optimal" policies; an improvement is what is sought. People are fond of saying there is plenty of room for improvement in management and almost any thoughtful attention to a management problem will produce some good results. This is undoubtedly true and there is much money to be made here. An overconcentration on this line of thought leads occasionally to the view that managers are not particularly intelligent. This, one suspects, if ever put to the test would turn out to be quite false.

The fact that we are after improvements in large measure frees one from any absolute standards of completeness or exactness. Likewise, we need not consider arbitrary standards of reliability or validity. The model need only be good enough to outperform the current method of decision making.

In some situations what one wishes to know is the general form of policy, rather than an exact specification of what actions are to be taken. Should a fixed inventory level be adopted for a product or should this inventory level be varied? Should the amount of a product produced depend on sales; on sales and inventories; on sales, inventories, and predicted demand; and so on? Should the number of salesmen's calls be increased or decreased? These and many similar questions can be usefully answered with rather rough predictions.[16] Indeed, it may be that the imprecision of one's own actions or control over what is done may render futile all efforts to produce increasingly exact models. One may simply wish to know that if things are moved generally in some direction what will go up and what will go down.

Again, a model may well have the final effect of confirming a policy toward which management is already predisposed. The function of the model is to provide a very rough confirmation of the effects which management suspects and to try to seek out any nonobvious aspects of the policy in question.

Ultimately, we are faced with the fact that no model of whatever sort claims to reproduce the real situation in all of its detail. Models have important uses in management science both in spite of and because of their simplifying nature. A model begins as an analytic statement, but its eventual usefulness depends on whether it can successfully be used as a synthetic or predictive statement. This need not be argued, since it is a matter of observation.

---

[16] H. I. Ansoff, "A Quasi-Analytic Model for Long Range Planning," in C. West Churchman and Michel Verhulst (eds.), *Management Sciences, Models and Techniques* (New York: Pergammon Press, 1960), Vol. I.

Chapter 7:

VERIFICATION

"Newton had the courage to venture and abstract explanation; but he had also prudence enough not to believe in it until an observational test had confirmed it."

—HANS REICHENBACH

Up to this point this book has gone to considerable trouble to insist upon concepts which can be operationally defined and to seek systematization of the relations among these concepts through mathematical models. The stage is now set for the confrontation of the model with the facts. A model, like any piece of logic or mathematics, is internally consistent; its conclusions are deductive consequences of its premises. Given a reasonable belief in the assumptions with which the model begins a reasonable belief in its consequences follows, because deduction is an analytic process.[1] It points out conclusions already contained in the premises, for the demonstrative process which connects them does not introduce doubts or uncertainties.

This kind of logical consistency is itself an important aspect of scientific advice for it is useful to help managers police their opinions and beliefs for consistency and to point out what actions are consistent with these beliefs. Science, however, tries to go beyond this to discover what beliefs are reasonable in view of the facts and data of experience. This is the process of verification or validation on which rests the claim of objectivity.[2] It is the historical result of the realization that the truth of synthetic statements could not be established a priori, and thus one must resort to observation and experiment as the source of knowledge.

Unfortunately this resort to experience and experiment does not preserve the freedom from uncertainty that exists within the logically consistent structure of a model and is necessarily a dis-

---

[1] R. B. Braithwaite, *Scientific Explanation* (New York: Cambridge University Press, 1955), p. 257.
[2] For a discussion of the validation of normative theory see T. C. Koopmans, *Three Essays on the State of Economic Science* (New York: McGraw-Hill Book Co., Inc., 1957), p. 134.

appointment to those who hope to thus establish general truths free from doubt, risk, or contradiction. We shall see in this chapter why this is so. As a basis for advice, science suffers from a need to point out these uncertainties by exhibiting in detail the evidence and reasoning on which its conclusions are based. Other kinds of advice need not make this full disclosure nor emphasize the uncertainties of their conclusions. Indeed, other sorts of advice tend to gain acceptance not so much through the demonstration of validity as through the projection of the image that their validity may be taken for granted.

The easiest reactions to advice are simply to accept it and act upon it, or reject it. The military concept of "completed staff work" aims at making the decision maker's job easy in this sense. It requires staff work be pursued to the point of actually recommending action so that the commander may simply sign the staff report or reject it in favor of further study. Scientific advice, however, provides explicit stimulation for all sorts of doubts and misgivings by showing what concepts were employed and what data were used, together with the specific steps by which inferences were drawn and recommendations produced. The decision maker is almost invited to raise questions at every step of the way, although impatience and unfamiliarity with the curious statements scientists often make may lead him to ignore this invitation. Indeed, as will later be suggested, the manager's reaction to scientific advice may be based on criteria quite apart from its specific investigation of its own validity.[3]

The process of examining the conclusions of the model for agreement with experimental data completes the essential aspects of the main thread of modern scientific procedure, the hypothetico-deductive method.[4] The hypothetico-deductive method advances an abstract explanation of the observed facts in the form of a mathematical model. If the experimental results can be deduced from the model, if we can reach the same conclusions by both the mathematical and experimental routes, then we say the model explains the data and the data tend to confirm the model. This process of verification matches the model with past and present data looking for agreement. Action-oriented managers wish, however, to know not simply about the past and present but about the future. What does the

---

[3] See Chapter 14.

[4] Hans Reichenbach, *The Rise of Scientific Philosophy* (Berkeley: University of California Press, 1959), p. 100.

model say about data we have not yet observed? Does the model predict as well as explain?

Here is the real importance of the hypothetico-deductive method and the role of the model as a producer of system in science. It is not enough for science to heap up mountains of facts; it must also give a systematized account of these facts, perhaps by way of a mathematical model. The model must contain testable concepts and propositions and be logically manipulable so one could make deductions with it. The reasons for all this include not only explanation but prediction as well. These indeed are the two chief functions of science.

What happens is this. If the deductions from a mathematical hypothesis agree with what has been observed, the observations lend support not only to the particular deductive consequences to which they directly apply but to the entire model. The facts vouch for the model, although they do not *demonstrate* its truth. This gives confidence in deducing conclusions from the model about what we might observe in the future and lends reasonableness to a belief in these conclusions. Thus, although experimental evidence tells one of the past and the present, it is reason and logic, through a mathematical model, that is used to look into the future.[5] We may well be wrong about the future, but the hypothetico-deductive method is widely accepted as the best available scheme for trying to look ahead.

Suppose, for example, we are studying a particular policy in current use by a management, and we attempt to describe this policy in terms of a mathematical model. Perhaps we can deduce from the model the expected consequences of the policy. Perhaps further, by collecting data on what the consequences of the policy actually are for the business, we can test the deductions from the model against these observations. If the two agree (agreement, as we shall see, is not a trivial matter to decide) it tends to confirm our belief in the model and thus in other deductions we might make from it. The great usefulness of this scheme is that we may now be able to deduce the consequences of various changes in management policy. Still further, we might deduce from the model a prediction as to the best management policy. We could not be certain of the truth of this prediction, but the support it carries because of its source is the essence of what is meant by scientific advice. System

---

[5] *Ibid.*, p. 80.

makes possible reasoning, and reasoning is essential for prediction.

Let us take a closer look at this process, not describing what a scientist might actually do but rather attempting an orderly reconstruction of an equivalent process. Suppose we begin with an initial mathematical model, produced or discovered as the result of abstracting some interesting features of the phenomenon under study. Once we have an initial model as a starting place we need give little attention here to how it was produced, although this will surely be of prime concern to the analyst.[6] The next step (see Figure 7–1) is to explore the logical implications of the model, attempting

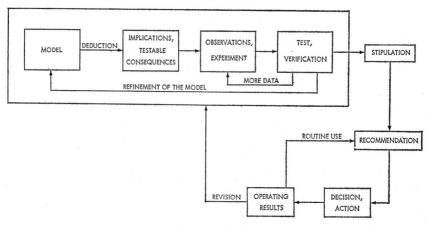

FIGURE 7–1

to deduce some testable consequences.[7] Having gone to some trouble to insist that the concepts in the model be operational, we know in advance that the consequences will be at least testable in principle. The question now is whether we are actually in a position to test them. Do the statements deduced from the model actually include some which are within one's experimental capability?

This poses problems for management science since the interesting deductions from the model are likely to refer to things that would happen to the firm if management adopted a particular policy. The ultimate empirical test requires that management actually try out the policy and that the firm itself become the experimen-

---

[6] J. Sayer Minas, "Formalism, Realism and Management Science," *Management Science*, Vol. 3, No. 1 (1956).

[7] For an alternate diagram see C. H. Coombs, H. Raiffa and R. M. Thrall, "Some Views on Mathematical Models and Measurement Theory" in R. M. Thrall, C. H. Coombs, and R. L. Davis (eds.), *Decision Processes* (New York: John Wiley & Sons, Inc., 1952).

tal material with which we work. This is both difficult and dangerous and not the sort of experiment enthusiastically supported by managers without careful reflection. Thus, a part of the skill of the management scientist is to gather as much evidence as possible within the limitations of time, money, power, and influence which prevent the firm itself from initially being at his disposal. Even when he later does real world experiments, two rather special difficulties crop up. It is the nature of management phenomena that they are subject to considerable variability from the viewpoint of the analyst. The basic notion of all experimentation is that the more variable the phenomenon the more replications of the experiment will be required to test a hypothesis about it. Or, what is really the same thing, if one tries to study complex phenomena using simple models it will take a large sample size to see the effects of those things included in the model through the haze of those left out. It is obvious that, difficult as it may be to do one experiment with the firm itself, it may be virtually impossible to achieve an interesting number of replications of an experiment.

Another difficulty is the tendency of certain kinds of experiments with policy to be irreversible. Management may well view an "experiment" to try out a new wage-payment plan in a plant as a commitment which cannot be altered.[8]

The management scientist attempts, therefore, to test his hypotheses with data which become available naturally during the ongoing progress of business. This is the basis for current attempts to reorient traditional accounting systems to produce this kind of data. It raises, however, all the difficulties well known to economists, of trying to achieve experimental control in observations which are not produced by manipulative experiments.[9] Parenthetically, it is well to note that many computer simulations of policy problems which are sometimes billed as laboratory experiments are tests in a very limited sense. The computer's output can only be a logically deducible consequence of its input, and thus the computer is really only an extension of the model itself.[10]

---

[8] The dangers of self-fulfilling assumptions, and the presence of the experimenter as a source of trouble, are well known. Organizations are not independent of the experiments done with them. See Elton Mayo, *The Human Problems of an Industrial Civilization* (Boston: Division of Research, Graduate School of Business Administration, Harvard University, 1946).

[9] Reichenbach, *op. cit.*, p. 98.

[10] There is an extensive literature on simulation. See, for example, R. W. Conway, Bruce M. Johnson and W. L. Maxwell, "Some Problems of Digital Systems Simulation," *Management Science*, Vol. 6, No. 1 (1959); Richard E. Zimmerman, "A

Finally, it is true some studies produce statements not even testable in principle. A lumber firm which plants seedlings today in anticipation of harvesting timber in seventy-five years has prompted the remark, "That's not planning, that's faith." Indeed, many long-range planning studies involve both assumptions and conclusions which apply rather strictly to the future and thus offer little or no possibility for experimental verification.[11]

Nevertheless, out of the deductions from the model an observation program is suggested and perhaps actually begun. After some data have come in (just how much is a crucial point) one makes a formal test of the hypothesis deduced from the model. In most interesting cases in management science, statistical tests are used. We shall see shortly the nature of these tests and what they yield in the way of results. For the moment, we will get on with an examination of the hypothetico-deductive method by suggesting that the results of this initial test are used as evidence by the analyst to choose among three alternatives.

1. Collect more data, leading to another test.
2. Modify the model, changing the concepts included or the relations hypothesized, or both. This will lead to a new data-collection program and a test of the modified model.
3. Decide against further data collection or modification of the model, and use the model as a basis for advice to management.

We must include in this, the analyst's decision problem, the special case in which the initial model is regarded as sufficiently well established so as to lead immediately to the third alternative. This occurs in the case of well-established general laws clearly understood to be applicable to the situation at hand. This is what happens in the more routine engineering problems.

Alternatives one and two in the scientist's decision problem keep him within the box in Figure 7–1 which represents staff activity prior to making a recommendation to management. What goes on is preliminary to making a prediction of the consequences of various management policies. The selection of alternative three involves

---

Monte Carlo Model for Military Analysis," in J. F. McCloskey and J. M. Coppinger, *Operations Research for Management* (Baltimore: Johns Hopkins Press, 1956); and J. Harling, "Simulation Techniques in Operations Research—a Review," *Operations Research*, Vol. 6, No. 3 (1958).

[11] Walter J. Strauss (Institute for Air Weapon Research Laboratories for Applied Sciences, University of Chicago), "The Validity of Operations Research Studies with Emphasis on Those Pertaining to Force Composition Studies," WADD TR 60–336, LAWR Report 60R3, Contract No. AF 33(616)–6824, February 1960.

such predictions and the actual production of a recommendation for management. (As shall later be noted, many prefer to stop with the prediction and make no recommendation explicitly. This point, while important, need not trouble us for the present.) We have called this step *stipulation* for it plays the key role in action-oriented research.[12]

To stipulate is to agree without further evidence or modification of the model that (1) the model and the data agree (more properly, they do not disagree), and (2) the model is acceptable as a basis for action.

The decision to stipulate, as shall be shown, is most difficult because the test does not demonstrate the model is necessarily true; one must make the decision in the face of partial ignorance or uncertainty. The decision that the model and the data do not disagree is, because of its technical nature, usually largely in the province of the scientist. The decision to accept the model as a basis for action falls to the manager who also finds he must make this choice under conditions of uncertainty and doubt. Understanding the stipulation decision is, of course, the very core of the process of advice for action. No clear and simple division of the activities of the manager from those of the staff adviser is possible, nor is it wise to suppose the model could become the sole basis for action. The term "stipulate" is used here in a sense similar to its legal sense. The parties agree that, without further evidence or demonstration, certain statements will be accepted and the proceedings will go forward as though these statements were true.

Assuming the analyst and the manager do agree on stipulation after some amount of effort in the staff work "box," the manager takes some action and results are eventually forthcoming. These results may either (1) lead to continued acceptance of the model as a basis for action, in which case it may be used again, perhaps even routinely, or (2) produce dissatisfaction with the model and thus require further staff action. The entire process may then begin anew.

To understand the assurances and uncertainties in this process, two points must be examined in more detail: the statistical tests of the model against the data, and the decision to stipulate. The scientist, like the manager, is faced with decisions under uncertainty. The only way the scientist can preserve objectivity is to spell out as well as he can the details of the decisions made.

---

[12] "Stipulation" is roughly related to Reichenbach's "posit." Reichenbach, *op. cit.*, p. 240.

To examine the nature of the statistical tests used to confront the model with the data, let us begin with the simplest case.[13] Suppose the model leads to an assertion of the general form, "*A* always implies *B*." Ordinarily, statistical situations arise when such statements involve probabilities and assert that "*A* sometimes implies *B*." The "always" statement may be thought of here as simply the special case in which *A* is said to imply *B* with probability equal to one. Statements with probabilities of one included in them are rather rare in management science, and when they occur they are often suspect. ("Using this inventory policy, you will *never* run out of stock." "If you build your plant of this size you are certain to have enough capacity for the next ten years.") If we could get data on instances in which *A* occurred, together with evidence on whether or not *B* also occurred, we would have the basic material for a test of the model's assertion.

Here we assume no possibilities for errors of measurement in observing or categorizing the events *A* and *B* are going to trouble us. Presuming this freedom from errors of observation, then a single instance in which *A* is observed and not *B* invalidates the "always" implication of a statement involving probability one. (This invalidation does not by any means assure that people will cease to believe it, for if the statement happens to have achieved some institutional importance a simple observation that it doesn't fit the facts is unlikely to destroy it. As has often been pointed out, theories, even in science, are unlikely to be dropped until they are replaced with better theories.)

On the other hand, the observation of a number of instances in which *A* and *B* both occur does not unquestionably establish what will be found in those instances of *A* which have not yet been observed. This is the problem of inductive inference which has greatly troubled philosophers. Although it is hard to establish the logical basis for our assurance that the sun will continue to rise each morning, it has not deterred us from acting on this belief. In the same way, the problem of induction has not deterred people from using observation and inference as a basis for the conduct of affairs. Our faith in the order of things as revealed by careful study has been often justified, and we continually enjoy its rewards.

Empirical evidence never proves a hypothesis in the sense that the hypothesis becomes a deductive conclusion or logical conse-

---

[13] Braithwaite, *op. cit.*, p. 198.

quence of the data.[14] The evidence may only make it reasonable not to throw out the hypothesis. The important point is that logic permits one of two conclusions as the result of an empirical test:

1. For the time being the model, or an assertion it makes, has not been contradicted or undermined by the data, and thus we have no reason to discard it.

2. The data contradicts or fails to justify further consideration of the hypothesis, and thus we dispense with it.

As long as the statements being tested are general statements which refer to instances not yet observed or in the future, no amount of empirical testing will ever allow us to assert their truth with certainty. These, of course, are the only kind of statements of any use as a basis for advice on choices among future courses of action.

The same situation prevails if the assertions deduced from the model contain probabilities other than probability one or zero, but with considerable additional complications. Probabilities enter the model whenever we recognize errors of measurement or try to study complex situations with simple models. This leads to data-collection programs in which we experience some important lack of experimental control. These features are widely prevalent in management science.

Suppose, for example, the model leads to an assertion of the form, "Under the inventory policy now in use by management, the probability of running out of stock on any day is p." For purposes of discussing logical structure, this is similar to the assertion, "The probability of heads when a certain coin is flipped is one half." As is often remarked about the coin statement, the inventory policy statement does not mean that if $p = .10$, we will run out of stock exactly one day in every ten or exactly ten days in every hundred. Nor does it say anything whatsoever about what will happen on a particular day, say tomorrow. Tomorrow we will either run out of stock or we will not, and the probability statement has no meaning at all in this context. What it does say is that if we use the policy in question for a very long time, the ratio of the number of days on which we go short to the total number of days is likely to (but not certain to) approach .10.

In getting data on how an inventory policy has behaved in the past, we might make a start by studying the last 100 days. Consider three of the many possible results of this observation program.

---

[14] *Ibid.,* p. 163.

1. We might observe that during the past 100 days we had never run out of stock. This neither proves nor contradicts the assertion of the model. All we can say is, *if it were really true* that $p = .10$, this is a very unlikely set of observations in the sense of being rare or of low probability.

2. We might observe that on twenty of the last 100 days, there was a stock shortage. We would conclude again neither the truth nor falsity of the assertion but only that if the assertion were in fact true the probability of the result we have observed is small. We can actually compute the probabilities of the various observational results if the model is rich enough in assumptions to relate the observations to the hypothesis by means of a probability law. (In this case, the binomial distribution.) The probability law permits statements of the form, "If in fact $p = .10$, then the probability of twenty or more days of shortage in 100 is about .001."

3. We might observe that on exactly ten of the last 100 days we were out of stock. Even this does not confirm the truth of the assertion.

The analyst behaves in this sort of situation as a decision maker who settles on a policy or decision rule and then goes ahead and applies it to whatever data are obtained. The policy in this case is a statistical test procedure which relates the observations to the conclusions the analyst may draw about the hypothesis. He adopts such a rule or policy because something can be said about its performance in the long run, although nothing can be said of its behavior in a particular instance of application. The form of the policy often used is as follows:

If the proportion of days on which shortages are observed is less than some number p_L, or greater than some other number p_U, reject the hypothesis, keeping in mind that if we got more data this rejection might be cancelled by a subsequent test.

If the observed proportion of days on which shortages are observed is greater than or equal to p_L, but less than or equal to p_U, do not discard the assertion.

The sense of such a rule of policy is argued very roughly as follows. Given a statement as to the relative frequency behavior of the observations under the assumption the hypothesis is true, and similar statements about their behavior under assumptions the hypothesis is false and some other one is true, then we can compute two important quantities: (1) the probability that the rule will indicate rejection when in fact the hypothesis is true, called the probability of a type 1 error; (2) the probability that the hypothesis will not be rejected under the rule when in fact another specified hypothesis is true, called the probability of a type 2 error.

These are measures of long-run behavior of the rule which was set up. They could be changed by alteration of the number of observations, *n,* and by alternations of the acceptance numbers, p_U and p_L. Basically, however, the process is to first select a rule and then to interpret the observations according to the rule.

For a given policy, that is for a particular sample size, p_L and p_U, we can express the conditional behavior of the rule under various assumptions about the value of *p.* This behavior is expressed as a conditional probability that the policy will lead to rejection under the assumption that *p* has a stated value. The general way this conditional probability behaves is suggested by Figure 7–2. In general,

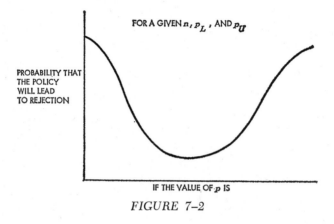

FIGURE 7–2

if the true value of *p* is close to .10, then the probability of a rejection under the policy tends to be small. If the true value of *p* differs from .10 then the probability of rejection under the policy increases as the difference increases. This is reasonable enough, but it does not establish the truth or falsity of the assertion nor does it establish the "probability that the assertion is true."

Several things are to be noted about this process.

First, it does not, of course, solve the problem of induction. It argues that if a reference class of events has certain properties the behavior of observations of events from the reference class may be described by a certain probability distribution. If the observations behave in "reasonable" accord with the probability distribution it is not "unreasonable" to think of them as having come from a reference class with the specified properties. The data which compose the evidence in support of the statement are viewed as a sample of observations of events in the reference class. Care must be taken to assure the observations are "representative" of the reference class. This means the biases of the observer or the process of observation must be prevented from restricting the observations to any particular subclass which could have a bearing on the results of the inference. This is called taking a random sample.

Second, it leaves one with some difficult problems in defining reference classes. When we wish to apply the results to events other than those observed—that is, to make a prediction—we would insist these events be predicted by members of the same reference class from which our original observations were taken. Let us take a relatively simple example. We study the annual sales figures of a company for the past few years and through the kind of verification process described come to accept the hypothesis that the annual sales in year t is a normally distributed random variable with a given standard deviation and with mean $A + Bt$. Now we wish to make inferences or predictions about years other than those observed. They may be past years or future years, but as long as they are not those included in our original sample the problem is the same. What characteristic must a year have in order to be a member of our reference class? If we literally had no other knowledge of the behavior of sales we might argue that all years are members of the reference class. But this is not so, since we obviously do not include years before the company existed, nor can we rule out the possibility the company might cease to exist in the near future. So the first defining characteristic of our reference class is made explicit. The process continues as we identify characteristics we think might be important. The years observed perhaps did not include war years. Can war years be thought of as members of the reference class? Strictly speaking, the answer is no, although we might or might not be willing to assume so. Our competition may have been stable over the years observed. What if it should change radically? The process goes on, *regressus ad infinitum*. The more knowledge we have the more carefully we can define reference classes, but at any given time for action we can only make judgments as to whether or not the events we are about to deal with are members of a reference class from which we have evidence. If we judge they are, then we are simply deciding to "act as if" they are. This, as we shall see, is a fundamental position which must be the basis for all action we want to call rational or premeditated.

Suppose further we have in hand a hypothesis about total company sales by months, based on observations of total company sales over a sample of months. Now, suppose we are willing to grant that a coming month is a member of the proper reference class but we learn that three of the firm's major customers have already placed definite orders for the month in question. What does this do to our original hypothesis? It is not at all clear that it makes sense to subtract the orders received from the total number suggested by the hypothesis. This is the basis for the saying that "Nothing fouls up a good statistical hypothesis like too much information."

Third, the process does not, as is sometimes supposed, tell one about the truth or falsity of the hypothesis, nor even about the probability of its truth or falsity. It simply indicates the long-run relative frequencies with which various kinds of mistakes will be made if the rule is applied to repeated sets of observations.

Fourth, to bring it off, we must be working with a "statistical" situation. That is, we must be able to state a probability distribution for the observations under the assumption of the hypothesis in question. In coin problems, this is the binominal distribution. If we cannot do this we are no longer working with a statistical situation, and it is unfortunately true that the vast majority of management decisions involve nonstatistical situations. For example, suppose we hold the hypothesis that the sales of a company over the next few months will be at a certain average rate. This hypothesis is challenged by the sales manager who confronts us with the observation that our major competitor has doubled his advertising budget for this period. Now, unless we have a statistical law relating the behavior of observations of his advertising budget to hypotheses about our sales, we cannot use this observation as a test of the hypothesis within the formal process of statistical inference. This differs from the reference-class problem only in that we are perhaps now willing to agree we have a new reference class to deal with and are raising the question as to what relation the observations have to our hypotheses about this new reference class.

Fifth, aside from any question of ultimate verification, this process does not really represent "completed staff work." That is, it does not go on to say what action would be sensible in the light of the observations we have in hand. In some contexts, among them "pure research," no real action is contemplated and one may provisionally reject or fail to reject a hypothesis, postponing indefinitely any behavior consistent with either conclusion. It is always assumed still more observations will be accumulated.

To do the job management science requires, it is necessary to reformulate the problems as an action problem. We sometimes slip implicitly into an action framework by assuming that if we fail to reject a hypothesis we will go ahead and act as though it were true.

This is a logical conclusion only if we can demonstrate that the hypothesis or its negation are the only possibilities, and that one of them must be true. More often the rejection of a hypothesis simply leaves one with an endless number of possibilities which have not been rejected. In management science work we usually assume the problem is to choose between a number of explicitly stated hypotheses, one of which must be true. Usually this assumption either is obviously acceptable or is stipulated in advance.

Once the problem is formulated as an action problem, the question of the proper or reasonable choices for sample size, p_L and p_U arises. One recognizes that data are costly to obtain but valuable in producing better advice. When does the cost exceed the value? In choosing p_L and p_U for any given amount of data, one can alter the shape of the curve of Figure 7-2. It would be helpful to know and consider the cost of acting as though the hypothesis were false when in fact it is true, and the cost of acting as though it were true when in fact it is false. As we shall see, modern statistical decision theory has reformulated this problem as an action problem.[15]

The nature of management science is such that sooner or later it has to recommend some action other than making more observations. Usually this comes sooner rather than later. Eventually it will suggest that action be taken consistent with either acceptance or rejection of the hypothesis. It will recommend management "act as if" the hypothesis were true or "as if" it were false. *Indeed, the fundamental question in management science may well be when to stop collecting data and developing the model, and when to produce a recommendation for action.*[16]

The nature of statistical tests has thus led us to use the term "stipulation" to describe the decision to go ahead and act, using the model as a basis. This decision must be made in the face of the residue of uncertainty empirical evidence leaves. Indeed, from the point of view of logic the scientist is in no better position than the man on the street with respect to the prior claims he can make for his predictions.[17] However, scientists believe there are ways of

---

[15] Herman Chernoff and Lincoln E. Moses, *Elementary Decision Theory* (New York: John Wiley & Sons, Inc., 1959).

[16] Churchman, speaking in much more general terms, calls this the "pragmatic problem of induction." See C. West Churchman, "A Pragmatic Theory of Induction" in Philipp Frank (ed.), *The Validation of Scientific Theories* (Boston: The Beacon Press, 1954).

[17] Otto Neurath, "The Foundations of the Social Sciences," *International Encyclopedia of Unified Science* (Chicago: University of Chicago Press, 1944), Vol. 2, No. 1.

looking at events which will make them appear orderly and ordered views of past events can be discovered which will ultimately be confirmed by future events. Management scientists believe this is true in managerial situations and they hope that as these regularities are discovered action consistent with them will be more successful than action which is not. This has been the case in physics while in economics and political science, for example, the demonstration is far less clear cut. Economists, however, do not conclude that because expert judgments can presently show better predictive performance than their formal theories this will always be so.[18] This is not to argue that statistical tests are futile but merely to suggest what they do and do not promise the man of action.

As a basis for decision making, one needs general statements which go beyond the observations of past and present events to make predictions of future events. Reasoning from observations to establish the "reasonableness" of general statements is inductive reasoning. Philosophers have long been concerned with providing a justification of induction, since its nature is quite different from that of deduction.[19] In deductive reasoning conclusions are produced which are already contained in the assumptions or premises underlying the model. Through the process of deduction a reasonable belief in the assumptions is transformed into a reasonable belief in the conclusions. Deductive conclusions cannot, however, refer to the future and thus be useful in decision making unless the premises also refer to the future. But the premises, if they do refer to the future, can only carry a reasonable belief by inductive reasoning, since induction alone can be used to produce such premises. The important points to be made about induction are these.

First, in producing predictive knowledge by inductive logic science does not produce *certain* knowledge. We must have inductions in order to make decisions, and thus we are willing to pay the price of acting in the face of doubt and uncertainty. Induction is not a demonstrative form of logic like deduction. We will make mistakes. Our statements about the future, based on empirical evidence, will sometimes be wrong, for empirical knowledge does not lead to certainty. The main thing however, is to find what we

---

[18] Cowles Foundation for Research in Economics, *Report of Research Activities July 1, 1956–June 30, 1957* (New Haven, Conn.: Yale University, 1958).

[19] See, for example, Reichenbach, *op. cit.*, pp. 215–51; Braithwaite, *op. cit.*, pp. 255–92; Bertrand Russell, *The Problems of Philosophy* (Oxford: University Press, 1912); C. West Churchman, *The Theory of Experimental Inference* (New York: The Macmillan Co., 1948).

might regard as reasonable statements about the future in the face of these difficulties. Neither managers, as they go about their decision-making tasks, nor advisers, as they produce what assistance they can, require certain knowledge as a basis for action in the conduct of their affairs. The basic question is perhaps, "How much uncertainty is, or ought to be, tolerated in decision making?" To put it another way, "To the extent that we have some control over the kind of mistakes we make, and the frequency with which we make them, how should this control be exercised?"

Second, a statement about the future is made in the sense of a trial and a decision based upon it must be regarded as an experiment. We do not know if a predictive statement is true but we may decide to act as if it were. If it turns out to be wrong we learn what we can from this experiment and prepare for the next trial. This view of the situation perhaps holds the key to understanding management's decision-making activities and the role of the advisory staff in the process. To see it as an *experimental* process may indeed be quite useful.[20]

Third, science tends to require its workers to be explicit or even exhibitionists with regard to the uncertainty introduced by induction. Other sorts of advice can hardly afford to do this.

Fourth, the problem of induction is perhaps usefully regarded as a problem of decision making in the face of incomplete knowledge. The scientist adopts a rule or policy for making inductions. Such a rule tells what connection there is to be between the observations which result from his experiments and the general ones which he suggests as reasonable. These policies are not matters of deductive logic, and one cannot establish in advance what would be the best policy or even say very well what is meant by "best" in such situations. About the rules or policies used in scientific work one may, however, say certain things.

1. They are explicit and thus in a position to acquire some degree of objectivity.
2. They all require empirical knowledge as a basis.
3. Scientists are in rather good agreement as to what policies should be used.
4. These policies may be justified on the grounds they tend to do what is expected of them. That is, they do lead often to general statements which turn out to be true. They work in the sense that they make good predictions, although not perfect ones. Nearly everyone will agree that the inductive policies used in science may claim to be justified on the basis of a better record than

---

[20] See Chapter 9.

other kinds of inductive rules (metaphysics, omens, crystal balls, hunches, rumors, and so on).

Returning to the key notion of stipulation, this involves two decisions:

1. The model, interpreted as a general or predictive statement, is a reasonable description of the data observed, or the data is reasonably consistent with the model. This is the decision involved in verification in its usual sense in science.
2. The model is acceptable as a basis for decision making. This involves the manager taking into account a good deal more than the scientist may have included in his model, and thus goes beyond scientific verification to more daring inductions.

The man who stipulates is perhaps saying, "Look, we will require no more evidence on this particular point nor will we reason further about it. The proceedings will go on and we will act as though its truth were established. We have, perhaps, other points subject to greater uncertainty at the moment to which we might better devote our evidence-gathering efforts." Just who in an organization does the stipulating is clearly of some importance. A manager may find that someone else is stipulating various things for him and thus preempting the decision. The importance of this process, which March and Simon call "uncertainty absorption," will be suggested when we take a closer look at the decision process.

Similarly, the concept of "management as if . . ." suggests some insights into the importance of stipulation. In one large company the producing divisions are given a sales forecast from company headquarters. They are expected to plan production on the basis of this forecast without raising too many questions about it. Headquarters is saying, in effect, "For the purpose of getting on with the job of planning production the company stipulates this forecast. Production is to be managed as if it were true." There are many other examples in which such stipulations, resulting in "management as if," are necessary and useful. Indeed, "management as if" is universal, although not always in its explicit form.

The question of when to stipulate thus raises the whole question of what bases are required for action. No amount of data can produce objective certainty about the future. In an interesting and difficult decision nothing like subjective certainty is obtained by reasonable men. Thus, ultimately one must stipulate the basis for choice, subject to a greater or lesser residue of uncertainty. Without insisting on it too much, it may be helpful to look for differences between the process we are calling stipulation and the somewhat more restricted process of induction in scientific work. Stipulation involves usually one decision or one class of decisions within the context of a particular firm. Scientists would like to make inductions to far more general statements, ultimately establishing support for completely general scientific laws. Induction in science involves the use of some explicit inductive policies which have the general support of scientists. Stipulation may or may not include these but generally includes other policies for induction which may be neither explicit nor scientific. These policies are vaguely mentioned under the general heading of managerial judgment. Stipulation may thus involve a complex fabric of inductions. In making inductions in science we try to be explicit about the policies used and our choices as to when to cease data collection and model enrichment. Stipulation involves what must ultimately be far less reasonable decisions which are required of us if we are to go on with practical affairs. Indeed, one might say that the scientist is experienced at inductive reasoning but managers are, by definition, those who have experience in stipulating. Management scientists work toward incorporating the process of stipulation into a view of verification appropriate for management science. A recommendation for action is produced which carries with it the following interpretation: "If the manager to whom this recommendation is made were himself to obtain the data and do the analysis on which the recommendation is based, he would make the decision in the way recommended." When a manager does accept a recommendation, in this sense verification occurs. The implications of this view are considerable for management science, as will be shown.[21]

To summarize the situation, it might be said that the necessity for stipulation arises from;

1. The problem of induction, or the residue of uncertainty empirical knowledge cannot remove from predictive statements.

2. The lack in management of statistical situations in which inductive policies may be quantitatively applied.

3. The incompleteness of the models used in management science, the attempt to understand complex situations with simple models.

4. The pressure of scarce resources, of which time is one, that limits the efforts which may be devoted to data collection, in the face of demands for action.

---

[21] See Chapters 10 and 16.

5. The lack of wide verification for general laws in the field of management science.

6. The difficulty in achieving repeatability, both experimentally and actually, in the phenomena to be studied.

7. The limitations imposed by our insistence on toughmindedness or operationality.

8. The greater variability of management phenomena as compared, say, with physical phenomena.

9. The difficulties involved in abstracting from the complexity of the actual situation a simplified model which will yield useful conclusions.

10. The finiteness of any piece of scientific work—some assumptions always remaining untested and perhaps even unstated.

11. The interest of management in studies which form the basis for long-range planning, in which both assumptions and conclusions are untestable even in principle.

12. The difficulty in doing manipulative experiments and the dangers of irreversibility and intrusion of the experimenter's influence in those which are done.

A very important question, of course, is whether guidance can be given as to logical or reasonable policies for deciding when to stipulate. Ideally, one would like to be able to say, in the tradition of marginal analysis, "Stipulation ought to occur when the marginal cost of further data collection of model enrichment would just exceed the marginal benefit the decision maker would derive from it." This would obviously require that a number of difficult concepts be made operational, and that we be able to predict what the results would be if we decided to collect more data or how beneficial it would be to modify the model in an as yet unspecified manner. We would then have to indicate how all this might influence the manager's decision and predict the ultimate gain from the resulting action. This is hardly a useful approach.

On the other hand, at least the form of a logic for deciding when one ought to stipulate exists in statistical decision theory. Here some assumptions are made about the probability distributions of the observations which might be obtained, the cost of making observations, the policy for relating observations to action, and finally the payoffs to the decision maker. Then, using averages or expected values, the marginal analysis may be done. The result, in practice, is a sequential sampling plan, but the principles seem more general. This will be examined more carefully later.

The guides this logic gives on when to stipulate are reasonable enough; however, they can be applied only in rather restrictive situations in which we know quite a lot and are willing to make the calculations. In these cases, though, the stipulation can be made rationally, even optimally with respect to an operational value system. This includes certain conditions under which the stipulation is in part a product of time pressure for time may, if its influence is well understood, be treated as a scarce resource.

In reality, however, many things happen:

1. We stipulate immediately a great many things which are taken to be obviously true.

2. Time, cost, and the impossibility of observation cause stipulation which is not necessarily a matter of choice to the decision maker.

3. The scientist and others in fact stipulate for the manager under conditions, the reasonableness of which the manager may not be aware.[22]

4. Many stipulation decisions are decisions under such ignorance they cannot be explained on the basis of logical principles.

Of special interest is whether the manager stipulates his entire basis for a decision without the need for any further data or analysis that might be provided by the staff. Chapter 13 will offer some hypotheses which may explain something of the way managers decide to stipulate.

Although this chapter has been at pains to emphasize the difficulties and uncertainties of verification and stipulation, this has been done only in an attempt to make clear what promises management science can make. Well aware of these troubles, management scientists have shown great skill in gathering data on the one hand and in developing important tactical schemes for mitigating their difficulties on the other. Sensitivity analysis is one such way of coping with the problem of stipulation, if not solving it.

This useful device consists of asking certain hypothetical questions of the form, "What would happen if . . . ?" Two cases of such questions may be distinguished. First, suppose we are interested in errors of prediction associated with one or more of the variables included in the model. Consider the case of a variable X in a model of the form

$$C_{aX} = f(a, X) = \text{cost of taking action } a \text{ given } X.$$

Suppose one has estimated the value of X to be E and wishes to explore what would happen if this estimate were in error. This might be done by asking a series of questions of the form: "What would be the result if the value of X were actually A and we had taken the action appropriate to E?"

---

[22] J. G. March and H. A. Simon, *Organizations* (New York: John Wiley & Sons, Inc., 1958), p. 165.

Let: a_A = the best action to take if X is A, as indicated by the model.

     a_E = the best action to take if X is E, as indicated by the model.

We may then summarize the situation in the matrix below:

		Value of X	
		A	E
Action	a_A	C_{AA}	C_{AE}
	a_E	C_{EA}	C_{EE}

Now suppose the evidence we have in hand seems to point toward E as the value of X and we propose to plan on the basis of this conclusion. We are only interested in what we take to be a relatively unlikely event, namely that X is A. Typically, one might ask, "Suppose our estimate is wrong to the extent that $A = .5\ E$ or that $A = 2\ E$, how serious would this be?" If X is A and we had known this, we would have chosen a_A. If X is A and in our ignorance we choose a_E, then when we have acted and learned the result we will regret our mistake. A measure of this regret is

$$C_{EA} - C_{AA}$$

That is, regret is measured by the difference between the cost which results from having taken the wrong action and the cost which would have resulted from having taken the right action. (These costs are, of course, the ones predicted by the model.) If the regret in this case is small we would probably argue that a_E is a good enough course of action because: (1) the evidence suggests it will be the best one; (2) even if it is based on a faulty estimate of X, the regret resulting from the mistake (using E instead of A) will be small. Now we might repeat this analysis for other values of A which seem reasonable ones.

This line of thinking may be extended directly to the case in which one is uncertain with respect to the value of X. That is, no evidence is available to indicate what the value of X may be. We may then ask the question, "In view of our ignorance as to whether X is, say, A or E, which action should we recommend?" This might be answered by computing the regret for each course of action and each possible value of X. If we restrict ourselves for the moment to two possible values of X, this regret matrix would be

	$X = A$	$X = E$
a_A	0	$C_{AE} - C_{EE}$
a_E	$C_{EA} - C_{AA}$	0

Then one might choose the action which would minimize the maximum regret. Such a choice might be acceptable if the maximum regret were small in the judgment of the analyst. If it were large, then the alternate decision might be to devote more effort to predicting the value of *X*. Examples of this sort of hypothetical question are prominent in the literature of management science.[23] The results of a sensitivity analysis can be of help in determining where one's efforts at data collection should be applied and thus in making a start at a reasonable basis for stipulation.

A second type of question, closely related to the first, asks, "Suppose, for whatever reason, we are unable to take the action suggested by the model. On the basis of the model, how serious is this?" This is equivalent to saying, "If we take *X* to be *E*, but do not take action a_E, what is the predicted cost increase or regret?" Here we would probably be considering two actions which are nearly similar and be interested in how sensitive predicted cost performance would be to which action we took.

Smith has used this sort of question to show that in developing truck-replacement policy it is possible to deviate from the best replacement life indicated by the model by a considerable amount, with a relatively small increase in cost.[24] In other words, if we do not in this case take the best action indicated, we can take an action quite different from it and predict only small regret. This is particularly useful when one wishes to explore actions different from those suggested by analysis because of considerations left out of the model's simplified picture. Manglesdorf has shown other situations in which regret increases both slowly and very rapidly as one deviates from a predicted best action.[25]

Situations of the sort exhibited by Smith have been found in enough management problems to provoke a highly speculative generalization which may be called, "the flat-top hypothesis." In its simplest form, it asserts there are an interesting and useful number of management problems in which the cost, profit, or criterion func-

---

[23] See, for example, Charles C. Holt, Franco Madigliani, John F. Muth, and Herbert A. Simon, *Planning Production, Inventories, and Work Force* (Englewood Cliffs, N.J.: Prentice-Hall, Inc., 1960); T. M. Manglesdorf, *"Waiting Line Theory Applied to Manufacturing Problems,"* in Edward H. Bowman and Robert B. Fetter, *Analyses of Industrial Operations* (Homewood, Ill.: Richard D. Irwin, Inc., 1959); and William T. Morris, *Engineering Economy* (Homewood, Ill.: Richard D. Irwin, Inc., 1960).

[24] Vernon L. Smith, "Economic Equipment Policies: An Evaluation," *Management Science*, Vol. 4, No. 1 (1957).

[25] Manglesdorf, *op. cit.*

tion is relatively flat in the neighborhood of the best action. Profit would appear graphically as a curve with a flat top in two dimensions or a mountain with a flat top in three. The chief reason for naming this observation is to invite exploration of it in as many management policies as possible.

In situations where the flat-top hypothesis holds, a few tentative corollary statements might be examined.

1. It should be fairly easy for management, working with the intuition born of long experience, to bring policies into the general neighborhood of the optimum.

2. If this is so, further analysis may result in only relatively slight improvement. This one might expect to find in well-developed, experienced, and successful firms. Further improvements may, however, be worth having, especially if large amounts of money and many repetitions of the decision are involved.

3. If it holds, the flat-top hypotheses would explain why relatively simple models and relatively rough measurements can closely confirm management decisions based upon experience.

4. If, however, management is not operating in the neighborhood of the optimum, then relatively simple models have a good chance of bringing about an improvement.

5. It implies the existence of many ways of making decisions that put one in the neighborhood of the optimum. A variety of actions and predictions may yield approximately similar results. There may be only one best way, but there are many good ways.

The emergence of statistical hypotheses in science and their central importance in management science emphasizes the problem of the repeatability of the situations science is to study. Objectivity is to be guaranteed by making it possible for investigators to repeat each other's experiments. The policies used to test statistical hypotheses are based on the assumption experiments can be reproduced. Indeed, it is often said that the competence of science is limited to the repeatable.

"Repeatable" here means an event can be usefully classified as a member of a larger reference class of events. In business situations one might argue that, looked at closely, all decisions are unique. On the other hand, looked at in the right way, a decision is not unique because it is an example of many reference classes. The way out is to ask if it is useful for the purpose at hand to consider an event repeatable. In management problems, replication of experiments is certainly most difficult. One hopes sufficient experimental control can be achieved so that the hypothesized effects can be detected in the face of the variability or "noise" resulting from the uncontrolled effects or errors. The lack of repeatability, or experimental error, must be such that a sufficient experimental program can be achieved to provide a satisfactory power function of the sort shown in Figure 7–2. Likewise, when a recommendation is made and applied the conditions of its application will, it is hoped, be sufficiently similar to the conditions under which it was derived and tested so that it results in a gain and not a loss to management. In management science, the assumed repeatability traditionally expressed in the "ceteris paribus" assumption is a forbidden luxury.

The trouble in many areas of management is that the really important decision problems are not repeatable in any obvious and useful way. The manager's intuitions are supreme in these cases. On the other hand, where useful repeatability has been obtained, say in the areas of quality control or inventory policy, management science has been rather successful. Problems rather obviously repeating in the ongoing course of business affairs tend to develop good management responses without the aid of staff advice. Yet small improvements in each instance will multiply, for there are many occasions over which to amortize the cost of advice.

The businessman's familiar remark, "But my business is different," supports the idea that repeatable situations among firms, rather than within firms, may be even less obvious. Indeed, it is a basic objective of management science to discover ways of looking at affairs which will reveal useful classifications. The general strategy of the analyst is to aggregate particular events into classes so that statistical hypotheses may be verified. This is very much like what a manager does when he undertakes a policy of diversification or buys an insurance policy.

The analyst's problem and the manager's problem with respect to repeatability are two sides of the same coin. The analyst looking for opportunities to verify a statistical hypothesis hopes first for a situation which occurs repeatedly in the firm, or can, at reasonable cost, be made to occur. Failing this, he attempts to enlarge the reference class by, perhaps, looking at other firms. Failing this, he may try to look at those aspects of his problem sufficiently general so that fundamental results in the basic sciences (psychology, sociology, or economics, perhaps) may have some relevance. Unfortunately, apparently these attempts to enlarge the reference class have so far met with quite limited success in management science. The essential dilemma of the analyst is the necessity for stating statistical hypotheses and the difficulty in achieving repeatable experiments for their verification.

The manager's problem is that as long as he must deal with relatively unrepeatable decision situations he must meet each situation on its own merits. There may be little in the way of statistical hypotheses to assist him; or, if there are such hypotheses, it is not entirely clear how statements which talk only about repeating situations can be reasonably applied to unique situations. On the other hand, as the repeatability of a situation increases the situation is viewed as one of a reference class or category. Statistical hypotheses become the basis for statistical policies which may be applied to the class of situations. Categorization becomes the basic mode of decision making. For example, as long as a firm deals with a relatively small number of customers few general statements can be used as a basis for deciding whether or not to extend credit. When a large number of customers are involved statistical hypotheses may be developed and verified. They then become a part of the basis for credit rating and policy emerges relating various characteristics of customers to the amount of credit to extend. In similar fashion, a salesman sees his customers as individual accounts while the sales manager works with policies for large classes of customers.

Out of this discussion one may draw the following points:

1. Empirical knowledge is characterized by a residue of uncertainty.
2. The problems of verification in management science are difficult, though by no means impossible.

Some of the consequences of this situation will be suggested in the following pages. It means that the methodology of management science must, for the present at least, involve something different from the development and application of general laws which characterize the mature sciences. Advice and its scientific bases appear to have uses in management not wholly dependent on the process of verification, and stipulation may occur on grounds far removed from the process of verification as the scientist sees it.

Chapter 8:

THE

PREPARED

MIND

"Give me a fruitful error any time, full of seeds, bursting with its own corrections. You can keep your sterile truth for yourself."

—VILFREDO PARETO

The burden of the remarks up to this point might be summarized in the following propositions:

1. There is difference between discovery and verification. Verification yields to a logical explanation while a psychological explanation must eventually be given for discovery. Discoveries are made by those who, among other things, have minds prepared to receive new insights, but verification is to some extent a learned trade of the scientist.

2. Management scientists insist on dealing with verifiable statements arising out of operational concepts. This insistence may almost become an obsession resulting in a good deal of data collection without any clear idea of what the data is for.

3. The difficulties of verification are great. One is forced into deciding when to stipulate the nature of a decision situation on grounds which are rational in the most limited of senses.

4. Management science is, at present, without any large collection of general laws. In any science the general laws function as hypotheses when one goes from the laboratory into the real world. This is the nature of induction, which leads one to expect some uncertainty in application. It happens however, that well-established general laws are not regarded a priori as hypotheses, do not absorb resources for their explicit verification all over again, and are stipulated immediately. The situation in management science does not differ in principle but in degree.

5. Models, although always incomplete abstractions from reality, provide useful logical structures which may be tested for their applicability in particular situations.

6. The success of science is in repetitive situations, while many important management decision problems do not appear, as we now see them, as members of large reference classes.

7. No practical problem is an isolated experiment. Each exists as a special problem within more comprehensive problems; each consists of a number of more specialized problems itself. The management scientist cannot embark on the solution of all these problems, regressus ad infinitum. He must stipulate

125

solutions immediately for most of them and operate on the remaining few. Hopefully, he chooses the crucial ones.

The conclusion seems almost forced upon us. *The function of management science, at least at this stage of its development, is to raise useful hypotheses rather than provide men of action with well-established general laws.* The work of the management scientist depends on his knowing or discovering hypotheses which, when tested in particular management situations, provide useful bases for decision-making advice. This method of procedure, emphasizing the lack of widely verified, generally applicable laws and the necessity of discovering and testing hypotheses in each particular instance, is called the hypothetical method.[1]

Lacking well-established general statements about the world of management, we have two choices. If we had time, and found ourselves quite free from pressure to render scientifically based advice immediately, we might simply wait until useful laws of management achieve substantial verification. Some feel this may never happen and it is not particularly the objective of management science to work toward this end. Without prejudging the ultimate achievements of the discipline, it does seem clear that it is unlikely to happen without considerable involvement of real managers of real firms. These men, in turn, have little motivation to become involved unless they stand to learn something about decision making in their own time. Our second alternative seems to be that of using hypotheses as fast as they become available or can be discovered, recognizing in each instance that they must be verified. At least they cannot be immediately stipulated as engineers stipulate the long-established laws of physics. This, after all, is what all sciences have done whenever the frontier of established knowledge was outrun by demands for application to immediate problems. The hypothetical method is not a method of empty-headed, methodological scurrying around. It requires a storehouse of relevant hypotheses which give structure to management problems and prepare the mind of the analyst to achieve useful insights. It requires the methodological skill to verify, and ultimately to stipulate, these hypotheses in

---

[1] For generally related discussions see Morris R. Cohen and Ernest Nagel, *An Introduction to Logic and the Scientific Method* (New York: Harcourt, Brace & Company, 1934); W. I. B. Beveridge, *The Art of Scientific Investigation* (New York: Random House, 1957), pp. 56–71; and P. L. Smith, "Management Science and the Meaning of Sociology," in C. West Churchman and Michel Verhulst (eds.), *Management Sciences, Models and Techniques* (New York: The Pergammon Press, 1960), Vol. I.

each management problem. Indeed, it requires that management science become a larger and more cumbersome cumulative body of knowledge than is necessary in a more mature field. In management science one must have several hypotheses and the means of verifying them, for every well-established law to which other scientists will immediately stipulate. There is little doubt, however, that the field will be restricted to hypotheses or quasi-laws for some time to come. The problems of formulating and testing general laws for a management science are imposing.

"A hypothesis" simply means an explanatory or predictive statement offered as a possible candidate for verification. It carries no particular explicit evidence of having been verified in other situations sufficiently similar to the one at hand to permit ready stipulation by the careful analyst. How do such hypotheses function in the hypothetical method of management science? A well-articulated collection of relevant hypotheses performs the function of figuratively sandpapering the fingertips of the analyst, as the safecracker does, to heighten his sensory input.

The general lack of established "laws" in the field means that in dealing with the phenomenon one must be equipped with a large number of hypotheses. These must be viewed as sensitizing ideas which tell one what to look for, what might be true, and what merits further investigation.[2]

For example, nobody takes the existence of various well-developed inventory models as equivalent to the existence of general statements about the nature of inventory management which could be applied in a wide variety of managerial contexts. Instead, these models are treated as hypotheses, performing several functions for the investigator:

1. Sensitizing him to inventory management as an area in which his efforts might be beneficial.

2. Giving him a context, a hypothetical set of variables and relationships in which to do his inital thinking about the problem.

3. Providing a basis for immediate consideration of the question, "In what ways, if any, is the situation under study not well described by the models in hand?" Having answered this question he may then go on to modify the existing models to suit his particular situation and purpose.

Naming the hypothetical method is intended to emphasize the importance of an over-all organizing concept with which to observe,

---

[2] See also Russell L. Ackoff (ed.), *Progress in Operations Research* (New York: John Wiley & Sons, Inc., 1961), Vol. I, p. 7; and Stafford Beer, "Cybernetics and Operational Research," *Operational Research Quarterly*, Vol. 10, No. 1, 1959.

sort, and classify the images one gets on confronting the phenomena. This is the meaning, in the best sense, of the term "trained observer." He does not photograph and mount in his album everything which he sees; rather, he has a series of over-all concepts into which he fits and organizes his impressions. In looking at an industrial plant one can easily note the difference between the "tourist" who simply sees sights and the engineer who assembles his views in terms of the flow of materials, for example. Most importantly, having once selected an organizing context one is led to look for and retain impressions which might otherwise have been missed.

As an example, one might examine the success of statistical quality control, say as applied to process control. Now, it cannot be denied that the prevalence of this technique is in some measure due to its relative age, having been developed in the 1920's. However, it might well be suggested that part of its success is due to the fact it embraces within itself the hypothetical method. In process control one raises the hypothesis that under certain conditions the output of a process could be well described by a probability distribution. This very notion immediately sensitizes one to the problem of process variability and the degree to which it can be controlled. The basic method in statistical quality control is simply to test this hypothesis continually. When it is found to be true it becomes, for the moment at least, something of a law which can be used to predict the characteristics of the output. However, within the context of the method, it is explicitly recognized that it will be true only some of the time. The essence of the method is the control chart which tests this hypothesis repeatedly.

The central function of hypothesis is suggested by the remark, "Theories are nets; only he who casts will catch."[3] The man who throws his net into the ocean does not know what he will catch nor even that he will catch anything at all. He does know that if he wishes to catch he must throw his net. Hypotheses function as tools leading to the discovery of useful insights rather than as ends in themselves.

The use of hypotheses to prepare the mind of the observer is well known. One must know what to look for and what questions to ask in a management situation or he will see nothing except the superficial routines of business. He need not know the answers in advance but he must know some questions. Hypotheses function basically to

---

[3] Novalis. Quoted by Karl Popper in *The Logic of Scientific Discovery* (London: Hutchinson Publishers, 1959).

structure the environment and to give conceptual order to the complex and confused experiences which confront us. They need not be correct to be useful as a conceptualizing device. In fact, it is probably more important that a hypothesis be useful in organizing experience and in suggesting other hypotheses than that it be right. It is a very old tactic in science that some models are kept on not because of their predictive ability as much as for their assistance in conceptualizing experience.

Indeed, part of what we mean when we think we understand something is that we can see a relation, however casual, between what happens and what is predicted by some hypothesis. Expectations and predictions are very difficult to formulate, both for scientists and for managers, and hypotheses are a great help in this regard. Perhaps one of the central purposes of management science is to help managers form expectations and secondarily to identify which expectations are reasonable.

Hypotheses may also form a link to well-developed logical structures. One most useful creation of management science is an inventory of models whose logical structure has been fairly well explored and understood. The tactic in many management situations is to be able to ask the questions which will reveal the extent to which one of these well-developed models applies to the problem at hand. Some sense can be made out of what happens in management science by supposing a kind of specialization of function among workers in the field. Some investigators have the function of proposing models or logical structures and exploring them deductively.[4] The remarks these people make about applications or generality are rather limited. Another group of specialists has the function of trying to relate particular situations to the models in this inventory, modifying where necessary and confirming them in the particular case at hand. The important thing is not so much that the model fit the situation closely as it is taken off the shelf but that it help to organize and stimulate an investigation. The process of studying how models fail to fit the situation suggests not only enrichments for the model but also brings better understanding of the situation itself. A case can be made that the difficulty in management science is not a shortage of empirical data, as some believe, but a far more

---

[4] It may be useful to ask if the universities should not do this while those in industry concentrate on the empirical side. A great deal of communication between two such groups is required. See Bernard Barber, *Science and the Social Order* (New York: Collier Books, 1962), p. 143.

serious shortage of hypotheses. The success of management science in recent years has been due to putting forth new hypotheses more than to the discovery of new facts.[5]

Science makes no rules as to the source of hypotheses. Indeed anyone who rejects the other sciences, history, managerial experience, the conventional management literature, and so on, cuts himself off from many important and useful sources of hypotheses. But it must be remembered that the hypotheses gained from these sources are just that, and little more can be asserted about them within the bounds of science without putting them to the test of experiment.[6]

One great difficulty remains, however, with, say, the conventional management literature as a source of hypotheses: the statements it contains are not often operational. Indeed, in some cases it is impossible to see how they could ever be made operational. Others might be made operational by constructing a sufficient array of operational definitions for the terms used, however it is seldom clear under what conditions the assertions are supposed to hold—that is, what controls must be held on the experiment.

If one accepts for a moment the idea of the hypothetical method the function of management science education becomes clear. The role of the universities must be to train the analyst in the procedures of verification, in the analysis and design of experiments. They must provide preparation in mathematical analysis and deduction to equip the management scientist with the language in which models are expressed and the tools for working out their testable implications. Perhaps most importantly, the function of education is to provide an arsenal of hypotheses, clearly labeled as such, with which management problems may be seen and structured. Perhaps some of the criticism of management scientists may be interpreted as saying

---

[5] For the importance of hypotheses as opposed to facts in altering beliefs, see Beveridge, *op. cit.*, p. 70.

[6] A useful source of hypotheses is the collection of "principles" or "rules of thumb" which have grown up in many management areas. These rough guides to action are useful in the absence of anything else because they simplify complex decision problems, allow decisions to be made quickly, and produce results which are generally acceptable, though very much subject to improvement. See William J. Baumol, *Business Behavior, Value and Growth* (New York: Macmillan Co., 1959); George Terborgh, *Dynamic Equipment Policy* (New York: McGraw-Hill Book Co., 1949); Gordon B. Carson (ed.), *Production Handbook* (New York: The Ronald Press Co., 1958); William T. Morris, *Analysis for Materials Handling Management* (Homewood, Ill.: Richard D. Irwin, Inc., 1961), pp. 12–23; and Vernon Van Dyke, *Political Science. A Philosophical Analysis* (Stanford, Calif.: Standford University Press, 1960), p. 216.

they are well equipped to do mathematics and design experiments but lack a rich collection of hypotheses.

Much traditional management education provided hypotheses, but unfortunately rather vague ones. As is now widely realized, the difficulties with this kind of education were that little training was given in the deduction and testing of assertions. Much time was devoted to hypotheses which were not labeled as hypotheses and were greatly lacking in operationality.[7] Then too, much of the students' time was taken up with institutional knowledge, definitions, and conventions. The case method of business education and its modern adjunct, the business game, seems largely to miss the point because it suppresses the making of explicit hypotheses which could form the major useful product of such activity.

In speaking of the hypothetical method one is really speaking of an engineering method, a method of application. For insisting the hypothetical method was actually to be the method of the ultimate science of management would be to insist on a level of predictability in organizational phenomena far below that which will eventually be realized.

One must be careful in this discussion to avoid taking too weak a position and insisting on really very little possibility of any general statements about organizational phenomena at all. The position taken here is more closely related to the state of the art than to the ultimate possibilities for general knowledge in the field. That is to say, at present there is a great lack of general statements but it is not supposed this will always be so.

The point is simply this. The prepared mind has organized previous experiences with which to draw analogies, overall organizing concepts within which to fit one's observations, and perhaps above all, a variety of hypotheses which suggest things to look for and relationships to think about and compare. The preparation of the mind by depositing hypotheses is the basic step in the hypothetical method.

---

[7] See Chapter 5.

Chapter 9:

MANAGEMENT
AS EXPERIMENT

"All life is an experiment. The more experiments you make, the better."

—EMERSON

If Emerson was serious, he expected a far more heroic detachment from our own affairs than most of us can manage. If, however, we invite a mature, professional manager to regard each instance of a decision, an action, and some results, as an experimental trial leading to further experiments, he may not find it so unreasonable. If we suggest this view, to a scientifically trained staff person, perhaps he would find this attitude compatible with his training and position in the firm. If Emerson was not only serious but right, then perhaps this notion is of some consequence in understanding management science.[1]

To suggest the ongoing operations of a business be regarded as a series of experiments is to suggest a rather important management concept. This is the proposition that a firm should be run so as not only to produce its products or services at a profit but also to produce information on how to improve its own operations. Organizations ought deliberately to produce among their various outputs in-

---

[1] This idea has been mentioned but not extensively developed by Salveson and is closely related to the ideas of Churchman and Littauer. See Sebastian B. Littauer, "Social Aspects of Scientific Method in Industrial Production," *Philosophy of Science*, Vol. 21, No. 93 (1945); C. West Churchman, "A Pragmatic Theory of Induction," in Philipp G. Frank, *The Validation of Scientific Theories* (Boston: The Beacon Press, 1954); C. West Churchman, *Prediction and Optimal Decision* (Englewood Cliffs, N.J.: Prentice-Hall, Inc., 1961); and W. W. Cooper, "A Proposal for Extending the Theory of the Firm," *Quarterly Journal of Economics*, February 1951. Mention of the idea is made in Melville Dalton, *Men Who Manage* (New York: John Wiley & Sons, Inc., 1959), p. 252; M. E. Salveson, "A Problem in Optimal Machine Loading," *Management Science*, Vol. 2, No. 3 (1956); and Roger Hilsman, *Strategic Intelligence and National Decisions* (Glencoe, Ill.: The Free Press, 1956), p. 160. It is consistent with the view of induction given by Reichenbach as well as the excellent practical discussion of Miller and Starr. See Hans Reichenbach, *The Rise of Scientific Philosophy* (Berkeley: University of California Press, 1959); David W. Miller and Martin K. Starr, *Executive Decisions and Operations Research* (Englewood Cliffs, N.J.: Prentice-Hall, Inc., 1960), pp. 415–34.

formation relevant for moving further toward their objectives. In less general terms, a production manager should seek to produce not only the products but also information on how the products and the production operations themselves may be improved. Each management action is to be treated as a test of the decision conceptualization upon which it is based, a test of a hypothesis which has been produced out of assumptions and simplifications and the truth of which is necessarily a matter of doubt and uncertainty. Ideally, the setting in which managers decide and act should be something like that of a laboratory.[2]

The need to view management as experiment derives from

1. The incompleteness of the models used.[3]
2. The impossibility of complete verifications, the need for stipulation.
3. The lack of well-established and practically reliable laws (this is a matter of degree and not of principle) which in turn leads to the hypothetical method.
4. The uncertainty of predictive knowledge (this is a matter of principle).

These tend to make the same point in slightly different ways.

The important thing for management science, however, is not to verify conclusions beyond all doubt nor to suggest immediately what is surely the best course of action. Its function is, rather, to provide a control system which will show as efficiently as possible whether a wrong decision has been made and suggest a better alternative on the basis of the most effective use of the evidence available. This is not entirely trivial since mistakes in decision making are not always obvious.

It has been argued here that one must stipulate and manage affairs "as if . . ." in the face of the residue of uncertainty necessarily present when one confronts practical affairs. It is now argued that the ongoing operations which result should provide some kind of test of the "as if . . ." statements. Each decision becomes an experiment which benefits from the results of the previous one. This is the essential, self-correcting nature of science in general, and perhaps the basic contribution management science will make to management. Managers certainly learn from experience and are self-correcting, but the aim of management science is to make these corrections quickly and economically, perhaps more quickly and more

---

[2] Churchman, *op. cit.*, pp. 321–38.
[3] *Ibid.*, p. 333. Churchman notes that a model may not fit the phenomenon closely but using it may be the best method of learning from experience.

economically than by any other procedures. The closed loop involving management action in Figure 7–1 suggests the process in mind.

It is thus this book's central theme that the ongoing operations of the business enterprise be viewed as experiments and that the idea of experiment here be intrepreted much in the way it is in all of science. Indeed, this attitude is the meaning of scientific management and considerable confusion about what can be scientific in management may be cleared up by exploring the implications of these data. It is important to note that the term "experiment here stands in sharp distinction to casual or naive experience.[4] It will be further argued that the function of the management scientist is to make experience into experiment, or to turn casual experience into "designed" experience. It must also be remarked that it is not supposed that anything like all of the operations of the business should or could be immediately subjected to this sort of treatment and interpretation. As the discussion of the requirements for scientific experimentation will try to show, the opportunities for explicitness, premeditation of design, control, and replication cannot be met in many important episodes in the existence of the business.

This idea should not be entirely foreign to the thinking of managers ready to recognize that the results of their actions could not be perfectly predicted in advance. Thus any action is, in a crude sense, an attempt at experimentation. What has often been missing, however, are those aspects of experimentation which make it scientific rather than casual, trial-and-error conduct of affairs.

To call for management to be viewed experimentally is not only to suggest staff people take this view and carry out the work it implies; it may also be quite productive for managers to adopt this point of view in their own thinking, and management education seems to show signs of moving in this direction. There are important consequences of the idea for both staff and management.

We may well imagine a businessman whose reaction to our suggestion—that the conduct of his business be regarded to some extent as an ongoing experiment—is the same as that of the outraged mother who screams, "No doctor is going to experiment with my

---

[4] No hard and fast line can be drawn between science and experience or common sense. In social matters every man sees himself as an expert and much of what he thinks is outdated academic theory. This important idea is discussed in R. B. Brathwaite, *Scientific Explanation* (New York: Cambridge University Press, 1955), p. 20; Bernard Barber, *Science and the Social Order* (New York: Collier Books, 1962), pp. 47, 312, 319; and John Maynard Keynes, *The General Theory of Employment Interest and Money* (London: Macmillan and Co., Ltd., 1954), p. 383.

child." The analogy may be pressed a little further, for it is precisely the task and contribution of management science to test out the treatment as completely as is reasonably possible before administering it to the patient. That is, management science makes its mark by trying to avoid the application of ill-considered policies to the actual conduct of the business. A prerequisite to the reasoned employment of management science by managers is thus the recognition that the manager, in the face of the symptoms perceived, is to some extent ignorant (or more positively, not as certain as he would wish to be) of the consequences of various policies or alternative courses of action he might employ. To advance on the "quest for certainty" with reason and caution he might then conclude, requires advice. Given some understanding of the sort of advice management science might produce, he may give it a prominent position among the sources of counsel to which he turns.

The kinds of experiments conducted with very little more prior consideration than "I wonder what would happen if we tried this?" or "Let's just try a lot of different things to see if they work" are not particularly suggested. Usually in the conduct of the affairs of business there is the desire to take actions believed to be effective, however limited the notion of effectiveness may be. At least the desire to "look before you leap" is presupposed.

The work of the management scientist is to refine the continuing sequence of consideration, choice, action, and the monitoring of results so as to make it an effective process not only for applying knowledge but also for producing more knowledge. The tasks involved include:

1. Raising good hypotheses and developing fruitful logical structures which can be made operational. This is the point of the hypothetical method. It is most important to note, however, that raising hypotheses is not exclusively the task of either the management scientist or the manager. If the world were perfect the vast weight of the manager's experience and intuition would be coupled with the objective output of the scientist to produce hypotheses consistent (insofar as possible) with both kinds of knowledge. Thus nobody is asked to worship at the shrine of any particular doctrinaire approach to management problems. Hypotheses may come from anywhere.

2. Making explicit a conceptualization of the management decision problem which provides the occasion for the inquiry. The most obvious, and widely neglected, precondition for an experiment is an explicit statement of the hypotheses being tested.[5]

---

[5] A major part of the work of producing hypotheses must fall to academic workers in management science since those practicing in industry must satisfy themselves with empirical answers to management questions.

3. The design of experiments, both in the "laboratory" setting and in the operations of the firm itself. As designer, the staff scientist must consider sample size, controls, and the economics of experimentation. He must work as well as he can toward an answer to the basic question of when to stop gathering data and stipulate. He must formulate explicit policies for deciding how the experimental results are related to future experiments. He must try to design experiments which will show not merely that something went wrong but what went wrong and what might be done about it.[6]

4. Management control systems, on the view taken here, are simply routinized experiments. One must decide what is meant by "under control" in connection with the operations of the firm. This implies the staff man must help the manager distinguish between controllable and uncontrollable variations in his operations. Some variations are not economically explainable and thus are best regarded as inherent variations while others can be economically explained and thus linked with causes which in principle could be removed. In short, if managers are to manage "by exception" some considerable effort may be required to decide what the exceptions are.

5. Interpreting the results of the experiment to management in terms of future management actions. (This is the same as saying "in terms of subsequent experiments.")

6. Showing as clearly as possible what aspects of each decision problem must depend on experience rather that experiment, thus emphasizing the competence of management science.

A basic limitation here is that the sorts of hypotheses one wishes to test will be statistical hypotheses. Thus, a single experiment or a single episode is of little value. It requires several replications of the experiment to get an idea of the variation of the results to be expected and to associate some probabilities with these variations. It is difficult to confirm or disaffirm a hypothesis with anything like scientific objectivity on a single trial. In addition, any particular management decision problem may well require that a number of hypotheses be tested before the required knowledge may be obtained. To the extent that these replications, with the necessary controls, cannot be undertaken, the contribution of science is limited. An important part of the work of the management scientist is getting the most knowledge from some given number of replications or minimizing the cost of the experimental program required to achieve some desired level of knowledge.

This view of management has several implications for managers themselves. Managers experience in common with all of us a need to be certain about the decisions they are making. The scientist who

---

[6] The principle of management by exception has long been used as a means of directing managerial attention to the operations which require it. Standards are established and the process of comparing the performance of the firm against them goes on continually. The suggestion here is that this scheme be refined and extended.

argues that the only scientifically tenable attitude toward management is that of experimentation clearly flies in the face of this need. In fact, one would suppose this view of the benefits of science to be something of a disappointment to managers, who may well have expected something more in the way of assurances about the conduct of their affairs. It seems that what science does is to display our ignorance more than it adds to our knowledge. This view is bound to be disappointing until one looks at alternate ways of doing things.

Overconfidence, strong predispositions, and the refusal to expect a variety of results from one's action are hardly compatible with the experimental attitude. Much of what passes for fact must indeed be regarded as hypothesis. For example, even the objectives of the decision maker or of his firm may turn out to be simply statements one stipulates and then puts to the empirical test. The tendency to make decisions and then refuse to look back on them or re-examine them in the light of emerging evidence will be challenged. March and Simon have hypothesized that the decisions managers make while they are planning and elaborating programs of action are seldom re-examined as the programs are executed.

Managers must, as is well understood, supply judgments as essential inputs to decisions. These may be the product of experience, hunches, intuition, or whatever, but their origin does not obviate the need to test and refine them. The experimental method is the only one by which they can be thus tested and improved. Hopefully, management science may eventually improve the operations of firms which suffer from lack of cumulative testing of managerial judgments. For example, decentralization has been a widely discussed point of management philosophy for many years. One could probably document cases in which firms have pursued an almost repetitive cycling from centralized management to more or less decentralized management. Such cycles have appeared in the history of the Soviet Union since the revolution—an excess of one policy giving way to an excess of another, producing a system which experiments without learning, experiencing costly oscillations.[7] Perhaps management science might help to bring such a system toward a state of control more quickly.

On the other hand, managers may well find that much of what seems common sense to them is in general agreement with the view here suggested. For example, when a new policy is proposed the

---

[7] Georg von Rauch, *A History of Soviet Russia* (New York: Frederick A. Praeger, Inc., 1957).

hypothesis is that the rate with which it is implemented is proportional to the increase in profits it promises. New policies in uncertain environments must be tried out gradually (experimentally) and the greater the difference between two policies the less experience is required to demonstrate this difference. This is all in at least rough agreement with the basic principles of experimental design in science.

There are important differences between experience, which all managers have, and experiment, which is the business of the scientifically trained staff man.[8] Experience may be regarded as loosely organized familiarity with the happenings of the past, out of which judgments and intuitions are produced. How these are produced out of the vast complexity of past perceptions is hard to say. The process is personal, subjective, partially subconscious, and not easily talked about. By contrast, experiments try to place what seems reasonable, plausible, or intuitive against the facts so that one may modify his judgments.

If one produces a product or service at a profit he may regard these happenings as business experience. If, at the same time, he can produce information on how his operations might be improved, then he has done something close to an experiment.[9] Experiments are purposeful tests of explicitly stated hypotheses. It is very important indeed that the hypotheses be made explicit, as well as the data collected, the experimental controls provided, and the rules for moving from the data to the conclusions set. Experience may be one source of hypotheses but experiment is the means by which these are tested, and experience must be rendered explicitly for this to be done. Although it would be foolish to attempt to draw a hard and fast line between these two, the sad feature of much management experience is that most of the knowledge that might be wrung from it is wasted.

This is a subtle feature of the hypothetical method. Unless we

---

[8] An especially interesting example of the intuitive experimental design some decision makers exhibit is the case of farmers and their trials of hybrid corn. See Zvi Griliches, "Hybrid Corn and the Economics of Innovation," *Science*, Vol. 132 (1960), pp. 275–80. On the other hand, there is evidence that some managerial behavior is directly opposed to experimental considerations. See James G. March and Herbert A. Simon, *Organizations* (New York: John Wiley & Sons, Inc., 1958), p. 187.

[9] Fritz Machlup has said, "If practical experience were sufficient to teach us what we need to know, science would be superfluous." Letter appearing in *Science*, Vol. 134 (1961), p. 639. A brilliant discussion of this general problem as it confronts biologists is given in Paul Weiss, "Experience and Experiment in Biology," *Science*, Vol. 136 (1962), pp. 468–71.

have an explicit hypothesis and submit it to a deliberate test with expected results, we will not be alert to the unexpected. Incurious experience, making no effort to produce information, may lead one to miss even the obvious. Perhaps good advice to an inexperienced manager would be this: "Formulate a policy to guide your decision making, even if you can't think of one you regard as very good. If you have an explicit hypothesis or policy then your experience becomes an experimental evaluation of it. If you change it, at least you know what you are changing from. This is the only way to learn without unnecessary waste of experience."

Two highly developed instances of management as experiment provide examples of these ideas. The whole field of management control systems is rich in cases of the experimental approach to management.[10] The basic difficulties of prediction lead to a need to control events. Control implies simply testing the actual results of ongoing operations for indications that a change in management action or policy is called for. It is clear that for effective operation the ability to detect the need for changes and to control events increases as one's ability to predict the course of future events decreases. In the dynamics of practical affairs prediction and control tend to merge, resulting in an experimental form of management on a routinized basis. So important is this kind of procedure it may well be suggested that intelligent confidence and success in management arise not so much through the ability to predict as through the ability to control affairs by quick and effective response to observed results. The movement toward forms of accounting, (sometimes called managerial accounting) better suited to management decision making may be understood in these terms. If the ongoing operations of the firm are regarded as experiments it becomes the function of management accounting to collect the data relevant to the hypothesis tests these experiments seek. The difficulties with accounting have included the lack of specific hypotheses. Thus, its emphasis has been, in common with other types of management control systems, on what happened (reporting the data) more than on why it happened and what changes in management policy and action are suggested by the data.

Statistical quality control is, from the point of view of scientific

---

[10] For a summary of the latest thinking in this field see Merrill M. Flood, "Adaptive System Models" in J. Banbury and J. Maitland (eds.), *Proceedings of the Second International Conference on Operations Research* (New York: John Wiley & Sons, Inc., 1961).

refinements in experimentation, the neatest instance of routine hypothesis testing in management control systems.[11] Indeed, it is, in principle, an exact reproduction in a management situation of the verification procedures examined in Chapter 7. As has been widely noticed, the application of these policies for testing statistical hypotheses is not limited to quality-control decisions alone. In general the problem is that of Chapter 7 moved into the real world of the factory or office. Management is currently operating on the basis of a particular policy which makes sense and is consistent with the truth of one or more statistical hypotheses. (The fraction defective of a production process is .05. The mean daily sales of product x is 200 units.) Data, made available through the control system usually on a sampling basis, are relevant to the truth of this hypothesis. The control system performs repeated tests of the hypothesis, designed so as to achieve various specified probabilities of type 1 and type 2 errors. As long as the hypothesis is not rejected it is taken to be sensible for management to continue its present policy. If the hypothesis is rejected then a policy change is presumably in order. This sort of scheme is perfectly general, applying to all situations in which a policy is chosen for its consistency with a particular statistical hypothesis and the rejection of the hypothesis would lead to a rejection of the policy. In statistical quality control, the policy change involves adjusting the production system so as to restore its behavior to that consistent with the hypothesis. It functions both as a prediction and a standard. On the other hand, the hypothesis may say something about customer behavior that may well lie outside the direct sphere of influence of the firm. In this case the policy change is an adaptive one, perhaps modifying marketing policy in the light of a new hypothesis about customers.

The second especially interesting and well-developed example of management as experiment is provided by the work of G. E. P. Box[12] resulting in a scheme known as evolutionary operation, or EVOP. It has been developed and applied most widely in the chemical industry but the ideas involved are of great generality. Box noticed that in chemical process design the engineering calculations and the pilot-plant experimentation on a small scale did not predict the results of full-scale operation to more than a good first approximation.

---

[11] Acheson J. Duncan, *Quality Control and Industrial Statistics* (rev. ed.; Homewood, Ill.: Richard D. Irwin, Inc., 1959).

[12] G. E. P. Box, "Evolutionary Operation: A Method for Increasing Industrial Productivity," *Applied Statistics*, Vol. 6 (1957).

This book has argued that this is precisely the situation in management science, but to an even greater degree. Thus, when a chemical plant is built the optimal operating conditions predicted for it only approximate the actual operation conditions for the real plant. As the plant is operated over the years, management ordinarily will experiment with it from time to time, taking advantage of new ideas, suggestions, and chance discoveries to improve its operation. Box simply suggested this process be routinized, speeded up, and conducted in an economically feasible manner. He did not suggest doing radical and costly experiments with the full-scale plant but planned an evolutionary process which would allow production to continue in an economical fashion at the same time information was being produced on how to improve the process.

Simply considered, evolution is a process which produces changes in organisms, adapting them as their environment changes. Two mechanisms are at work: small genetic variations due to various agencies such as mutations, and natural selection. This, Box suggested, was a process the management of chemical plants should imitate. Small variations should be introduced in the process and favorable variants selected as the basis for new operating conditions. His technique suggests a carefully planned series of experiments in which very small changes are made in the operating conditions of the plant. The effects of these small changes are inevitably masked by errors which cannot be controlled in full-scale plant operation. However, since production is going to continue in any case, and since these changes are not large enough to influence seriously the cost or volume of production, the experiments can be repeated many times. With a sufficient number of replications the effects of the planned variations may be detected with the statistical tools Box devised. This information becomes the basis for a change in the operating conditions and the initiation of a new series of similar experiments. EVOP is only a more powerful, concentrated, and carefully designed form of the natural evolutionary process of management. It represents a high order of refinement in the experimental attitude toward managing.

Chapter 10:

OBJECTIVES, VALUES, AND THE CRITERION PROBLEM

> "The extent to which people act with a clear idea of their ends, knowing what effects they are aiming at, is easily exaggerated. . . . To a very great extent people do not know what they are doing until they have done it, if then."
>
> —R. G. Collingwood in
> *The Idea of History*

Traditionally, scientists assisting decision makers limited themselves to supplying facts intended to indicate the outcomes of various actions being considered. This was based partly on the assumption that decision makers knew their objectives and could easily evaluate the predicted events with respect to these objectives. Management science attempts in many cases to go further and to produce a positive recommendation of which course of action the decision maker "ought" to choose. To do this, it is obviously necessary for the advisor to incorporate some knowledge of the decision maker's objectives in his analysis of the choice problem. This program has run into some well-known difficulties, all of which have to do with the general question, "In what sense can the consideration of the goals of a decision maker be scientific?" or, in other terms, "To what extent can the management scientist's recommendation contribute scientifically to the evaluation of outcomes?"

To raise this question is to confront the management scientist with a host of troubles. It opens problems which are among the most important of those that lack solutions in management science and which have led to considerable confusion about the role of science and its relation to management. The historical position of science was that it produced knowledge but the scientist was neither concerned with nor responsible for any uses that happened to be made of the resulting knowledge. This freed scientists from any direct concern with questions of values and goals and they attempted to maintain a safe distance between themselves and anyone who did apply their knowledge. Management science has raised these questions, however, since they cannot be avoided by those directly concerned with action and its prudential bases. As long as management scientists accept any responsibility for the results of their recommendations, a more direct consideration of the objectives of those whom they advise is required.[1] Simply supplying "the facts" to a decision maker assumed to know what he wants is a difficult position to maintain.[2] Decision makers are not so clear on what they wish to achieve, but they do want recommendations from management scientists on what course of action they should elect. This chapter undertakes the task of showing the present competence of science in this regard.

The problem of expressing a decision maker's values is a very old one. As Schumpeter explains, it goes back at least as far as Aristotle.[3] The main stream of development since the late eighteenth century has been in economics, although more recently psychologists who study decision-making behavior have become involved, as have management scientists themselves. Some flavor of the ideas can be grasped from three contributions, somewhat widely spaced in time.

In 1730, Daniel Bernoulli proposed the honored and still useful hypothesis of the diminishing marginal utility of money.[4] It gives mathematical expression to the following ideas about decision makers and their relationship to money:

1. A decision maker prefers more money to less of it.
2. The more money he has the less value he attaches to additional dollars. Wants are satiable.

Bernoulli regarded the truth of these remarks as derivable from introspection, but one could design experiments to verify them empirically. From the diminishing marginal utility hypothesis some important consequences for business policy may be deduced.

In Chapter 2, Jeremy Bentham (1748–1832) was introduced as author of the astounding proposal that man's goals consisted of seeking pleasure and avoiding pain. Furthermore, said Bentham, a calculus of pleasure and pain could be established. Certainly one

---

[1] J. Sayer Minas, "Science and Operations Research," in J. Banbury and J. Maitland (eds.), *Proceedings of the Second International Conference on Operations Research* (New York: John Wiley & Sons, Inc., 1961).

[2] See C. West Churchman, *Prediction and Optimal Decision* (Englewood Cliffs, N.J.: Prentice-Hall, Inc., 1961), p. 240.

[3] J. A. Schumpeter, *History of Economic Analysis* (New York: Oxford University Press, 1954).

[4] For a useful historical study see George J. Stigler, "The Development of Utility Theory," *Journal of Political Economy*, Vol. LVII (1950).

should choose among actions according to their consequences, and this calculus would permit their mathematical calculation. Bentham proposed what the management scientist always seeks for his mathematical representation of a decision, a mathematical criterion function. His logic was simple enough, calling for the addition and multiplication of various numbers, but it was not at all clear how the numbers were to be obtained in the first place. Bentham seemed hardly concerned about this, but he appears to have assumed that the numbers were arbitrary judgments or some obvious proximate measure such as money or human lives.

Modern excitement about the problem of value measurement seems to have been stimulated by the work of von Neumann and Morgenstern in developing an important and subtle theory of values.[5] Their work was in the form of a system of axioms which referred to the preferences of a decision maker among gambles. The axioms seemed intuitively reasonable and presumably could be tested. Further, it was possible to deduce some surprising and useful consequences about the decision maker's preferences by this scheme.

This axiom system suggests the following interpretation.[6] If a decision maker's preferences among gambles behave in certain "reasonable" ways which agree with the axioms, then a scale for measuring values or utilities may be deduced. These utilities have two interesting properties of major importance in the theory of decision making.

1. Values are measured on a utility scale having an arbitrary zero point and a constant unit of measurement. This, if it turns out to have empirical meaning, is encouraging to many who had felt values could only be represented in terms of rankings. It means that the resulting measurement could be multiplied by probabilities and added to form expected utilities.

2. If utilities are measured according to this axiom system, it is *logically consistent* to choose always so as to maximize expected utility. This single measure would provide a consistent expression of the decision maker's preferences. Logically, it is not necessary to consider variances or to be concerned with how many times the decision is to be made.

We will shortly examine this set of axioms to see how all these things happen and look at the possibilities for making some sort of verification of it.

To bring the problem of evaluating the consequences of action

---

[5] John von Neumann and Oskar Morgenstern, *Theory of Games and Economic Behavior* (Princeton, N.J.: Princeton University Press, 1953).

[6] For a very clear explanation see R. Duncan Luce and Howard Raiffa, *Games and Decisions* (New York: John Wiley & Sons, Inc., 1957).

within the competence of science would seem to require that, at a minimum, several things be accomplished. An explicit statement of the objectives of the organization or the decision maker would have to be produced. This would presumably indicate the existence of multiple objectives in most cases. Knowledge that these objectives were stable or a prediction of how they were changing would be needed. The scientist would then have to develop some method of value measurement, that is, some method of measuring the extent to which an event represents progress toward the attainment of each objective. A common unit of measurement would have to be obtained to permit the resolution of conflicts among objectives. Usually, an outcome advances some objectives at the expense of others. Thus a single number is required for the "value" of the event so it can be compared with other events. Finally, all this must go on within a conceptual scheme which permits the verification of these measurements in the same sense other statements are verified in science. Here is the basic structure of the tasks involved. Work toward their accomplishment appears to have been the subject of great misunderstanding. Among the many confusions abroad, three can be mentioned.

1. The impression that advice as to what a manager "ought" to do is some traditional form of moral or ethical directive proceeding from the personal moral beliefs and assumptions of the advisor. If this were the case the adviser's claim to objectivity in its most interesting form would be destroyed. To the extent that his advice is implemented, the management scientist would then have assumed the traditional management prerogative of determining the goals of the organization. Indeed, a strict divorcement of the scientist's own moral views from the recommendations he makes is the significant feature which sets off management science from the other sorts of advice available to decision makers. How this is to be assured and whether it is wise at all have been the subject of considerable interest in the case of physical scientists and their role in government.

The problem of ethics arises for the management scientist, however, just as it arises for anyone else, when the objectives of his organization appear in serious conflict with his own. How is he to make peace in this sort of conflict?

On joining an organization a scientist may have little information about the ethics of the organization beyond the usual public relations pronouncements. Indeed, it may be some time after joining that he begins to get any inkling. Ethics are held by individuals in the organization. They are seldom made explicit; they are seldom discussed among members of the organization. Thus, acquiescence to action is the manner in which they are shared. Ethics are not revealed verbally but in terms of acts.[7]

---

[7] See Philip Selznik, *Leadership in Administration* (Evanston, Ill.: Row, Peterson & Co., 1957). Recent discussions have been stimulated by happenings in the elec-

The scientist may, through the processes of induction into the organization or adjustment to the life in it, "internalize" the goals of the organization, thus making the ethics of the organization his own. This is probably a very common result and is certainly sought by many organizations. On the other hand, he might simply accept the goals with reservations, because the definition of his job and the system of promotions and rewards require him to do this. He may accept with the belief this will lead to promotion which will in turn lead to an opportunity to do something about the organization's objectives. The scientist, like others in an organization, accepts some limitations on the scope and responsibility of his efforts. He can work only where management lets him work, and thus may find his job description putting him out of the realm of establishing organizational goals.

2. That the problem is solved, either in terms of the decision maker's ultimate evaluation or in terms of a staff recommendation, by the conventional calculations of cost and profit. Certainly these calculations are approximately relevant and they perform yeoman service in ignorance as to alternatives. They do not, however, express with any completeness the considerations which determine the decision maker's actions, nor do they exhaust the management scientist's interest in the matter.

3. That an essential element for the continued existence and progress of an organization is an *explicit* statement of objectives, shared and agreed upon by its important decision makers. A further confusion holds that an organization must have the sort of scientific rationalization of values suggested above and that the achievement of objectives will necessarily be improved because of it. In politics this confusion leads to socialism and central planning.[8] The fact that few organizations have anything like an explicit statement of shared objectives is sufficient to demonstrate it is not essential.

What makes the problem of value measurement so difficult? Why not simply ask the chief executive what the objectives of his organization are? Why is this important information not provided in a memorandum to every decision maker in the firm? One might hypothesize several interrelated reasons for this difficulty.

1. In an organization, power and decision-making responsibility is dispersed among individuals and groups in more or less complicated ways. To expect shared and mutually agreed upon statements of the organization's objectives is to presume a great deal about communication, persuasion, and community of interest. Likewise, the organization finds itself imbedded in a complex society which has some bearing on the objectives of the organization in little-understood ways.

2. To produce a statement of the firm's objectives considerable time and thought must be invested. To some extent, when one says managers do not know their objectives he is saying they haven't gone to the trouble of making

trical industry. See John Herling, *The Great Price Conspiracy* (Washington, D.C.: Robert B. Luce, 1962).

[8] Frederich A. Hayek, *The Road to Serfdom* (Chicago: The University of Chicago Press, 1944).

them explicit. This is not the same as saying objectives do not exist or that, given the right sort of help and stimulation, managers would be unable to make explicit statements. The modern manager is much more concerned about his goals than his nineteenth-century predecessor as a result of repeated attacks asserting his ends were opposed to those of society. The notion of "management by objectives" has encouraged the tendency to produce explicit statements, but the problem is far from solved in a way generally useful to the management scientist.[9]

3. It seems reasonable to suppose an organization's goals change from time to time, or perhaps even continuously. The firm's objectives in a peacetime economy are, at a decision-making level, different from those it seeks in a wartime economy. Changes in management bring changes in objectives, and the achievement of some goals leads to the formulation of new ones.

4. The goals are, in general, multiple and conflicting. No simple statement of a single objective will suffice.

5. The relationships between means and ends are not unique. There may be many means to a given set of ends, and a given course of actions may indeed serve a variety of ends. The whole problem would be considerably simpler if more were known about the relation between means and ends, but this is a substantial part of management science's task.

6. It is difficult to find a satisfactory conception of the meaning of goal statements which will permit assessment of their reliability and validity.

7. Every decision maker experiences some degree of conflict between his individual values and those of his organization. He finds, quite naturally, that his attempts to resolve these conflicts eventually make it extremely difficult to separate the two.

8. Traditions, ideologies, and moral conflicts discourage discussion of objectives, or force a strict custom of secrecy upon them. Many statements of goals are carefully calculated public relations utterances and not statements of fact. The whole subject is to be discussed with a relatively few top decision makers who guard their prerogatives carefully.

9. Nonlinearities, satiable wants, and aspirations tend to upset the simple maximization models with which first approaches to the problem have been made.

10. The goal statements which are available and serve the manager satisfactorily are of small benefit to the management scientist since they are not operational statements. The manager may well assert his objective is "a healthy future existence" for his firm and feel this is all that need be said on the subject. His everyday task is to make implicit judgments about the relation between actions, outcomes, and this objective. He gets along rather well without making the problem any more explicit.

The basic question to be clarified here is, "What is the impact of the recommendations produced by management science insofar as they include consideration of a decision maker's objectives?"

---

[9] Peter F. Drucker, *The Practice of Management* (New York: Harper & Bros., 1954).

What does a management scientist mean when he suggests that a manager ought to adopt a particular policy?

Actually, of course, management scientists take several positions on this question, sometimes addressing it directly and sometimes leaving the answer unstated. The position of a staff adviser depends both on the circumstances which force him sooner or later to stipulate a model of a decision and on the state of competence management science has achieved in this connection. He may, in a traditional fashion, regard himself as simply a data collector; the manager is presumed to know what data he wants and the scientist is sent to get it. No recommendation is made, and perhaps no attempt to conceptualize the decision is possible for the analyst. If, however, the scientist draws inferences from the data to produce predictions useful in deciding, then this conservative position is in trouble. Since any policy for inference making involves (more or less explicitly) statements about the costs of errors, the analyst who makes predictions must become involved in questions of value. In spite of the fact that these questions may be suppressed or answered with conventional assumptions, it remains true that a reasonable policy for making inferences depends in part on what it costs to make mistakes in the context of the particular decision for which the prediction is required.

The supposition that the decision maker knows or has time to specify what data he wants and what inferences are required is exceedingly naive. As soon as the scientist finds himself in a staff position he is of necessity drawn further and further into trying to answer for himself the question of what is important to the decision maker.

Consider a statement of the form, "In every decision, this firm ought to choose the action which will yield the greatest profit." If the truth of such a statement could be established it would provide the necessary basis for recommendations of the form, "The firm ought to choose x, since it is the profit-maximizing alternative in this decision." If grounds were produced by the staff for stipulating that x indeed promised the greatest profit among the alternatives considered, then the recommendation would carry considerable force when coupled with some demonstration of the truth of the previous statement. Further, if the truth of the first "ought" statement could be demonstrated (in the sense that science verifies statements) it would function as a general rule for processing the data of any decision problem into a recommendation and would be called a principle of choice.

There are immediate difficulties in making the concept of profit operational. Efforts to do this, as will shortly be seen, require so many judgments that the resulting definitions are highly arbitrary. This difficulty aside, the basic question is, "How is the management scientist to regard such a statement?" On what basis can he arrive at the point of stipulating that the firm indeed ought to maximize profits? What is to be done to resolve contradictory assertions that the firm must consider all sorts of intangibles in addition to simply profit?

The statements with which science likes to work are, as has been said, either analytic or synthetic. Analytic statements are not predictive but are merely self-explanatory definitions. Is there any sense in which the "ought to maximize profit" statement can be regarded as analytic? If we were, for example, to consider the profit-maximizing imperative a part of the definition of the term "corporation," we could claim it was analytic for any corporation. But not many people will agree with this. They will say that we have simply backed the basic question up one step and postponed facing the meaning of "ought." For now we must answer questions like, "Why ought this firm accept your definition of corporation" or "Why ought this firm be a corporation in the sense of your definition?"

The basic nature of the problem remains and can never be removed by such analytic exercises. These attempts to regard principles of choice as analytic do not help much in finding a basis for stipulation.

The classical view of such statements was to regard some of them as synthetic a priori statements. They were not analytic nor were they subject to empirical investigation. Their truth was given by introspection and intuition. As we have seen, modern science makes a very strong rejection of the synthetic a priori.[10]

This leaves us with the possibility that the profit-maximizing statement makes a prediction which can, at least in principle, be verified. The statement is thus the ordinary but interesting synthetic type. What experiment could one conceive to demonstrate its truth or falsity? Unfortunately, as the principle now stands it doesn't seem to make any prediction of the form, "If you do this, then you

---

[10] Hans Reichenbach, *The Rise of Scientific Philosophy* (Berkeley: University of California Press, 1959).

will see such-and-such." It cannot be dealt with by science this way either.

One approach is to say that the profit-maximizing principle and others like it simply will not do, in the form we have given them. A new statement is to be substituted for it which expresses more adequately the meaning a management scientist attaches to his recommendation. The sense of a recommendation is to be taken from the statement, "If you want to maximize profit, then you ought to choose action x" or more generally, "If you wish to achieve A, then you ought to do B."

This form of recommendation consists of a conditional phrase and an assertion.

1. "If you want to achieve A."
2. "B is an effective action for achieving A."

The assertion is clearly a synthetic statement. It makes a prediction about the relationship between means and ends, between actions and objectives. If an operational definition of objective A can be given, as well as of the word "effective," then we have a prediction conceivably subject to verification by experiment. Thus, this part of the recommendation falls within science. Its verification is regarded by many as the sole task of science in connection with recommendations.[11] Science must investigate the relations between actions and objectives, and what it reports in the form of recommendations is simply knowledge of these connections. Of course, this is no easy task. The difficulties of giving operational definitions for interesting objectives are great, and a less naive view suggests that the scientist limit himself to studying relations between actions and those particular objectives which can be made operational. Clearly, to the extent that firms are interested in other objectives, the work of the scientist will be somewhat beside the point. These notions of effectiveness have problems of their own, but they are suppressed in practice.

What is to be done about the other part of the recommendation, the conditional phrase? The analyst may simply say the phrase must remain as a condition on the recommendation, since there is nothing he can do about it professionally. The recommendation itself is not subject to verification by the staff and thus carries the corresponding residue of uncertainty along with its "ought." The function of science is to explore the relationships between actions and objectives, and

---

[11] *Ibid.*, p. 279. Anatol Rapoport, *Operational Philosophy* (New York: Harper & Bros., 1953).

this alone. This sort of knowledge is very useful, however, especially if the study contains a large number of recommendations showing the relations between a variety of actions and a variety of objectives. This is one contribution of sensitivity analysis. In providing such knowledge to the decision maker, there is no basis, on this view, for limiting it to a single recommendation. The results of the work of the staff may be to suggest the relation between several actions and a single objective. Often, however, it is more useful to work with several objectives, discussing each in turn. The scientist then works with a profile of measures for each policy, rather than a single number to represent its worth to the decision maker. Ideally, the next step would be to collapse this profile of measures into a single one by assigning weights to each and adopting some method of combining them. It is at this point that the problem becomes excessively difficult.[12] The manager too finds great difficulties when the attempt is made to provide a single criterion measure for a portion of his organization.

It is difficult to maintain any permanent distinctions between means and ends since today's objectives may simply be the tools for the achievement of tomorrow's objectives. The task of science may, however, begin with the study of synthetic statements about the relations among what are commonly called objectives. What relations are there among profit, return on investment, share of the market, rate of growth, technological leadership, employment security, and so on?

However, if a decision is ever to be made on the basis of the recommendation, someone must stipulate that management does indeed wish to achieve objective A. This does not fall to the staff analyst; to do so would be to sacrifice his objectivity in a most important area. As long as the manager himself can and does stipulate a statement of objectives which is sufficiently operational, the scientist may confine his work to the relations between means and ends while still functioning effectively as a source of advice. Action-oriented research can neglect the problem of stipulating objectives only so long as it remains true that managers know what they want. Management science has found itself involved not only with finding out how to achieve certain ends but also with finding out what ends are really sought by decision makers. The efforts to deal with this

---
[12] V. F. Ridgway, "Dysfunctional Consequences of Performance Measurements," *Administrative Science Quarterly*, Vol. 1, No. 2 (1956).

problem have led to a second position relative to the conditional phrase in a recommendation.

Some of the factors which make it difficult for the manager readily to produce useful statements of the firm's objectives have been guessed at. Operational definitions of goals are not easily arrived at and they do not leap immediately into the mind of the manager. The vagueness with which goals are commonly discussed seldom provides the management scientist with the working material he would like to have. Multiple goals must be made explicit and relative weights attached to them so they may be combined into a single measure of effectiveness. There is certainly nothing in this which recalls any routine processes of conscious thought for the ordinary decision maker. When the manager sees how toughminded the scientist wishes him to be in connection with goals, he may welcome some assistance. Indeed, there is little reason to suppose he can do without it.[13]

Now, it must be emphasized that the work of the management scientist, even if limited to the study of what actions lead to what ends, may be of considerable help to the manager. Such explorations may very well stimulate thinking and clarify to a great extent the structure of the firm's objectives. However, the management scientist may find it necessary to go further. It might be emphasized again that underlying every prediction is a policy for drawing inferences. Such policies, as discussed in Chapter 7, require the answering of value questions. Even predictions based on the so-called "best-fit" straight line for some data involve making the assumption the cost of errors is a quadratic function of their absolute magnitude. The technical details of inferential policies and the context in which such value considerations arise make it useful for the manager to have assistance from his staff. It is no small task to explain what he is supposed to stipulate for purposes of making inferences. The analyst thus cannot avoid helping the decision maker formulate his targets.

How is this to be done without getting involved in the nonscientific meaning of "ought"? The answer is simply that management's objectives are to be considered evidence similar in principle to any other sort of evidence. Data on objectives are to be observed, theorized about, or modeled; predictions are to be made; and hopefully verifying experiments will test these predictions. Natural as this may seem for the management scientist it represents a consider-

---

[13] See Chapter 15.

able departure from conventional scientific problems and raises serious difficulties. At present, this is a program being studied by management scientists rather than a method clearly within their competence.

Let us see how such a program might be carried on, first in the simplest possible case. Suppose we return to a model introduced in Chapter 6. "If outcome A is preferred to outcome B, and if outcome B is preferred to outcome C, then it follows that A is preferred to C." This model is a relation called transitivity. Now suppose we go to a decision maker, hoping to observe his preferences between A and B. We might simply ask him, more or less directly, which he would prefer if confronted with a choice between the two. Alternatively, we might confront him in a "laboratory" situation with A and B, and observe how he chose. Finally, we might look for an actual instance of decision making in which he had chosen between A and B. These three methods are not suggested as equivalents, and serious questions must eventually be answered about their respective reliabilities and validities. However, the result is observational data for the management scientist.

Suppose the results of the observation program are that indeed A is preferred to B and B is preferred to C. The management scientist might then assert that the data together with the model suggest a prediction that, in a choice between A and C, the decision maker will choose A. An experiment might be performed to verify this prediction. If it is not verified, then one or both of the following conclusions are possible:

1. The decision maker's preferences are not transitive, and the model does not fit.

2. The experimental conditions under which the data were obtained are not sufficiently like those under which the verifying experiment was done. That is, good experimental control was not achieved. The model was too simple and by leaving out all sorts of other considerations which influence preferences it has been simplified beyond the point of producing useful predictions.

All this is again exactly like the process suggested by Figure 7–1. The problems are great but are those we have encountered before in trying to use simple models and do experiments where control is difficult. If it were to succeed, however, it would mean the scientist, having obtained data on certain preferences, could predict choices in situations as yet unobserved. This prediction could conceivably be verified.

Suppose now, that the data are observed as before and indicate the decision maker prefers outcome D to E and E to F. The management scientist then might say, "In a decision between D and F, I recommend you choose D." The meaning of the recommendation is thus, "If the model fits your preferences and if the choice situation is sufficiently like the conditions under which the data were obtained, I predict you would choose D." A recommendation is thus a prediction of how the decision maker would act under certain conditions.

The difficulties involved in this scheme have been studied with great care by C. West Churchman.[14] The program Churchman develops can be roughly stated as follows: The function of science in connection with values is to predict what choice a person would make if he chose under the conditions which prevailed when the scientist measured his values. Verification of this prediction is then possible under the standard conditions. The meaning of a recommendation is then, in Churchman's words, ". . . a prediction of behavior when the decision maker acts in a state of complete knowledge, either knowledge that predicts with certainty, or knowledge of the true probabilities of the outcomes. As an aid to the decision maker the scientist must do two things: he must try to improve the decision maker's state of knowledge, and he must try to find out how he would act if his ignorance were removed."[15]

In the very simple procedure described above the scientist might have used a slightly different model. Having observed that A is preferred to B, he might associate a number x with A, called "the utility of A," and a number y with B so that y is less than x. Some number z might be assigned to C so that z was less than y. Since the utility of C, z, is less than the utility of A, x, he would predict that A would be preferred to C. This process is called scaling, since the model establishes a scale on which utilities are associated with preferences. He would have a wide choice of possible numbers for z, y, and x, since all that is necessary is the proper relationship among them. The numbers 1, 2, and 3 would be obvious choices, thus establishing a ranking of the outcomes. The important point is that these numbers or utilities are not inherent in the outcomes, nor are they inherent in the decision maker. They are simply representations of the relations between decision makers and outcomes. They represent preferences.

Let us next examine a more complex example of the experimen-

---

14 Churchman, *op. cit.*
15 *Ibid.*, p. 19.

talist view of values. As a part of their famous book on game theory, von Neumann and Morgenstern introduced an approach to the axiomatization of values which attracted considerable attention. Since this book is interested largely in the possibilities of interpreting their approach as a possible method for obtaining a value scale which would represent a decision maker's preferences, we will be content with a rather rough presentation of the ideas involved.[16]

Suppose we have three outcomes, θ_1, θ_2, and θ_3. We begin by asking the decision maker to rank these outcomes from the most preferred to the least. Let us then reassign the subscripts so that they correspond to the ranks. Thus θ_1 is now the most preferred of the three outcomes. We may now arbitrarily assign the following values to θ_1 and θ_3:

$$V(\theta_1) = 1$$
$$V(\theta_3) = 0.$$

The question is how to express the value of θ_2 on the scale we have just established. About the only requirement we must meet in expressing this value is to select a number in the range zero to one so as to preserve the original preference ordering.

To do this, suppose we confront the decision maker with the following choice:

$a_1 : \theta_2$ with probability 1
$a_2 : \theta_1$ with probability p_2 and θ_3 with probability $1 - p_2$.

We try various values of p_2 until we find the decision maker is indifferent between the two alternatives. Since our only requirement for assigning a value to θ_2 is that the number used lie between zero and one, and since p_2 is such a number, why not let $V(\theta_2) = p_2$? Since p_2 fills the bill neither better nor worse than any other number, let us use it. Suppose we repeat this process with three additional outcomes and obtain the results:

$$V(\theta_4) = p_4$$
$$V(\theta_5) = p_5$$
$$V(\theta_6) = p_6.$$

Note that in doing this it is not at all necessary the outcomes be preferred to θ_3 but not preferred to θ_1. If, for example θ_4 is preferred to θ_1, we then confront the decision maker with the alternatives

---

[16] Luce and Raiffa, *op. cit.*, pp. 12–38; Churchman, *op. cit.*, Chapter 8; and Herman Chernoff and Lincoln E. Moses, *Elementary Decision Theory* (New York: John Wiley & Sons, Inc., 1959).

$a_1 = \theta_1$ with probability 1

$a_2 = \theta_4$ with probability p_4 and θ_3 with probability $1 - p_4$.

Clearly here the value assigned to θ_4 must be a number larger than one in order to preserve the preferences. Thus we might select $V(\theta_4) = 1/p_4$. Now we might multiply all the values by p_4 so as to keep them in the interval zero to one. A similar process may be used for outcomes ranked below θ_3 in preference.

Let us now assume values have been assigned in this way and all values are in the interval zero to one, with θ_1 the most preferred and θ_3 the least preferred. Consider the following decision under risk.

	P_1	$1 - P_1$
	s_1	s_2
a_1	θ_2	θ_4
a_2	θ_5	θ_6

Consider a_1 which will result in θ_2 with probability P_1 and θ_4 with probability $1 - P_1$. The decision maker has already indicated indifference between θ_2 and θ_1 with probability p_2 and θ_3 with probability $1 - p_2$. He has also indicated indifference between θ_4 and θ_1 with probability p_4 and θ_3 with probability $1 - p_4$. It might then be possible to say that he would be indifferent between a_1 and θ_1 with probability $P_1 p_2 + (1 - P_1) p_4$ and θ_3 with probability $P_1 (1 - p_2) + (1 - P_1) (1 - p_4)$.

Now our original scheme for assigning values was to find a "prospect" or "gamble" involving θ_1 and θ_3 and let the value be equal to the probability of θ_1. Using this same idea we would assign a value to a_1 which would be

$$P_1 p_2 + (1 - P_1) p_4.$$

This, however, is equivalent to

$$P_1 V(\theta_2) + (1 - P_1) V(\theta_4)$$

which is simply the expectation of a_1.

Now the remarkable feature of the von Neumann–Morgenstern method emerges. If we use this method of assigning values it becomes perfectly natural to use the expectation principle of choice. The expectation principle is perfectly consistent with the decision maker's preferences and there is no necessity for becoming entangled in any of the arguments which involve an empirical interpretation of the principle. Thus, this method not only provides a means of value measurement but the values obtained lead directly to the expectation principle of choice.

This conclusion is so important that it will be restated. If we use this process of assigning values, then in decisions under risk the decision maker will be acting in a manner consistent with his own expressed preferences if he selects the alternative which maximizes expectation. Nothing need be said about long-run limits or frequencies. The expected value or expectation becomes an index of preference over probability distributions which agrees with the decision maker's answers to the questions posed above.

The axioms which lead to this method may be very roughly stated as follows:

1. The decision maker can make a complete and transitive ranking of the outcomes.

2. Any prospect of gamble involving equally desirable outcomes is just as desirable as either outcome by itself.

3. If outcomes A, B, and C are ranked so that A is preferred to B, B is preferred to C, and A is preferred to C, then there exists a gamble involving A and C which is just as desirable as B.

4. If A and B are equally desirable then the gamble $pA + (1 - p)C$ is just as desirable as the gamble $pB + (1 - p)C$.

If these axioms hold the existence of the value scale can be shown. The question of interest is whether these axioms do hold in the firm and whether the decision maker can answer questions of the sort indicated above. There is not yet sufficient evidence to argue conclusively one way or the other on these questions.

The difficulties are great and, in the opinion of some, insurmountable. The basic objective of this sort of program is clear. If people behave according to such a set of axioms, the measurement of some "simple" preferences would make possible the prediction of choices in more complex action situations. The meaning of a recommendation would then be a prediction.

All this will seem incredibly naive and complicated to those who feel that what can be done is to be done practically through the use of predictions of cost and profit as an explicit value scheme. Unquestionably, a great amount of useful analysis is done by management scientists in terms of cost and profits.[17] Adam Smith was held in high regard by businessmen because his work could be

---

[17] For some excellent remarks see Roland N. McKean, *Efficiency in Government Through Systems Analysis* (New York: John Wiley & Sons, Inc., 1958).

interpreted as showing the relationship between the firm's profits and the "good society." It seemed possible to argue that the firm which indeed sought to maximize its profits would be making a positive contribution to social welfare—a classic case of the work of science in exploring the relations between actions and objectives. This is nothing more than a somewhat oversimplified interpretation of the invisible hand theorem, but it could free managers from uncertain reflections as to the importance of other goals.

Without maintaining that profit maximization is in fact the objective of all managers, several arguments are commonly given to suggest it serves adequately as a measure of value for management decision making:

1. Although management indeed has other goals, the attainment of these is well correlated with the attainment of profits. Profits thus serve as a useful proximate measure of value.

2. Profits constitute a rule of thumb by which the busy manager simplifies very complicated affairs. He need not absorb all the details of the operations of his firm nor the complexities of the decisions he must make. Profit predictions provide him with a useful basis for simplifying his environment. Managers find it easiest to decide questions which they believe are decidable in terms of accounting dollars. They thus welcome any attempt to express the values of events in dollars and any ideological exercise which supports the convention that dollars are indeed the appropriate measure.

3. If one goes about looking toward the maximization of profits other objectives will "take care of themselves." This may be interpreted as saying that profit is in some rough sense the most important objective and certainly the most easily quantified. Specific attention to other goals may be suppressed and dealt with in an implicit fashion. This in turn supports the conventional position that the staff should concern itself with predictions of cost and profit exclusively. The staff, on this view, has not the competence to go beyond these considerations, and the evaluation of events relative to other goals is the task of management. But this calls attention to the existence of other goals and shows where staff work stops and managerial judgment takes over. With this common view of the problem, no great surprise attaches to the refusal of management to accept the staff recommendations. Unfortunately, however, the experimental feedback from such refusals seldom indicates whether the differences are concerned with other aspects of the decision. This view simply suggests another way in which management science models simplify the management situation. They try to be of service by answering questions as to how a manager might choose if profit were his objective.

4. Profit is simply an intermediate goal. It provides a mechanism for greatly simplifying the way in which a variety of objectives are brought to bear on a choice problem. This is to argue that if the firm makes plenty of profit it is clearly in a place to accomplish whatever other objectives it may have. This position argues that while it may be impossible to specify the relationship between, say, research and development and profit, it is possible to argue that

if the firm has plenty of profit it can if it wishes undertake R and D. Profits represent the power to achieve other goals, including public service and so on. Typically, it is argued that an objective of the firm is to survive and grow and that profit is a necessary condition for this.

5. The most important and subtle argument in favor of the use of cost and profit in decision making suggests that it is a basis for achieving decentralization or delegation of decision making without loss of coordination. To run a business of any size it is necessary to delegate, but in order to avoid burdensome costs of coordination some effective control scheme must be devised. If every decision maker is given a score in the form of profit or cost and told to maximize or minimize his score, it is hoped the problem of coordination among decision makers will automatically be solved, resulting in effective operation of the firm. The use of cost and profit calculations in the firm's decision making thus provides an internal price system. By analogy the allocation of resources in the firm is to be handled by a "market mechanism" similar to that of the economy. This raises all the fascinating questions of the possibility of a rationally designed system of decentralized decision making. Cost accounting makes a beginning in this direction but great difficulties remain which require the attention of management science.

On the other hand, there are a wealth of arguments to the point that a simple theory of profit maximization will not in fact predict the choices made by managers.[18] While profit can be made operational it presents one with some difficulties in the process. One of the most troublesome of these is the allocation of overhead, which requires judgment on the part of the calculator of profit. Many other such judgments are required to produce an operational definition, giving it a rather arbitrary character. One must couple with assertions of the profit motive the answers to several difficult questions:

1. How far in the future are profits to be calculated in a given decision? How are future profits to be related to present profits?

2. What is the relation between profit and risk or uncertainty? How is one to combine profits and probabilities in making a choice? To understand risky decisions it may become necessary to translate profits into utilities. The theory of diminishing marginal utilities suggested it was necessary to consider both the mean and the variance of the probability distribution of profit in making a decision. On the other hand, if in a decision relatively small sums are involved profits may reasonably be assumed to be linearly related to utilities and the latter may be neglected.

3. What explanation is to be given for the three following instances of management decision-making behavior?

---

[18] Churchman, *op. cit.*, pp. 51–52; Talcott Parsons, "The Motivations of Economic Activities," *Essays in Sociological Theory* (Glencoe, Ill.: The Free Press, 1949); James G. March and Herbert A. Simon, *Organizations* (New York: John Wiley & Sons, Inc., 1958); Hayek, *op. cit.*; and Ludwig von Mises, *Bureaucracy* (New Haven: Yale University Press, 1946), pp. 31–36.

a) Managers do not select the profit-maximizing alternative and engage in policies apparently antithetical to the maximization of profits.

b) It is possible to show a manager ways of making more profit which he will decline. Not all means of making a given amount of profit are equally acceptable to a manager.

c) Managers explicitly use other goals than profit in their work. For example, they are concerned with such measures as sales volume, rate of growth, share of the market, and industry position. They are also given to considering such objectives of a less operational character as the good corporate image, satisfactory labor relations, job security and satisfaction, and public service. Either these are objectives quite distinct from profit maximization or they are simply intermediate goals which managers believe will lead ultimately to profits.

It may well be that the most sensible view of profit calculation the management scientist may adopt at present is that it provides a language in which his hypotheses may be operationally stated. The hypotheses he tests must include not only predictions about the relations between actions and objectives but also predictions about the goals of managers. If profit is not a satisfactory measure of objectives the first step is to discover this experimentally.

This latter comment suggests the position which seems appropriate in view of the management science of today. Just as the problem of verifying the relations between actions and objectives led us to regard management as experiment, so the problem of stipulating objectives is to be regarded as an experimental problem. In other words, the idea of management as experiment is to include experiments relative to hypotheses about objectives. Once again it must be emphasized that ways of looking at the problem and problems to be solved by management science, rather than its accomplishments, are being described.

Ideally, the experimentalist's program would test hypotheses at two levels, one from the viewpoint of the analyst and the other from the viewpoint of the manager himself. A recommendation by the analyst is to be considered, as has been said, a prediction. It asserts that under certain conditions the decision maker will choose policy *x*. This prediction is based in part on an attempt to measure the manager's values, establish a theory about how these values behave, and then deduce a prediction about his choices. If, in an actual instance of choice, the decision maker does not choose policy *x*, then something is wrong. Perhaps the measurements were wrong, perhaps his values do not behave according to the theory, and perhaps the conditions that the measurements and the theory assume do not hold in the instance at hand. Which is the case is what the analyst would like to learn from each actual instance of decision making. If the experiment does not confirm his hypothesis he asks why.

Suppose a recommendation has been accepted by management, confirming in a sense, hypotheses of this sort. Suppose further, action produces ultimately some attainment of the goals held by management at the time of choice. The second sort of experiment is that which management performs, asking whether experience confirms that the objectives they seem to want are those really wanted. The experiment may show that having achieved the ends, they have been modified in favor of others. True preferences are subtle things. They cannot be known on the basis of incomplete information and intuition. Their emergence depends on the development of complete information and they are best known through actual experience. Experience not only provides knowledge about relations between ends and means but also provides the decision maker with knowledge of what it is he wishes to achieve. Knowledge of goals emerges experimentally as a result of action. We decide what we want, act, reflect about what we have achieved, and act again. Our actions are experiments to find out what we want. We learn from our mistakes and know only after something has been achieved whether we wanted to achieve it.[19]

Once one begins to think in the rational and experimental terms which characterize management science, it is natural to wonder how a firm can get along at all without an explicit, shared, operational statement of its objectives. How can anything so complex as a modern corporation be designed and operated without detailed planning of its operations? How can the firm act without knowledge of what it seeks? These same questions applied to economic systems have occupied economists extensively. We have experimental demonstrations that explicit planning toward stated social goals is not a necessary condition for an effective economic system. Some hypotheses suggested below might bear investigation in the case of the firm, mainly to preserve an experimental attitude toward the usefulness of explicit goal statements.

1. The bit of logic which asserts that one cannot possibly decide what to do until one decides what one is after is empirically false when applied to groups of people, including business firms. The functioning of every group

19 Reichenbach, *op. cit.*, p. 296.

in which more than one person participates in decision making tends to demonstrate that people can very often agree on what actions are to be taken without agreeing or even discussing very much what ends these actions are supposed to serve. Indeed, one can perhaps think of the actions taken by the firm as a collective experiment in which all of its decision makers seek to improve their knowledge. Only a very small number of firms feel the need to reflect collectively on what their long-run objectives are.

2. As the organization thus evolves the members share common experiences of working together and the result is a large degree of implicit agreement on objectives for the organization. Indeed, the basic purpose of executive training programs is to transfer to upcoming executives this implicit agreement on the goals of the firm.

3. To the extent that such common views of what is to be achieved do not emerge, the process of decision making for the firm becomes essentially competitive rather than cooperative. Various decision makers in the firm compete with their associates according to their power and responsibility. Each works hard for the objectives he feels are important. The pressures of taking some sort of action if the business is to survive prevent a deadlock. If this competitive process works out well the firm prospers and decision makers are promoted, thus reinforcing what has been learned as a result of the competition. In short, it would seem that any useful view of the firm's decision-making operations must involve both cooperation and conflict.[20]

4. One might even postulate that, drawing a parallel to economic planning, the competition among decision makers may be guided by some "invisible hand" toward the continued existence and prosperity of the company. It is probably true that no single group is sufficiently informed to make adequate plans for the firm, that it is possible to "overplan," and that it is possible to lose both the flexibility and experimental attitude toward goals this book has argued for.

---

[20] March and Simon, *op. cit.*, pp. 113–35.

PART III **Line and Staff Dynamics**

Chapter 11:

DECISIONS AS
CONCEPTIONS

"Look before you leap."

Managers will receive with mixed emotions the news that psychoanalysis has begun the study of the reasons why they make business decisions the way they do.[1] The psychoanalyst works from the hypothesis that management decisions are largely influenced by mental processes outside of the realm of conscious control and awareness and to understand them one must formulate theories of what goes on in the unconscious mind. This may turn out to be an important tool in the study of decisions. This book does not, however, propose to lead an amateur excursion into the complexities of psychoanalytic concepts, although it does seem that a few hypotheses well established in psychology may be highly suggestive. There is a useful parallel, to be noted in passing, between the program of psychoanalysis and that of management science. Psychoanalysis works toward developing an awareness in conscious thought of the unconscious mental processes. Once this awareness is developed the person can deal with these processes so as to adapt better to his environment. Management science proposes to take a manager's thoughts from his conscious mind out into view by expressing them in words and symbols. Then these thoughts can be tested and enriched by others, leading hopefully to decisions in better accord with reality. The aim in the following sections is to indicate how this view helps one to understand the way in which advice can influence action.

In examining the way managers think the standards of tough-mindedness discussed previously will be kept up in order to avoid getting into the position of adopting hypotheses which could only be verified by the figurative adventure of lifting off the top of the

---

[1] Herbert Holt and Melvin E. Salveson, "Psychoanalytic Processes in Management," in C. West Churchman and M. Verhulst (eds.), *Management Sciences, Models and Techniques* (New York: Pergammon Press, 1960), Vol. I.

manager's head and looking inside. This can be done by insisting that whatever hypotheses one sets out on mental processes lead to some predictions about observable actions. The mind is conceived of as a "box" into which go the sense data of experience and out of which come the responses or actions these stimulate. It was at one time hoped the box could remain a "black box" in the sense that behavior could be predicted by studying the relations between stimulus and response. This was of limited value because it was soon noticed that different people give different responses in quite the same situation. To explain this, one must say something about what goes on inside the mind, that is, to illuminate a little of the interior of the black box. In doing so, however, the hypotheses must be kept anchored in observations about the stimulus situation and the responses to it. Of course, one can only argue that such a hypothesis, even when confirmed by these observations, explains thinking in the sense that a person "behaves as if" he thought in a certain way. This very trouble was encountered before in examining the problem of establishing measures of value which would explain behavior in choice situations.

Plainly, much of what is called the "responses" of managers will be what they say to people. If one must know something of how a manager views the future prospects for his business he generally cannot wait for the future to become the present and observe the manager's actions. He must ask him. Although psychologists are becoming increasingly clever at asking questions, one must still face the age-old danger that words do not make simple and direct connections between thoughts and actions. Will a man say what he thinks? Will he act as he says he will act? The first of these problems can be dealt with by putting him under oath or establishing a relationship which encourages direct expression. The second is met only by correlating words with actions.

It is well known, for example, that part of the skill of managers is the facility for expression which persuades and motivates associates. One cannot help but notice that much of what is said is consciously or unconsciously aimed at marks other than clear and full expression of thought. If one listens, as he must, there are no kitchen recipes for reading between the lines. Nobody knows how big a problem this is nor very much about how to deal with it. It seems to have always been true, however, that advisers have tried to cultivate candid discussion with those whom they advised.

The basic premise taken to be the beginning of wisdom in the study of decisions is simple enough: A DECISION IS A CONCEPTION OF A CHOICE SITUATION AND ACTION IS DETERMINED BY THE CONCEPTION. "A decision" means here the way a person thinks about a choice situation. His conception of it is the basis for attempts to explain the fact that different people act in different ways when faced with what are objectively the same problems of choosing. To work with decisions is to work with conceptions. Professor Boulding has called a man's conception his "image" and has written a fascinating book pointing the possibilities for studying images as a guide to empirical research which might help considerably to unify the sciences.[2] The conception has been variously referred to as the chooser's "model" of the choice situation, his frame of reference, or his definition of the situation.[3] In military doctrine the term is "the commander's estimate" of the situation. The military approach, as one would suspect, is to try to have the commander make his conception explicit by filling out a form.[4]

Psychologists might suggest we look at the manager as a complicated information-processing system. The information which forms his conception of a decision situation comes in part from external events by the process of perception and in part from his memory by recollection of the information previously stored there. The job of putting information into the memory's inventory is called learning. Two important properties of this sort of information-processing system are, first, that all the information in the memory is not a part of the conception which is determining behavior at any given moment. The outside events perceived have the effect of calling up from the memory only certain items of information stored there. Second, not all of the outside events which are available at any moment are perceived in the sense of becoming a part of the conception. These two processes, perceiving and recalling, are thought to influence one another. The selection of what is recalled from memory depends on what information is coming in by way of perception, but the selection of what is perceived is dependent on what has been recalled from memory. In sum, the product of thinking is a conceptualization of the choice situation.

---

[2] Kenneth E. Boulding, *The Image* (Ann Arbor: The University of Michigan Press, 1956).

[3] James G. March and Herbert A. Simon, *Organizations* (New York: John Wiley & Sons, Inc., 1958), p. 139.

[4] William A. Reitzel, *Background to Decision Making* (Newport: The United States Naval War College, 1958).

This conception is produced by perceiving and recalling, processes that are both interdependent and selective. The information-processing system has indeed a limited capacity for handling data. In these terms, a basic function of management science is to work toward increasing this capacity.

One might almost imagine that the mind, viewed as an information-processing system, develops ways of economizing in the use of its capacity. Habits are simply actions taken in response to perceived stimuli without the necessity of using much capacity for conscious thought. We brush our teeth in the morning without really thinking about it and while we shave we can ponder the problems the day will bring. Bruner and his associates have studied the thinking process of categorization.[5] They take categorization to mean the strategy of coding our perceptions so that things one could distinguish as different are made equivalent. For example, one forms the category "organization man" and then classifies a large number of discriminably different people as such. This strategy of thought economizes the information-handling capacity in two ways. The environment is greatly reduced in complexity, because instead of perceiving a mass of unique persons, objects, or events, perception is in terms of categories which collect stimuli into classes. Categorization also reduces the necessity for learning anew the properties of events. For example, classifying a person in the "organization man" category is presumably done on the basis of certain attributes noted in him and taken to be criteria for admission to the class. The class has associated with it other attributes that may be ascribed to him without actually going to the trouble of learning whether or not he possesses them. Of course, mistakes are made when this is done and the invention of categories must be looked at in terms of these mistakes.

Categorization is basic to thinking at the conceptual level as well, and very shortly the task will be taken up of forming conceptions of decision situations into categories which have some usefulness from the point of view of management science. Policy making is a form of categorization which has the benefits of economizing the information-handling capacities of the manager. Policy may be read, "When decisions which fall into category x are encountered there is no need to do anything more than apply

---

[5] Jerome S. Bruner, Jacqueline J. Goodnow, and George A. Austin, *A Study of Thinking* (New York: John Wiley & Sons, Inc., 1956).

the rules which have been established for this category." Policy is not usually as simple as this nor very satisfactory if it is, but this attests to a lack of skill in the invention of decision categories for which rules can be premeditated. The point of policy is both to economize the information-handling capacity of the person using it to think about a choice situation and to economize that of his associates who may categorize him as a user of policy and thus know something of his decision-making behavior without actually perceiving it.

One fact of modern organizational life looms in trying to make operational the ideas of an executive acting as a decision maker. It is often difficult to determine which particular person in a large organization actually makes a given decision. Indeed, in tracking down the decision maker one may run into some sort of group decision process. The decision was made by a committee or at a meeting or by informal consultation among a number of people. One comes to talk about an institutional mind and the company's decision. We often hear that General Motors or the Pentagon has made some decision or other. This conception of organizational choice is primarily useful in looking at an organization from the outside. An ability must be presumed to go inside the organization and make at least a crude analysis of the process whereby individuals interact to produce the decision. This analysis involves some look at the structure of power, influence, and communication within the organization. Ultimately, however, we want to think of conceptions as existing in the minds of individuals, for an adviser cannot address himself to an institution. He cannot give advice to General Motors, but only to particular individuals in that organization. As will be shown later, the ways these individuals behave in organizations play a major role in what actions are finally chosen; however, for a while the discussion must be of *a* decision maker or *a* manager. He may not be deciding what the organization will ultimately do but for the moment at least he is deciding what he thinks it should do.

Consider now the elements of a manager's conception of a choice situation and suppose these elements can be classified as alternative courses of actions, possible outcomes or results associated with the alternatives, and goals or objectives which give values to the outcomes. The supposition is not that every conception has elements in each of these classes, for conceptions will be discussed consisting of, say, alternatives only.

The second basic premise is that managers are not satisfied with conceptions limited to alternative courses of action only. They insist, at least in the cases taken up here, in conceptualizing the consequences of their actions and in evaluating these consequences. In short, they want to "look before they leap." This desire to consider the consequences of one's action is the weakest meaning of the term "rational choice." People do not always do this, for many instances of "snap" decisions, made "off the cuff," would be hard to classify as habitual responses or as involving much consideration of possible outcomes. It is not the thesis here to insist they ought to do this nor can it be proven they will be better off if they do. Thomas J. Watson said, "Think," but Roger Stevens, highly successful in real estate, said, "Whenever I think, I make a mistake."[6] The suggestion is only that the need to calculate and evaluate the possible consequences and is a precondition to seeking decision-making advice, and one widely shared among managers.

Whenever it has been necessary to predict the behavior of managers, as it has been in economics, for example, hypotheses have been set forth about the conception the manager had of his choice situations. These conceptions have been given appropriate names, the oldest of which is *economic man.*[7] Classical economic man achieved perfection in conceptualizing his opportunities for choice. It was supposed he had complete knowledge of the alternatives open to him, knew exactly what result would follow from each one, and was able to establish a complete rank ordering of the desirability of the outcomes and thus of the actions. Modern economic man knows all the alternatives but is not quite so sure exactly what outcome will result from each. He does, however, know all the possible outcomes associated with an action and the probabilities of each of them. To each outcome he attaches a value and then chooses the action which maximizes the sum of the values times the probabilities, over the outcomes.[8] The notion of expectation, defined in this precise way, comes from the theory of probability. Soon this discussion will return to the question now an active subject of research, namely, "What is the relation between

---

[6] The editors of *Fortune, The Executive Life* (Garden City, N.Y.: Dolphin Books, 1956), p. 171.

[7] Martin Shubik, "Some Theories of Decision Making," *Administrative Science Quarterly,* Vol. 3, No. 3 (1958).

[8] Boulding, *op. cit.*

mathematical expectation and conceptual hope for the manager?"[9]

Boulding has eloquently summarized one point of view on these hypotheses as to the nature of the manager's conception. "Alternatives do not usually have the courtesy to parade themselves in rank order on the drill ground of the imagination. Our relational image is faulty at the best. Our image of the consequences of our acts is suffused with uncertainty to the point where we are not even sure what we are uncertain about. The economists have tried to deal with the problem of uncertainty by supposing that each of the alternatives in our image presents itself to the mind not only with utility tags attached but also with whole probability distributions. Economic man, clever fellow that he is, now maximizes the expected value of his acts, a feat of mathematical agility which it would take centuries of experience and enormous electronic calculators to perfect."[10]

Hypotheses have run to the other extreme as well. The least complimentary but possibly the most romantic is *heroic man,* who without hesitation chooses among any group of actions having not the slightest idea nor care about the consequences.[11] Not much of a theory can be deduced from the postulate of heroic man since his behavior is bound to appear quite random.

Somewhere in the middle ground is *administrative man,* whose conceptualizations are less well defined but more in accord with the information-handling capacities postulated by psychologists. He has a more limited estimate of the situation and looks not so much for actions which are provably the best of all possible actions but for those which are simply satisfactory. In psychological terms, he looks for actions which, by some rough conception, appear to promise the satisfaction of his aspirations. Administrative man or managerial man can best be viewed as a name for hypotheses which try to bring the results of psychological theory to bear upon the study of how managers make decisions.

The central features which emerge from this view of the manager's conceptualizations are:

---

[9] Chapter 16. See also George Katona, "Expectations and Decisions in Economic Behavior," in Daniel Lerner and Harold Lasswell (eds.), *The Policy Sciences* (Stanford, Calif.: Stanford University Press, 1951); and R. M. Cyert, W. R. Dill, and J. G. March, "The Role of Expectations in Business Decision Making," *Administrative Science Quarterly,* Vol. 3, No. 3 (1954).

[10] Boulding, *op. cit.,* p. 84.

[11] Shubik, *op. cit.*

1. Because of the limited information-processing capacities of the mind, and because of the selective character of both perception and recall, the manager's concept is incomplete. He does not know all of the alternatives open to him, he may have only a rough picture of the outcomes, and his abilities to evaluate them are something less than perfect.

2. His estimate of the situation may have the qualities of vagueness, uncertainty, doubt, or confusion. For example, as he tries to conceive of events further and further into the future, these qualities may increase to the point of what may crudely be called complete ignorance.

3. The dynamics of the decision process begin usually with some external event which evokes the first elements of the conception and initially categorizes the situation as one involving choice among managerial actions. The subsequent complex process of perceiving, recalling, and thinking may add to the conception, clarify it, or even completely reorganize it. Eventually the manager either elects, or is forced by the pressure of affairs, to stipulate the conception as it is and select an action.

Subsequent chapters will suggest some hypotheses for the elaboration of this outline.

We are, of course, especially interested in administrative man when he recognizes the limitations of his estimate of the situation, finds himself unwilling to stipulate, and seeks advice. He may seek advice in specific ways, with respect to specific elements of his conception. For example, he may seek out an expert in the discovery of new alternatives. Presidential staffs, advertising agencies, and research groups all have their "idea men" whose chief function is to think up new alternatives and who have quite limited roles in predicting and evaluating consequences. He may seek a predictive expert who is asked, "What events will take place if we do this?" He may look for more facts from a "leg man" who digs them up, or from a "fact man" who has them in his head. He may ask for help in analyzing the data or in evaluating particular outcomes, and so on. Each of these modes of seeking advice falls short of asking for a recommendation as to what course of action he should choose. We will suppose, however, that this is what he asks for from management science. It would be foolish to pretend that management scientists are always asked to produce a recommendation for action, or that they can always produce one if they are asked. One can only say this is the kind of goal management science has set for itself and the kind of output sought in most management science studies which appear in the literature. It is overwhelmingly action-oriented.

The obvious consequence is that the management scientist as adviser must, if he is aiming for a recommendation for action, work with a conception of the decision himself. Indeed, it is almost a definition of management science to say it is as an activity which tries to produce an explicit conception of the decision situation the manager faces. The advice-producing process might now be pictured in several steps.

1. The manager, stimulated to an initial conception of the choice situation, develops his concept to the point where he recognizes a need to supplement his view with advice.

2. The manager, seeking out his advisers, communicates to them something of his view of the situation.

3. The advisers, beginning with the stimulus provided by the manager, develop an explicit conception of the decision. They then supplement, clarify, and reorganize this explicit conception or model, using the tools of their scientific trade.

4. The manager, through a complex process, receives the explicit model which hopefully has some impact on his own model. He then criticizes and makes suggestions about the explicit model. There may be several cycles of such interaction or perhaps none at all.

5. The advisors ultimately come to the point where they elect to, or are forced to, stipulate as to their model and submit it to the manager for whatever effect it may have in changing his conception.

This view of the advice-giving situation brings us to the important point of alternative purposes in the formulation of models of the choice situation. The psychologist and the economist take as their primary objective predicting human behavior. They are not, in their usual roles as scientists, concerned primarily with offering advice. The models they produce are called descriptive models because the aim is to describe and predict the decision maker's behavior. Management scientists, on the other hand, aim at producing advice. The models of the choice situation developed in this context are called normative models because they offer recommendations as to how the manager "ought" to behave. Starting with the model of administrative man we might agree we had a model useful for descriptive purposes. This view tries to say how the manager will choose. The adviser, whose job it is to supplement administrative man's limited view, does not produce a model of what the manager will do or would have done prior to seeking advice. In fact, the criterion for success in management science is not whether the manager's choice is predicted but whether it is influenced as a result of the recommendations produced.

Descriptive models are produced as a consequence of a scientist's desire to predict decision-making behavior. No scientist in this line of work would inform his subject of the model he had developed, for this would clearly invalidate the experiment. Normative models are the result of the seeking and giving of advice. They arise ultimately out of the manager's need for aid in developing his estimate of the choice problem. This distinction is one of objectives held by the developer of the model. It is a distinction often confused because:

1. The same models are sometimes used for both purposes. Economic man, which started out as a descriptive model, has considerable value as a recommendation or at least as a target toward which recommendations might aim. The theory of games has been used both as a theory which will predict how people will act if unadvised in conflict situations and as a theory which forms the basis of advice on how to act in these situations.

2. Advice expressed in terms of a normative model contains the results of descriptive models. If, as the preceding estimate of the process of advising suggests, the adviser begins with the manager's view of the situation, then this is essentially a descriptive beginning. Many recommendations are made with respect to actions to be taken by the manager involving other persons. Advice must predict the behavior of these other persons and attempts to do so often with descriptive decision models. For example, advice on marketing programs may involve predictions of consumer behavior which arise out of descriptive models. Advice on wage incentive systems includes a descriptive theory of employee decision making, and so on.

3. The objectivity requirement for advice involves both normative and descriptive considerations. The meaning of objective advice is that the adviser tries to be an extension of the manager's mind in the sense of producing recommendations consistent with the objectives of the manager. The adviser makes every attempt not to permit his recommendations to be biased in favor of some of his own goals for the organization. He takes the position of not questioning the goals of management but simply assisting in their attainment. Another way of putting this is that the adviser tries to produce recommendations the manager would find as his own conclusions had he but the time and skill to obtain the data and perform the analysis. He tries to produce recommendations the manager wants to accept. The adviser then is confronted with the problem of how the manager would choose if he were more fully informed, which is in a sense a problem in descriptive or predictive decision theory. The distinction, however, is important. A prediction of how a manager will choose without the benefit of scientific assistance is quite different than a prediction of how he would choose had he been able to do the work of the management scientist himself.

For purposes of study it is useful to divide the decision process into two phases: the establishment of a conception and the selection of a course of action as a result of the conception. The emergence of a conception will occupy the remainder of this chapter and the next one. Later these two phases will be put together in an examination of the decision process as a whole.

Our task as management scientists is to work with the development of the manager's estimate of the decision situation. We propose to do this by making an explicit model of the choice problem. Such a model is usually couched in terms which are recognizable as alternatives, outcomes, and values. It may well be emphasized again that this attempt to work with a model of the choice situation is a distinguishing mark of management science. The advice given by other sciences is more likely to concern specific elements of the choice problem and make little effort to deal with it as a whole. One must be careful not to claim too much for management science. To work with the decision situation is what management scientists would like to do and what they will do when the opportunity presents itself. It is the objective of much of the basic research done in management science, that is, research not limited to a single actual instance of management decision making. It is certainly true that management science does not always succeed, and many of its conclusions can only be viewed as relating to specific elements of decision problems. Nevertheless, policy is a central phenomenon in management science while it plays a background role in most other sciences.

At this point the hypothesis should be interjected that much of the relationship between adviser and manager can be talked about and trouble spots identified in terms of this traffic in models called the process of advice giving. It is necessary to take some pains to draw distinctions here, and the particular distinctions now emphasized are those relevant to misunderstandings which take place in advice giving.

In order to get things off the ground, some categories for models of decisions are useful. Management science, with its normative intentions, has come to employ several systems of categorization which are useful for its own attempts to move toward explicitness, consistency, and validity. For example, the management scientist may discuss his working conception of the choice problem in terms of:

1. Functional categories of management, such as marketing, production planning, or inventory decision models.
2. The analytical framework of the model itself, such as linear programming, game theory, or queuing theory models.
3. The degree of information completeness, such as decision models based on complete or assumed certain information and decision models reflecting various degrees of uncertainty or incomplete information.

For the moment, category system three, based on information completeness, will be used. Professor Knight suggested a categorization which has been widely adopted for discussions of decision models that reflect incomplete information.[12] A decision under certainty is one in which the model associates a unique outcome with each alternative. Choosing among outcomes is equivalent to choosing among alternatives. It is normally supposed when such a model is stipulated as a basis for choice that all the alternatives are presented and that values, at least in the form of a rank ordering, are available. This is the category into which economic man's conceptions would fall. A decision under conditions of risk implies that more than one possible outcome is associated with each alternative and that probabilities are stated for the outcomes. The introduction of probabilities into the model is an event of major consequence, not only for the usefulness of the result but also for the baggage of confusion which comes with it.

Finally, decisions under uncertainty recognize more than one possible outcome associated with at least one of the alternatives, but the model contains no statements of probabilities. It is to be emphasized that the word "uncertainty" now takes on a more precise and limited meaning than it has in ordinary discourse. To work with conceptions that fall into one of these latter two categories does not imply there is universal agreement as to which alternative is to be selected but only that for the moment the concern is with the conceptualizations themselves.

A fair amount of confusion results if one loses track of what these models of the decision process are supposed to represent. These are categories which describe the working models used by management scientists. For example, a good deal of work on the problem of inventory policy conceives of the predicted demand for a commodity as a random variable with a probability distribution. That is, the management scientist's model is one of a decision under conditions of risk. Out of this model he may produce a recommendation of the form, "Choose the inventory level which will minimize the long-run average of the costs of carrying inventory plus the costs of running out." The criticism that this is not the way it is done in industry, or that this is not the way managers think, is misplaced. The model is a normative one and is not intended to reproduce the way managers think. It is very interesting, however,

---

[12] Frank H. Knight, *Risk, Uncertainty, and Profit* (Series of Reprints of Scarce Tracts, No. 16) (London: London School of Economics and Political Science, 1933).

to reflect on the differences between the way a manager approaches such a problem and the way in which the management scientist conceptualizes it. Certainly we must understand something of such differences if the management scientist is to see the problem the manager wishes to solve, and if the manager is to make the resulting recommendations a part of his own conception of the decision.

While one may grant that models of decisions under risk, involving probability distributions, may well have great value in predicting the behavior of business decision makers, it does not seem reasonable that they do anything more than indicate that the behavior can be thought of as if the manager explicitly dealt with the probabilities. It does not appear reasonable to suppose that it reflects the manager's conscious conceptualization. Among other things, it appears to presume a greater amount of memory capacity, calculating ability, and reasoning power than can be ordinarily expected from the unaided human mind. Certainly it would seem that if this were the sort of conceptualization used explicitly by managers one would have heard more about it from them. Perhaps one of the more interesting reasons why managers may seldom deal with risk explicitly is the insufficiency of language in which to express it.

In order to make statements operational one relies heavily on the language he has available. This is especially relevant to the problem of making risk an operational concept. Clearly, managers and all of us recognize decisions made in the face of risk and speak about more or less risky future events. To translate these remarks into operational hypotheses one must have within his vocabulary the concept of probability, which is the means by which science makes risk operational. In other words, the predictive content of statements involving ideas of risk can only be specified by giving directions for the measurement of risk. The interpretation of probability theory in terms of events in the conduct of business affairs is essentially the specification of a set of operations for measuring risk.

One would hypothesize that the terms "probability," "risk," and "the law of averages" are, in the ordinary usage of the person untrained in the theory and interpretation of probability, not fully operational. Thus, the manager who holds no operational conception of risk is at considerable disadvantage when it comes to making explicit his reasoning in risk-taking decisions.

This points up a central task of the management scientist and indicates what has perhaps been a major contribution of management scientists in recent years. The task has been to provide managers with an operational language for expressing risk and to set up data-processing systems within the operations of the firm which do in fact carry out the instructions for the measurement of risk. The accomplishment has been the general public recognition of risk in operational terms.

Anthropologists have argued and indeed demonstrated persuasively that what we take to be reality and the content of our thought—which in turn determines the way we act—are importantly conditioned by the language we have available.[13] Clyde Kluckhohn has said, "Concealed in the structure of each different language are a whole set of unconscious assumptions about the world and life in it. The anthropological linguist has come to realize that the general ideas one has about what happens in the world outside oneself are not altogether 'given' by external events. Rather, up to a point, one sees and hears what the grammatical system of one's own language has made one sensitive to, has trained one to look for in experience. This bias is the more insidious because everyone is so unconscious of his native language as a system."[14] Indeed, it might be further suggested that much of the difficulty in communication between adviser and manager revolves around how risk is to be made operational, how its operational definition is to be interpreted in distinction to the everyday rough usage of the term, and the mixed blessing of making a clear public recognition of the term risk.

Having agreed that what is meant by "a decision" is the conception of a choice situation, one is led to some obvious cautions about the good old practice of hindsight estimates of the goodness of decisions. It is hard to argue with judgments of decisions based on observations of their results. If affairs do not go well, we commonly agree some bad decisions have been made. If an undertaking is singularly successful, someone is given or claims credit for being a very clever decision maker. Certainly it is results that ultimately count.

The question of more concern here is whether or not the observation of the results of a decision permit one to make a connection with the conception the chooser had. Can one learn from

---

[13] There are two notions of this. The cloak theory sees language as a cloak which conforms to thought. The mold theory views it as a mold which determines thought.

[14] Clyde Cluckhohn, *Mirror for Man* (New York: McGraw-Hill Book Co., 1949), p. 124. See also Harold Lasswell, *Politics* (New York: McGraw-Hill Book Co., 1936), p. 193.

after-the-fact results anything about before-the-fact conceptions which will permit one to make good decisions more consistently? Suppose we begin by trying to identify good decision makers, who will be defined as *consistently* successful. While this is possible in laboratory situations and in certain highly repetitive business situations, one always has the classical luck v. skill problem in the *ex post* study of a decision. In a long series of decisions luck and skill tend to be separable, and something can be said about the decision maker himself. In decisions considered unique or seldom repeated, it is more difficult to do this. Decision makers realize this difficulty and tend to construe it to their own advantage, ascribing success to skill and failure to luck. If a decision succeeds management will tend to regard it as a clear and certain act of choice, the undoubted result of the chooser's skill, experience, and unfailing foresight. If it does not turn out so well, it will tend to be regarded as a calculated risk with justification based on long-run effects. "We took a chance, and we lost. You can't win them all. That's the breaks. It's really nobody's fault." There is a natural human tendency to rationalize results by the reconstruction of one's original perception of the choice situation.

Reconstruction is also made difficult by the tendency for success in the management of affairs to stem not so much from a decision which determines action for any extended period of time as from a whole series of decisions. Typically, a major decision is made to launch some sort of program of action. As action gets under way many other decisions are made to compensate for unforeseen circumstances and to make a success out of whatever the original decision may have been. In this sense it is less important to be a good decision maker than it is to be fast on the feet in making a decision turn out a good one. This is a very important factor in actual management decision making. It clouds any judgment as to the goodness of the original decision which launched the program.

If working with decisions is taken to mean working with conceptions, then surely one must judge the effectiveness of decision making in terms of the conceptions used. Suppose the results of some decision are unsatisfactory. What can be learned from the way in which the decision was conceptualized that can be of future use? A prerequisite here is obviously being able to recreate the conception, a task immeasurably easier if the conception is a matter of record. Here, indeed, management science makes an important contribution by providing an explicit record of conceptions. Given this opportunity, there are two questions to be asked:

1. Given the conceptualization used, was the decision a good one? In light of the alternatives actually considered, the evidence used, and so on, was the chosen alternative reasonable? More precisely, the question is that of making the best use of the inputs which were actually available for the construction of the estimate of the situation.

2. Should the conceptualization of the choice situation have been changed, added to, or reorganized? Should other alternatives have been sought out, more data gathered, more or different analyses performed, and so on? Here one must distinguish what reasonably could have been known from what could not have been known by the chooser. Here too one must consider the aspiration level nature of the stipulation process. It is reasonable to draw any conclusion *ex post* from the fact that a few thousand additional dollars spent for research might have revealed a better but unforeseeable course of action? The pressure of events and resources which are limited must be reckoned with in judging the adequacy of a conception.

The problem here is verification of the conceptualization of a decision on the one hand and on the other the hard law of management that says, "Results count, not good intentions."

The presumption at this point is that if advice is going to be given and if it is going to bring about any change in the manager's estimate of the situation, two things must be true:

1. The manager must develop a dissatisfaction with his own conceptualization, either as a result of his own thinking or, more usually, as a result of suggestion.

2. The possibility must exist of changing the manager's estimate of the situation through the methods of management science.

Given for the moment the first of these conditions, it is well to note that the second is not entirely trivial. One must admit that the plodding, deliberate, and explicit processes of science are at present of very little use to those masters of the art of political, military, or managerial decision whose conceptions, if conscious at all, are far richer and based upon the integration of far more experience than anything science can reproduce. Such men are masters of the art of knowing and responding to subtle influences and disorganized experience which have no understandable relation to the orderly processes of science. Some gifted decision makers seem to have the classical ability called *trompe d'oeil*, the kind of mind that can see immediately, as if at a glance, a whole complicated choice situation and consistently elect a course of action which is successful. The kind of advice in mind here is going to be of very limited use to those who have mastered so well the art. Indeed, one would suspect such men would tend to use their staffs to relieve them of routine decision making and to work out the details which show clearly why the action chosen is the right one.

On the other hand, not all people are so blessed and the idea of the human mind as an information-processing system with rather severely limited capacities fits some situations quite well. As has already been hypothesized, the possibility for advice to have an impact on the manager's conception arises because:

1. The conception often lacks sharpness, definition, and order. It is characterized by doubt, uncertainty, and confusion. The basic problem of planning or decision making is sometimes taken to be the problem of endowing one's conception of the future with the concreteness of the present.

2. Advice may provide a language for the expression of, say, the uncertainties of a situation, thus refining them and making them an explicitly reckoned element of the chooser's model.

3. More alternatives may be discovered, more data collected and analyzed, more computations performed, and more factors considered when the mind is supplemented by the facilities of staff assistance.

4. The manager's conceptualization is subjective in the sense that the perceiving, recalling, and thinking of all men is controlled by feelings and motivations, wishes and drives. This is true of scientists and advisers of all kinds, but great efforts are made to produce scientific advice that is objective in the sense of freeing conceptualizations from the control of any particular individual's wishful thinking.

Psychology has been much concerned with the effects our needs and motivations have on our thinking, especially where these effects are not those of which is aware.[15] It may be useful to consider in this connection three rough hypotheses.

1. Habitual ways of viewing a decision situation arise because a conception which meets the needs of one situation is uncritically applied to others. Habits might be thought of as ways of economizing the limited capacity of the mind. Rather than develop a conception which tries to account objectively for each individual choice situation, one simply resorts by analogy to customary conceptions or tends to fit decisions into categories previously developed. Organizations develop such habits and they tend to get formalized into policies or routines for decision making. These habitual conceptions are perpetuated because they satisfy one's need to respond to the pressure of affairs which overtax the conceptualizing capacity of the mind. Habits also help to

---

[15] An excellent discussion of these issues for the nonspecialist is given by Gardner Murphy, *Human Potentialities* (New York: Basic Books, Inc., 1958). Interesting current research closely connected with decision making is discussed in Ward Edwards, "Utility, Subjective Probability, Their Interaction, and Variance Preferences," *Journal of Conflict Resolution*, Vol. 6, No. 1 (1962).

satisfy the need for being able to defend a decision in an organization. Certainly a widely used defense for an unsuccessful decision is the claim that it was based on "the way we always do it," or that it was placed in a category for which a policy was already determined. The problem of extinguishing habits which satisfy these sorts of needs is often referred to as the problem of overcoming resistance to change. The particular mark of a habitual conception which has begun to lose its objective relation to the choice situation is to answer the question, "Why did you choose this way?" with the explanation, "Well, I guess because we always do it this way."

2. One's conceptions of choice situations tend to move toward a view of the situation as the person would like to see it, and not necessarily as it is. Expectations are not independent of desires and conceptions play a part in satisfying needs when actions prove inadequate to the task. If a person finds himself in very limited control of a situation, to some extent quite powerless to act in a satisfying way, then at least he can remake his conceptualization of the situation so as to view it more satisfactorily. The next chapter will outline a special instance of this hypothesis which plays a central part in management decision making. If the need for certainty and confidence in decision making cannot be achieved through predictive knowledge and the ability to control events, then perhaps conceptions will become subjectively free of doubt and uncertainty in response to this need.

Perception is a selective process which tends to give structure to the vastly complicated situations encountered in experience. In perceiving a situation, some elements of it "stand out" more clearly than others. The psychological term is "figure and ground," the figure being those elements perceived most clearly against the suppressed background of the remainder. The psychologist goes on to hypothesize that the elements which tend to stand out as figure are at least in part controlled by needs, in the sense of having previously been perceived in satisfying situations. This, of course, works as the result of fears as well as desires. This kind of hypothesis seems to have great possibilities for sensitizing one to the kind of subjective images managers might be expected to work with. At the most obvious level one would expect the part of the environment which stands out in a manager's perception to depend upon such things as whether or not he had been making decisions during the Great Depression, the labor strife of the thirties, the Second World War, the postwar booms and recessions, and so on.

3. Finally, conceptions of choice situations get distorted because of the social and organizational processes which lead a person to view things in ways accepted by his associates. Socially shared views, which come not so much from contact with reality as from the need to agree, to belong, or to avoid questioning the views of a group, are part of most decisions. John K. Galbraith has called this "conventional wisdom," David Riesman has described it as "other-directed" rather than "inner-directed," and the crude stereotype of the man who sees things as his company sees them is currently called the organization man.[16] Gardner Murphy assesses its importance this way: "The world of

---

[16] John K. Galbraith, *The Affluent Society* (Boston: Houghton Mifflin Co., 1958); and David Riesman, Nathan Glazer, and Reuel Denny, *The Lonely Crowd* (Garden City, N.Y.: Doubleday & Co., 1953).

social immediacy—frequently the world of the unstructured, the confused, the rapidly changing, the world of uncertain norms and of value conflict—is the world in which need-determined thinking reigns supreme."[17] This kind of social deception also plays a central role in organizational theories such as that of Robert K. Merton.[18]

Merton was particularly interested in what he called the dysfunctional consequences of organizational forms and procedures. We might interpret his analysis this way. An individual decision maker, a part of an organization, experiences a demand from his superiors that his behavior be reliable, predictable, and in a general sense within control. They need to know how he is going to make decisions so they can account for, and plan on, the basis of his behavior. He thus finds it increasingly necessary to conform to the organization's way of conceptualizing decision situations or to follow the organizational rules. The rules and conventions tend to become important, no longer because of their original objective effectiveness for achieving organizational goals but rather for their own sake. It becomes less important to make a decision so as to advance the objectives of the organization and more important to make a decision acceptable in the organizational process. This leads to viewing decisions as falling into one or another of a relatively small number of organizationally sanctioned categories. Thus, conceptualization of choice situations becomes a rigid process. This may well mean the decisions are less and less successful at the same time they are becoming more reliable, predictable, and defensible within the organization. Merton's general conclusion is that such an organizational process has a good chance of not only failing to correct socially shared perceptions of decisions but actually reinforcing them and perpetuating their existence.

The point has been to suggest that what is meant by a decision is a conceptualization of a choice situation, and that one commonly experiences sufficient difficulties in forming these conceptions to warrant the sort of assistance management science offers. The next two chapters will suggest the rudiments of a dynamic theory of the decision process, looking always from the role of the staff adviser in these dynamics.

---

[17] Murphy, *op. cit.*, p. 120.

[18] A useful summary of Merton's work in this connection is given in March and Simon, *op. cit.*, pp. 37–41.

Chapter 12:

THE QUEST FOR

CERTAINTY

"I am not a bit anxious about my battles. If I am anxious I don't fight them. I wait until I am ready."

—Viscount Montgomery of
Alemein

John Dewey once wrote a book in which he deplored the tendency of men to seek, in pure thought or philosophizing, a refuge from the uncertainties which are inevitably associated with the outcomes of action in practical affairs. He called his book *The Quest for Certainty*.[1] He clearly was not talking about managers, for they have long prided themselves on their singleminded attention to action, to the nearly total exclusion of any exercises in abstract thought. R. H. Tawney remarked of the English, a nation of devotedly successful businessmen, "It is a commonplace that the characteristic virtue of Englishmen is their power of sustained practical activity, and their characteristic vice, a reluctance to test the quality of that activity by reference to principles. They are incurious as to theory, take fundamentals for granted, and are more interested in the state of the roads than in their place on the map."[2]

Nevertheless, managers certainly must be included in the generalizations about the prevalence of anxiety as a prominent state of mind these days. Freida Fromm-Reichman states it in the most sweeping terms: "The most unpleasant, and at the same time the most universal experience, except loneliness, is anxiety."[3] Freud seems to have gotten people started thinking about how anxious they are. He distinguished between objective anxiety, which he took to be a reaction to conceptualization of anticipated danger, and neurotic anxiety, which was a kind of free-floating anxiety lying in

---

[1] John Dewey, *The Quest for Certainty* (New York: Minton, Balch & Co., 1929).

[2] R. H. Tawney, *The Acquisitive Society* (New York: Harcourt, Brace, & Howe, Inc., 1920), p. 1.

[3] Frieda Fromm-Reichman, "Psychiatric Aspects of Anxiety," in Maurice R. Stein, Arthur J. Vidich, and David Manning White, *Identity and Anxiety* (Glencoe, Ill.: The Free Press, 1960), p. 129.

wait in the mind ready to influence estimates of choice situations on the very slightest encouragement.[4]

Whatever one may think of Freud, it is certainly true that he made people aware of their ignorance as to why they do the things they do. So fascinating are the possibilities which would result from understanding motives in depth that amateur psychoanalysis may be among the more popular national pastimes. Scientists, who saw the operational view of physics as the guardian of objectivity in their craft, have tended to be dubious about the usefulness of adventures into depth psychology and have insisted on the observation of behavior as at least the starting point for understanding people. Freud himself was careful to point out there was a large measure of vagueness and ambiguity in the term "anxiety." The task is to capture the insights which come from this postulate in a version which has more of the necessary toughmindedness.

Without an entangling mass of definitions, let us agree that anxiety is a mental state produced by uncertainty[5] and insecurity. Uncertainty refers to the lack of knowledge which prevents a person from taking action confidently, while insecurity suggests an inability to control the outcomes of his affairs. The point is that we find a choice situation that is characterized by uncertainty and insecurity an unsatisfactory choice situation and that we all share a basic human need to do something about this. The quest for certainty is really behavior motivated by the fundamental need for survival, safety, security, or certainty.

This fundamental postulate, the instinct for self-preservation and the need to feel that other needs will continue to be satisfied, provokes little argument. Nearly everyone concerned with explaining and predicting human behavior has found it not only acceptable but useful. Its uses even range to establishing the foundation for one view of ethics by Anatol Rapoport who postulates survival and security as invariant human needs, along with the need to belong

---

[4] Sigmund Freud, *A General Introduction to Psychoanalysis* (Garden City, N.Y.: Doubleday & Co., 1953), pp. 400–418.

[5] The term "uncertainty" is used in two senses. The technical definition which refers to a model of a decision in which the probabilities of the possible futures are known has already been suggested. This will be referred to in subsequent discussions as technical uncertainty. Without the adjective, the word "uncertainty" refers to models of decisions in which various elements are unknown and which are characterized by various degrees of acknowledged ignorance. The latter use is more general and thus includes technical uncertainty as a special sense.

and the need for order.[6] Harold Lasswell takes politics to be the process of deciding how the available values are to be divided up in society, and these values, he says, are deference, income, and safety.[7] The postulate can indeed be supported almost endlessly by reference to authorities.[8]

This can be said another way. A general human need exists to achieve conceptions of certainty in decision situations. Such decisions are easiest to make, they involve no conflicts in the mind of the decision maker, and they are not occasions for anxiety. No one would suppose, of course, that this need to achieve conceptions of certainty is all-consuming. It conflicts with other needs and one trades certainty for other values continually. A businessman who wanted to be really certain his new product would achieve some given sales volume could spend all his money for market research and delay its introduction indefinitely and still he would have no objective basis for certainty. As will be suggested, a great deal of business decision making can be understood in terms of a trade off between profit and certainty.

Perhaps the process of making a decision can be explained in a way which will place the need for a conception of certainty in the role of an intervening variable between the situation itself and the action with which the chooser responds to it. Suppose the process begins with some event which stimulates the formation of an initial model of the choice at hand. This first conception may well have the qualities of vagueness, doubt, uncertainty, and confusion. One does not choose immediately, but rather supplements and reformulates, either gradually or dramatically, the original conception. This happens as the result of perceiving or recalling additional information, and thinking it over. To ponder the situation is to organize,

---

[6] Anatol Rapoport, *Operational Philosophy* (New York: Harper & Bros., 1953), p. 94.

[7] Harold Lasswell, *Politics* (New York: McGraw-Hill Book Co., 1936).

[8] An interesting empirical study is Melville Dalton, *Men Who Manage* (New York: John Wiley & Sons, Inc., 1959), pp. 241–59. A review of related research is given by James G. March and Herbert A. Simon, *Organizations* (New York: John Wiley & Sons, Inc., 1958), pp. 112–35. The importance of uncertainty in interpreting economic history is suggested by Max Weber, *General Economic History* (New York: Collier Books, 1961). For other examples see John K. Galbraith, *The Affluent Society* (Boston: Houghton Mifflin Co., 1958); Charles O. Hardy, *Risk and Risk Bearing* (Chicago: University of Chicago Press, 1923); Frank H. Knight, *Risk, Uncertainty, and Profit* (Series of Reprints of Scarce Tracts, No. 16) (London School of Economics and Political Science, 1933); Robert A. Gordon, *Business Leadership in the Large Corporation* (Washington, D.C.: The Brookings Institution, 1945), p. 71; and N. Kaldor, "The Equilibrium of the Firm," *Economic Journal*, Vol. 44, No. 3 (1934). See further note 16 of Chapter 15.

transform, and compute; the results are reflected in changes in the way the situation is viewed. This sort of thing does not, at least for the man of action, go on indefinitely. Eventually a conception is developed to which the person is willing to stipulate. Here again stipulation simply means one is willing to agree to act as if a particular model of the situation were in fact true, or representative of the actual situation. Such an explanation seems to be consistent not only with theory but with certain empirical results in psychology and economics.

As long as the decision maker is unwilling to choose he is thought of as being in a state of conflict, in the sense that his inclinations toward the actions open to him are in conflict with one another. He may see the available actions as indiscriminately acceptable or indiscriminately unacceptable. The donkey had trouble deciding which pile of hay to enjoy, and the prince presumably experienced some conflict over which door led to the tiger, even after the signal from the princess.

The conflict results from his dissatisfaction with his model, his estimate of the situation. In terms of the elements of the decision model we might analyze the possible sources of his dissatisfaction.

First, it may be that his whole view of the situation is vague, confused, and characterized by doubt and lack of concreteness. One basic problem of planning future actions is to endow conceptions of the future with something of the concreteness with which the present is seen. As the model becomes clearer, dissatisfactions might become more specific. The array of alternative courses of action which are seen might be unsatisfactory. This may be because:

1. None of those being considered meets the decision maker's requirements for an action he is willing to choose. It is not a question of which action under examination is preferred since all are unacceptable.

2. He may believe that there are other alternatives reasonably available that are worth searching out since they have some possibility of containing something better than those currently considered.

3. It may also be that the other sources of dissatisfaction can best be treated by looking for additional actions.

The decision maker may find his conception deficient as well in the predictive knowledge he has of the outcomes which will result from the various actions. Here uncertainty returns as a word employed in its technical sense. The rough stages of one's views about the outcomes might be:

1. No idea at all, or vague ideas about some of the possible outcomes.

2. A statement of the possible outcomes associated with an action, perhaps not in detailed breakdown but hopefully in collectively exhaustive and mutually exclusive categories. One can always begin by using categories like, "Next year's sales will be either greater than a million units, or less than or equal to a million units." When the outcomes are all stated in this fashion one has technical uncertainty.

3. A statement of the possible outcomes together with the probabilities of each. How one gets these probabilities is, as has been repeatedly emphasized, a problem. In what sense it can be asserted that managers form conceptions which contain probabilities is also a problem. Nonetheless, the technical name for such a view of the future is risk.

4. Finally, by certainty is meant a prediction that a specific outcome will happen with probability one. It is the only possible outcome. Here again is the model ascribed to economic man.

Using certainty and uncertainty in the technical sense for just one more remark, the quest for certainty is the progression up this ladder of increasingly complete conceptions about which the future holds in the way of outcomes for possible actions.

Finally, the decision maker may view with dissatisfaction the evaluations he is able to make of the outcomes. Again, in exactly what sense one can think of the manager as forming value statements for the outcomes in his estimate of the decision situation is not clear. It may be he deals only with preferences among actions, or it may be that he can best be thought of as attaching single measures of value to each outcome and using these measures in a computational process which leads him to the selection of an action. It may also be that one can best think of him as associating with each outcome a series of measures or a value profile. These questions need not be decided here, for the point is that the kinds of views a decision maker has about the goodness or badness of outcomes may be a source of dissatisfaction leading to an unwillingness to stipulate. For example, if two investments appear at rough calculation equally profitable, one response to this conflict might be to refine the estimates of profit in an attempt to reveal a difference on which choice could be based.

As has been suggested, the sources of dissatisfaction may not be attacked head-on. Dissatisfaction with predictive knowledge may be met by looking for other alternatives for which one can make better predictions. The same sort of thing is true for unsatisfactory evaluations. Likewise, an unsatisfactory array of alternatives may lead one to seek better predictions and evaluations. The point is, however, that explanations such as these may be used to understand responses to the choice situation other than choosing.

Such responses may include gathering additional information, the search for new alternatives, thinking it over, and, importantly for us, seeking staff advice. These dissatisfactions, or rather the need which is unsatisfied, here is called the need for certainty. The assumption is that behavior in choice situations can to some extent be understood in terms of movement in the direction of satisfying such a need.

Businessmen, it is supposed, do not rush off halfcocked but pursue at least to some extent this quest for certainty. Their aspirations in this direction determine the point at which they will stipulate their estimate of the decision in part, but they must also reckon with the cost of attaining certainty, not only in money but in time. The pressure of affairs forces many a choice upon an unwilling chooser. To be forced into an unwilling choice is, to close the loop, a source of some considerable anxiety.

The kind of explanation being worked toward is one which will connect some observable conditions of the decision situation (the stimuli) with observable behavior which results (the responses), by means of the postulated need for certainty (the mediating process or the intervening variables). Let us first take up some examples of the types of responses one might take to be connected with the amount of uncertainty or dissatisfaction associated with a decision maker's model of the situation and the strength of the need to resolve the conflict of choice. The following general hypotheses are offered.

1. The greater the dissatisfaction with a conceptualization the longer will be the time required to make a choice. Given that a decision situation has been recognized, one would expect delay, inaction, and postponement to characterize unsatisfactory models. This has been carefully confirmed in simple laboratory choice situations by psychologists and it seems to agree in a rough way with much everyday experience in managerial situations.

2. To a manager, time is usually a scarce resource, for he has many matters competing for his attention. It is often true as well that advantages to his firm which result from quick decisions are sacrificed when decisions are delayed. More generally, one might postulate that the greater the amount of dissatisfaction the greater the amount of scarce resources which will be devoted to efforts to achieve better conceptualizations. The resources may include money, both in terms of cash outlays and in terms of incomes forgone, manpower, materials, and so on.

3. One would expect the decision maker to express his dissatisfaction with his conception in terms of his doubts, fears, and remarks on the difficulty

of making the decision. As will be suggested later, these kinds of remarks may represent a considerable personal sacrifice on his part. There is often a need to maintain a self-image of confidence and certainty in decision making as well as to project such an image both to his superiors as an indication of "executive ability" and to his subordinates to inspire respect and confidence in leadership.

4. A decision maker, dissatisfied with his own conceptualization, might adopt various devices for transferring responsibility for a decision. For example:

a) The decision may be put before a committee formally organized for the purpose, or before a group having no particular formal position in the organization. The committee and, indeed, the organization itself may become devices which serve to spread the burden of uncertainty over large numbers of people.

b) The decision may be referred to his superiors, or even to someone else not necessarily above him in the organization. It is difficult to distinguish between deliberate "buck passing" and legitimate surrendering of the choice into more capable hands.

c) The decision maker may abdicate all responsibility for developing his own conceptualization in favor of a rather unquestioning acceptance of the recommendation of some expert, adviser, or specialist. The average person, consulting his doctor, seldom tries to participate in decisions concerning his health but simply does what the doctor suggests.

d) The decision may be forced into some policy category or routine choice process. Here again it will be difficult to decide whether or not a decision should or should not have been subsumed under a particular policy. Tendencies toward elaborate justification for categorizing a decision, especially after it has turned out to be unsuccessful, might be taken as indicating this kind of transfer of responsibility. Here the use of habitual decision-making routines, policy, or categorization is interpreted as in part a result of the need for certainty. One would predict the extension of this kind of decision process beyond the range of its effective functional consequences.

e) The decision maker may permit, accept, encourage, or deliberately promote practices which tend to insulate him from uncertainty. One such practice, for example, might be called "management as if." One large food-processing plant makes a production program up for an entire year's operations. Although the program is clearly subject to considerable uncertainty because of the impossibility of giving an exact prediction of sales, the head office of the firm provides the plant with a very definite sales forecast and says literally, "Manage the plant as if this were known to be the actual sales for the coming year." Even though the production program has to be revised continually as unforeseen sales patterns emerge, all planning continues on the same "as if" basis using determinate sets of numbers for sales forecasts.[9]

Another very general practice of this sort is uncertainty absorption.[10] Typically, higher-level managers are furnished with aggregate data, averages, summary statistics, and so on which tend to filter out all the variations and uncertainties actually present in the phenomena these data describe. Uncertainty absorption results whenever a mass of data or evidence is used to draw

---

[9] In connection with "management as if . . ." see also Chapters 7 and 16.
[10] March and Simon, *op. cit.*, p. 165.

conclusions and these conclusions are communicated to the decision maker without the evidence itself.

Still another practice which tends to insulate the manager from uncertainty is that of taking predictions to be promises. A large supplier of industrial products requires the sales department to make a prediction of each month's sales in each sales territory. If, toward the end of a month, it begins to appear that the predictions will not be realized, the sales department is held responsible for getting sufficient additional business so that the predicted volume is achieved. It is clear that such a system will soon evolve to produce a rather close match between prediction and attainment.

5. Finally, in the interests of completeness, the widely held hypotheses which suggest various physiological correlates to unsatisfactory models of decision situations can be mentioned. These range all the way from small nervous symptoms such as perspiring hands to general nervous tension with the classical manager's ulcer.

In his provocative discussion of economic security, or the elimination of economic uncertainty, John K. Galbraith has stated the explanatory usefulness of the quest for certainty in strong terms. He notes the traditional resort to the need to maximize profits as a hypothesis for explaining managerial behavior and he calls this unfortunate since, he says, "The development of the modern business enterprise can be understood only as a comprehensive effort to reduce risk."[11] His thesis is that the greatest source of uncertainty was the market, characterized by the possibility of unexpected actions by competitors, the uncontrollable fluctuations of market prices, the vagaries of consumer tastes, and the rapid obsolescence of products. Much has been written about the rarity with which competitors actually surprise one another, the infrequency with which a manager becomes involved in provocative price policies, and the success with which firms have been able to reduce the effective uncertainty about each other's pricing and product policies. Great expenditures for market research, advertising, and new product research and development have increased the predictability and controllability of technological evolution and consumer demands. Diversification of product line has been one of the great modern policies, which can most sensibly be understood as a method for reducing risk and uncertainty.[12]

Through vertical integration the manager has removed much of the uncertainty that formerly surrounded the supply of raw materials. Their price and availability are far more within his control and

[11] Galbraith, *op. cit.*, p. 101.

[12] William T. Morris, "Diversification," *Management Science*, Vol. 4, No. 4 (1958). See also Knight, *op. cit.*

thus far less a source of uneasiness for him. Whatever the difficulties he may experience as a result of his relations with his labor union, he is no longer uncertain as to the price of labor or the conditions of employment which he will have to meet. All this, of course, takes no note of the older and seldom considered devices by which the government, together with the insurance companies, eliminate for him all the risks of natural disaster, social instability, and revolution which in earlier times were the prime source of uncertainty for businessmen.

Clearly, many actions chosen by the manager can be understood in terms of this need for certainty. His success in achieving this has been great, but there remains still the uncertainty of the business cycle or booms and recessions to be reckoned with. It is clear too that success has been achieved far more by big firms than by small ones. Although big firms seldom fail, small ones and new ones often do. Great security is enjoyed by the large firms in any industry, but industrial firms in general have a chance of only 24 per cent of surviving five years, and of only 19 per cent of being in business ten years after their beginning.[13]

Nor should the quest for certainty be taken as a "single-cause" explanation for managerial decisions. Nearly every opportunity to reduce uncertainty may be taken advantage of only at a price. Indeed, the need for certainty usually conflicts with the need for gain, and these two together form the basic explanatory hypotheses of economic decision making. It has always been a fact of economic life that one has to choose between more certain but often less profitable opportunities such as bonds, and less certain but usually more profitable opportunities such as common stocks. If a manager chooses to reserve the decision on the launching of a new product until after elaborate research and test marketing, he may well increase the certainty with which he views the decision, but he pays for this in the price of the investigation, a price which is often notably expensive not only in dollars but in time. One really needs the notion of a trade-off between certainty and gain or other values to understand decision making in modern management. (More will be said about this trade-off.)

In the realm of economic security, some rather acceptable explanations are available for a hypothesis of increasing willingness to sacrifice gain in favor of certainty. Many years ago a study

---

13 *Survey of Current Business*, U.S. Department of Commerce, Office of Business Economics, December, 1954.

sponsored by the Twentieth Century Fund produced the conclusion that big business was not necessarily more profitable but was clearly more stable.[14] Thus it is clear the bigness reduces uncertainty in the economic sense. It does this by means of three general mechanisms:

1. Using diversification strategies involving many products, many customers, many suppliers, many stockholders, many decision makers in management, and so on.

2. Having the ability to devote considerable resources to the control of its economic environment involving advertising, lobbying, arrangements with competitors, and product development.

3. Having available resources to devote to predicting the outcomes of decision, for example, through the employment of staff advisers and experts.[15]

This is complicated by the fact that, although bigness reduces uncertainty, uncertainty must be reduced in order to achieve or maintain bigness. The marshalling of funds and talent necessary to conduct large-scale business enterprise is impossible without the ability to achieve a measure of certainty in the minds of a rather large number of decision makers. No manufacturer can tool up and staff up for high-volume production without some considerable certainty as to the outcome.

The organizational process utilized by big firms is in itself a source of predisposition toward certainty. What is now called bureaucratic organization is not conducive to high-risk decisions. Modern corporate decisions are hardly the long gambles the fast-moving, risk-taking entrepreneur of the early industrial revolution was accustomed to taking.

Bigness breeds professional managers, and professional managers find in their own personal positions a tendency to favor certainty and slow-but-sure growth and profit as against the high-risk decision. To suggest but one example, Meyer and Kuh have carefully investigated the way capital-investment decisions are made.[16] One of their conclusions is that there is a strong bias in favor of internal financing of capital investment programs through depreciation and retained earnings rather than through external borrowing of funds. This means that capital investments tend to be limited to the amounts internally available and some presumably profitable

---

[14] Alfred L. Bernheim (ed.), *How Profitable Is Big Business?* (New York: The Twentieth Century Fund, Inc., 1937).

[15] Again, it might be emphasized that scientific advice is not always characterized by certainty. Indeed, it may increase the manager's uncertainty. See Chapter 14.

[16] John R. Meyer and Edwin Kuh, *The Investment Decision; An Empirical Study* (Cambridge, Mass.: Harvard University Press, 1957).

opportunities must be forgone. Indeed, the market rate of interest, which has long been supposed to have a basic relevance for the capital investment decisions of a firm, turned out to be of little importance. One explanation, which tries to look at the investment decision from the manager's own viewpoint, suggests that if a major investment fails the consequences are far more serious if the investment is externally financed. Indeed, these consequences may include drastic measures to meet the debt, eventual bankruptcy, and a strong possibility of the replacement of the management by the stockholders. If, on the other hand, the investment is internally financed, a major failure may bring only a slight reduction in dividend payment which may be of small consequence to the managers who own but little of the firm's stock themselves.

There is also the simple and acceptable hypothesis, which is consistent with a good deal of theory and empirical evidence in economic life, that the more one has the more he stands to lose and the more diligently he avoids risks. A number of decisions can be understood in this light. Big companies are loath to risk their reputations and market positions with untried and untested new products, while small, new companies tend literally to risk their existence on the roughest sorts of indication that a product will sell.

It must be noted, however, that managers exhibit some behavior widely interpreted as running somewhat counter to this notion of the quest for certainty. In fact, it is often suggested that businessmen are perfectly at ease with uncertainty, on such grounds as the following:

1. Efforts by managers to create the public impression that they are great risk takers and do, in fact, take great risks. This has considerable truth but does not indicate any lack of desire to reduce the risks involved. It is interpreted by some, on the other hand, as a perpetuation of a nineteenth-century myth as a justification of profits.

2. Discussions by managers of "running the calculated risk." In these situations the risk is almost never calculated in any interesting sense. Many such discussions can be better interpreted as ex post facto explanations of decisions which were not successful rather than rational integration of risk and uncertainty into the decision process.[17]

3. The observed decisiveness of managers, or their ability to make quick, confident decisions.[18] This may indeed mean that experienced managers have learned to live with uncertainty and doubt. This is, however, a tolerance developed out of necessity rather than choice. It is also widely known that managers realize that after stipulation and choice the thing to do is to forget

---

[17] See Chapter 16.
[18] See Chapter 15.

the uncertainty of the conceptualization since it is no longer relevant to action. This tends to reduce anxiety and focus on taking care of the future, the old rule of letting bygones be bygones.

Galbraith has gone on to suggest that a sufficient measure of uncertainty reduction in the economic field has been achieved by large business firms so that it is not a matter of major preoccupation with the managers of these firms. He states a proposition that might be reinterpreted this way: The measures one takes in an effort to reduce economic uncertainty are subject to sharply diminishing returns. That is, after the major hazards have been eliminated, to go on to further reduce uncertainty requires such a large expenditure or sacrifice that it is no longer judged worth it. Knight has argued extensively that if one were able to reduce economic decisions to certainties there would be no possibility of profit at all. This is, of course, based on the assumption that if one person sees an opportunity as a sure thing, others do also and thus the price offered for such an opportunity is bid up to the point where it equals the return known to be possible. The point is simply that it makes some sense to think of business firms as tackling the big uncertainties first, the uncertainties arising out of price and competition. Those firms who tackled the big ones first succeeded, those who did not failed. Having pushed their efforts to reduce this kind of economic uncertainty reduction to the point of diminishing returns, the reasonable thing to do is to turn toward other sources of uncertainty. These might be thought of as internal sources.

To suggest that after solving the problems of economic security businessmen turned to the internal problems of their own organizations and thus to management methods for the reduction of internal uncertainty, is, of course, to oversimplify. However, the major sources of economic insecurity seem to have had a natural prior claim to the resources which managers were willing to devote to reducing their uncertainty. The situation, as Chapter 3 suggested, has other important dimensions as well. Some evidence was found there for the hypothesis that the amount of effort devoted to the reduction of uncertainty from within may depend on the size of the firm, its age, the amount of uncertainty involved, and the availability of techniques for uncertainty reduction. For example, it was suggested that the firm had to reach a moderate size before it chose to devote sufficient effort to internal uncertainty reduction to justify staff groups for this purpose. Size increases the amount of money which can be devoted to reducing uncertainty and, by permitting the use of the resulting information over a larger number of decisions, may greatly reduce the cost per decision. This raises the familiar "make-or-buy" problem in the case of information. Should the firm create its own staff for this purpose or employ outside groups on a short-term basis?

It appeared also that attention to uncertainty reduction was a function of the age of the firm as well. While the firm is very young its main attention is directed toward the threats from its external environment; only when these are sufficiently neutralized does internal uncertainty receive attention.

It would seem also to be almost obvious that the greater the amount of uncertainty perceived by a decision maker the greater the amount of effort devoted to meeting it. Likewise, as the competence of management science to handle internal uncertainty increases the greater the amount of effort devoted to such work.

There is, of course, the simple basic demand on the part of management for reliability and controlability in the performance of men, machines, and materials. A manager must be, in the large sense, in control of his organization. The history of scientific efforts in management may in part be read as the history of the development of techniques for increasing the reliability, predictability, or controlability of all the things which happen in the plant. The systems for control of production, inventory, quality, productivity, and so on, together with incentive systems, job design, and job evaluation, represent progress toward the elimination of internal sources of uncertainty.

One of the major factors in recent business-activity fluctuations has been inventories. Manufacturers have found their inventories have become increasingly important as the speed with which goods reach the customer tends to increase. If price becomes less and less of a basis for competing, and product differentiation as well tends to disappear in some lines, then service and availability must grow increasingly important. Speaking generally, obsolescence, reluctance to finance inventories with outside funds, and their use (as in the case of steel) as an instrument of labor-management relations, have all tended to emphasize their role in the firm. Inventories are also the main device with which management tends to insulate the production process from the uncertainties of the market. The inventory is used partly to decouple the firm from its environment. Automation, mass production, less flexible labor contracts, and the like have tended to increase the need for certainty as to levels of production, which can, in part, be assured through inventory policy. Thus it is small wonder that a very large part of recent work in management science has concentrated on the problems of inventory policy. Much of this work appears to have been very well received by managers, and this can be understood in terms of the search for certainty.

As was also suggested in Chapter 3, size itself produces complexity and specialization of function in the organization which serve to further increase internal uncertainty. As delegation takes place and communication becomes more and more of a problem, each manager finds it increasingly difficult to be aware of what is going on in the other subunits of the firm. To the extent his decisions must include consideration of the activities of others, coordination becomes a central problem and lack of it creates uncertainty. It has even been suggested this source of uncertainty may eventually operate to limit the economical size of the organization. The bureaucratic form of organization, designed essentially to overcome the limitations of individual decision makers, carries with it this inherent difficulty. Max Weber, one of the earliest scientists to study this kind of organization, saw that the ideal form of bureaucratic organization would have to be rather rigid in order to mitigate this effect. Weber's ideal organization was supposed to operate on principles like these.

Operations are governed "by a consistent system of abstract rules . . . [and] consist of the application of these rules to special cases." This system of standards is designed to assure uniformity in the performance of every task, regardless of the number of persons engaged in it, and the coordination of different tasks.[19]

Of course, Weber was talking about an ideal, not an actual instance of organizational design. He felt that, "Experience tends universally to show that the purely bureaucratic type of administrative organization . . . is from a purely technical point of view, capable of attaining the highest degree of efficiency. . . . The fully developed bureaucratic mechanism compares with other organizations exactly as does the machine with non-mechanical modes of production."[20]

Later empirical studies of large organizations have shown that this sort of organization tends to perform the function of reducing internal uncertainty but unfortunately at the expense of certain other

---

[19] From *Essays in Sociology.* Quoted by Peter M. Blau, *Bureaucracy in Modern Society* (New York: Random House, Inc., 1956), p. 28.

[20] *Ibid.,* p. 31.

quite unwanted consequences. Thus the problem of internal uncertainty continues to remain a central issue in the work of management science.

Many of the responses which have been suggested here to the
need for certainty may be understood in terms of the manager's
willingness to devote some of his resources or give up some opportunities for gain in return for a reduction of the uncertainty in his
conceptions of decisions. These actions can be roughly viewed as
objective and reasonable in the sense that many people would
agree on the presence of uncertainty and the general effectiveness
of the efforts to reduce it. There is at least some measure of interpersonal objectivity. These efforts to reduce uncertainty are perhaps
pursued until some rough calculations of the diminishing returns
from further efforts suggest they be terminated. There are, however,
more subjective responses to the quest for certainty.

As was outlined in the previous chapter, if one cannot achieve
something like certainty in his decision models through objective
means, but external operations of prediction and control, then he
might simply remake his image of the decision. Perhaps if the need
for satisfactory estimates of the situation were strong enough, his
perception, recall, and thinking processes would simply suppress the
uncertainties in the choice situation. In short, he might achieve a
view of the decision situation to which he was willing to stipulate,
not by objective means but by the selective character of perception,
and recall as well as the need-controlled thinking process which
produces the conception. Long ago the philosopher Vico said this
in particularly harsh terms: "Men ignorant of the truth stick to certainty. Not being able to satisfy their intelligence with knowledge,
they are content to have their will supported by the consciousness
of certainty."

Several hypotheses might be suggested relative to this subjective attainment of certainty.

1. Certainty represents the traditional academic view of many business
decisions, and this may reflect a tendency to fit things into academic formulae
and modes of thought.

2. Certainty may be associated with personality characteristics such as
boldness, aggressiveness, confidence, success, self-assurance, and feelings of
power.

3. Certainty is surely related in part to the lack of language for thinking
about and expressing uncertainty noted before.

4. Certainty may be a part of an individual's need to preserve a self-image
of the assured, confident, and successful man of affairs.

5. Certainty may in part explain the appeal to all manner of hunches, cues, habits, and rules of thumb with which a decision model may be simplified.

6. Most important, certainty may help to explain some of the nonrational relationships psychologists have pointed out between evidence, experience, and beliefs. Facts alone are seldom sufficient to change people's minds.

We are dealing here with a widely observed human tendency to convert assumptions into facts, doubts into certainties, and to revise images of decision situations so as to meet the need for certainty.

Let us return to the original examination of the quest for certainty as a postulate and look in general at the responses the decision maker may make to it. Consider, for example, the case in which the manager is dissatisfied with his knowledge of the outcomes associated with the various alternatives in a particular decision. He is unwilling to make a choice because he does not have satisfactory predictions of what might happen as the result of the possible actions he might elect. The array of responses open to him would include:

1. Getting more evidence and performing more analysis to improve his predictive knowledge of the relevant future events.

2. Taking some action to control what happens or developing some power over these future events.

3. Searching for new courses of action, the results of which are more certain in his view.

4. Suppressing consciously or unconsciously, or denying the uncertainty.

Consider only the first three of these responses, those which tend to be more objective than subjective. Each response is both potentially costly and potentially profitable, and the question of which to utilize and when to stipulate and choose is a question of some consequence to the manager. Here again is raised the basic question of stipulation which first emerged in the analysis of verification in Chapter 7. From a normative or logical viewpoint it was asked, "When should the decision maker stop enriching his conception of the situation and proceed to take action?" The hypothesis is that the manager finds a different answer for himself than perhaps his scientific staff would suggest for him, although both find it a difficult problem. We might try to understand this process of utilizing one or another of these responses up to the point of choice in two ways.

1. It might be hypothesized that stipulation occurs at a point where the calculation of the marginal costs of getting more data, exerting more control, or searching for other alternatives is found to be roughly equal to the marginal benefit expected from the response.

2. It might be hypothesized that the decision maker is characterized simply by an acceptable level of certainty which must be achieved before stipulation will occur. The process is thus one of an aspiration level nature.

The first of these requires the decision maker to have some idea of the trade-off between uncertainty and profit as well as the ability to make some exceedingly difficult predictions. It is necessary to predict the cost of continuing the response together with the changes in uncertainty and the changes in profit to be expected as a result of this continuation. This is clearly the form of the process which is supposed in statistical problems, where the point at which one ought to stipulate can be determined in a highly reasonable fashion. As has been seen, it is a model of the process which the staff would like to achieve but seldom realizes in important problems. As an explanation of how the decision maker solves his own problem, it seems overly rationalistic. While it may well be true that managers do estimate the costs, say, of getting more data and something of the benefits expected from it, there seems little likelihood this is their major consideration or that they are consistently effective in making the necessary predictions.

One would probably do better to hypothesize that stipulation with respect to knowledge of future events is an aspiration level phenomenon. This does not mean the need for certainty is divorced from the desire for gain. The trick in making a useful theory of how managers stipulate is to say how their aspirations relative to uncertainty are determined. It would seem to depend on such considerations as:

1. The order of magnitude of the gains or losses that appear possible in the decision. One tends to require more certainty in "big" decisions than in "little" ones.

2. A very rough but dynamic perception of the gains and losses from extending a response, based largely on accumulating experience. If, for example, one finds that in a particular decision it turns out to be increasingly difficult and expensive to get additional data, then perhaps one's aspiration level with respect to uncertainty comes down.

3. Perhaps most importantly, the many personal and situational factors (of the sort suggested earlier in the present chapter) that influence a manager's aspiration level for uncertainty.

The following chapter will try to place these hypotheses in a somewhat larger context and work toward making them more specific and operational. For the present, it will simply be suggested that the matter of stipulation lies at the center of the kind of assistance which the staff can provide for management and the kinds of disagreements which arise between them.

This chapter may be summarized by suggesting that one of the functions of advice is to assist the manager in the development of his conceptualizations of decisions from doubt and uncertainty to explicitness and greater certainty. In particular, the functions of advice include:

1. Collecting and analyzing data for prediction.
2. Discovering new alternatives.
3. Exploring means of controlling future events.
4. Helping to clarify values, goals, and objectives.
5. Making uncertainty explicit.
6. Providing objective and operational measures of uncertainty in the form of probabilities.
7. Helping to distinguish between objective and subjective uncertainty.
8. Improving the process of determining the point at which the decision maker stipulates the evidence and proceeds to take action.

Roger Hilsman's statement of the situation in international affairs applies equally well to business affairs. "To the anxiety created by having to choose between values which seem equally dear would be added the anxiety of knowing one's knowledge is not trustworthy and that either action or inaction may bring consequences that are terrifying precisely because they are unknown. From this double anxiety only the dogmatic and the opinionated—the irrational—would be free. For those who strive for rational decisions and who know when they do not know, it would be a familiar companion."[21]

---

[21] Roger Hilsman, *Strategic Intelligence and National Decisions* (Glencoe, Ill.: The Free Press, 1956), p. 160.

Chapter 13:

DECIDING

"The effective businessman is invariably able to make up his mind, often on limited evidence, without uncertainty as to his own wisdom. It is a part of this talent not to reflect on past mistakes, or even to admit that a mistake has been made."

—JOHN K. GALBRAITH in
American Capitalism

Deciding is a chore we do so often that we become quite incurious as to how we do it. How business decisions are made is a subject which has aroused much curiosity but remains to a great extent a mystery. One can stereotype the outward manifestations of decision making, seeing some managers as table pounders and others as window gazers, but insights are hard to come by. Managers, when asked, find difficulty in making what they do explicit. Their reponses may include such remarks as, "I don't think businessmen know how they make decisions. I know I don't," "You don't know how you do it. You just do it. It is like asking a pro baseball player to define the swing that has always come naturally to him," and "Whenever I think, I make a mistake."[1]

This is not because managerial decision making is easy. Decisions classically consist of low uncertainty, low-profit alternatives, and high uncertainty, high-profit alternatives. Choosing between the two is not a trivial exercise. There are very few alternatives without some risk of loss, and the experienced decision maker somehow learns to live with this.

The study of decisions is, as has been indicated, broadly divided into normative investigations which produce advice and descriptive investigations which produce descriptions and predictions. Beginning with the descriptive side of things, the problem is that of trying to understand how managers actually go about making decisions. Much of what is often said on this question is essentially a static

---

[1] The editors of *Fortune, The Executive Life* (Garden City, N.Y.: Dolphin Books, 1956).

description relating a particular conception with a particular choice. It is much like the older psychological theories which hoped that for every stimulus there would be a predictable response. Given an event, the theory predicts what action managers will take. The prototype of this is perhaps the sort of theory which says that a manager, faced with a decision among alternative capital-investment opportunities, will apply some particular rule of thumb or other and come to a conclusion about his investment plans. Perhaps this is so, but perhaps also there is more to it than this. All theories begin with static problems, but it may well be time to move on to some attempts to understand the dynamics of decision making.

So far the hypothesis involves the decision maker's estimate or conceptualization of the choice situation. It has been argued that to study and understand decisions is to study and understand these models which are in "the eye of the beholder" rather than phenomena which can be observed with interpersonal objectivity. The manager who, from a hindsight position, berates his subordinates for making the "wrong" decision may be judging them against a divine, rather than a human, standard. One can only ask useful questions about what managers should do or will do in terms of the limited conceptions of choice situations out of which their acts are born. March and Simon have given this notion a useful name: "the cognitive limits of rationality."[2]

As the basis for a general picture of the process of deciding, then, is a hypothesis involving the decision maker's estimate of the situation. His estimate is limited in several ways. It cannot be in any sense complete because his experience is not complete. In addition, even his limited experience is picked and chosen by the selective processes of perceiving and recalling. His estimate is limited in its objectivity as well, because of the power needs and emotions have over his thinking. It may well be that at a given moment the model or estimate of the situation with which he finds himself is not a satisfactory one. He is unwilling to base his choice on so inadequate a conception of the nature of the affair. At this point a second basic postulate is introduced which ascribes to him a need to reduce the general quality of uncertainty in his model. Perhaps this need might lead him to seek or accept advice. Eventually the resources he is willing to devote to the reduction of uncertainty would seem more costly than the results they promise, and thus

---

2 James G. March and Herbert A. Simon, *Organizations* (New York: John Wiley & Sons, Inc., 1958), pp. 137–72.

finally he would stipulate, agreeing to act as if his conception were reality. Thus the action would be selected.

The need now is to bring back as a postulate one of the more warmly human attributes of administrative man. His rule for choosing an action is based simply on a criterion which distinguishes acceptable actions from those not acceptable. The criterion or standard which an action must meet to be judged satisfactory and acceptable is called an aspiration level. This seemingly uninteresting platitude is important because with it comes the idea that decisions are seldom explainable in terms of "best" actions. It is not supposed that decision makers either try or succeed in choosing an optimal action, that is, one which is demonstrably the best of all possible actions. In fact, many situations can be understood only if one assumes limited efforts are made to choose the best of a more restricted class of actions, say the class included in the model at the time of choice. If the decision maker is considering a number of actions, all of which are satisfactory to him, and there are only small differences in his preferences for the actions, he may well choose the act which attracts his attention first or to which he is drawn by some extraneous cue.[3]

This assumption of satisficing rather than maximizing behavior means further that one can give some dynamic qualities to a description of choosing. No longer is it the classic study of choice which began with a list of fixed and given alternatives among which the chooser was to select. Instead, the process takes on a time dimension which brings with it both some "face validity" and some opportunities for putting the hypotheses to the test of observation.

One might make a stab at a dynamic theory this way. The episode begins with some event which alerts one to a choice situation and evokes an initial image or estimate of the problem. The triggering events may be as important as the awarding of a major contract or as seemingly unimportant as a chance reference read or heard. If the evoked estimate contains an acceptable action, the choice may be made immediately. For this to happen the decision maker's model must be both sufficiently clear and certain and indicate an action which promises acceptable consequences. These conditions lead to immediate stipulation and choice. If no acceptable alternative is present in the evoked estimate, the decision maker will supplement, refine, and reorganize his view. He may

---

[3] *Ibid.*, pp. 140–41.

choose to reduce his uncertainty with respect to the set of alternatives initially evoked, in hopes that as the estimate improves one of
them will emerge as meeting his aspirations. Instead of this, or if
this fails, he may search for new actions. As these are discovered
and become a part of his estimate, he evaluates them. It is supposed
that the new actions are found singly or in small groups, and that
they are immediately evaluated to see if they are acceptable actions.
The decision maker does not accumulate a list of actions before
making the evaluation.

As soon as an action is discovered which meets his aspirations,
the decision maker stipulates and acts. This long the process will
continue, and no longer. Thus, if this notion is correct, one should
be able to tell something about the decision maker's model by
simply noting how long it takes him to make his choice. Psychologists have done just this with considerable success and shortly
their results will be drawn on.[4]

Of course, the pressure of deadlines and limitations on the resources available for reducing uncertainty may intervene and force
the decision maker to act before he has achieved his aspirations
with respect to his model and an acceptable alternative. This common event can be woven into the hypothesis by permitting his
aspirations to be changeable over time. For example, one might
hypothesize that:[5]

1. In the face of time pressures one tends to lower the standards for an
acceptable alternative as well as the standards for the certainty of one's decision
model. Likewise, the greater the accumulated drain on one's resources for
reducing uncertainty the less demanding one is with respect to estimates and
alternatives before stipulation and choice.

2. If acceptable acts are difficult to discover, aspiration levels will come
down.

3. If acts which are more than acceptable seem easy to find, one's aspirations may go up.

4. If it appears difficult to reduce uncertainty as the decision process
progresses, the requirements for certainty are lowered, and the contrary.

Eventually one develops a conceptualization of the decision one is
willing to stipulate.

---

[4] D. Cartwright, "Relation of Decision Time to Categories of Response," *American Journal of Psychology*, Vol. 54 (1941); D. Cartwright and L. Festinger, "A
Quantitative Theory of Decision," *Psychological Review*, Vol. 50 (1943); and L. Postman and C. Zimmerman, "Intensity of Attitude as a Determinant of Decision Time,"
American Journal of Psychology, Vol. 58 (1945).

[5] March and Simon, *op. cit.*, p. 141; William T. Morris, *Engineering Economy*
(Homewood, Ill.: Richard D. Irwin, Inc., 1960), Chap. 22.

Another view of the time dimension is also suggestive. Information is often most valuable as a basis for choice when it is fresh, current, and relevant. Its value tends to drain away as it grows older. The decision maker faces the unfortunate fact that if he takes time to refine his conceptualization and to search out new alternatives the value of the information on which his original image was based is declining. He would, if he were a calculating superman, find the point where the increasing significance of the new information was just matched by the rate at which the older was declining in value, and at that very point he would stipulate and choose. In actuality, the hypothesis here is that this process does go on but in a much more rough-and-ready fashion.

Right now, the hypotheses about the work of deciding should be made more explicit, and then one can look for the role of advice in the process.

Experimental psychology sometimes operates in a stimulus-response framework, however a conception is something which falls between stimulus and response. Such things are said to mediate between the stimulus and response, and might be grouped under the heading "higher mental processes." Thus one has a mediation theory.[6] Applying this idea in as simple a fashion as possible to management decision making leads to something like Figure 13–1. External stimuli, interacting with the decision maker's memory, constitute the process of evocation which leads to the formation of a first conceptualization of the choice situation. The contents of his memory determine what external events are active as stimuli, and these external events in turn determine what parts of all that is stored in the memory will form the conceptualization. In connection with the evocation process one might wish to consider variables like

experience	pressure
training	complexity
need for certainty	repetitiveness
optimism	operationality of goals
self-image	rewards system
habit	availability of policy categories.

The left-hand list might be called personality variables, while the right-hand one consists of situational factors.

These factors combine to evoke in the manager's mind an image or conception of a choice situation. Perhaps to begin with, this

---

[6] Jerome S. Bruner, Jacqueline J. Goodnow, and George A. Austin, A Study of Thinking (New York: John Wiley & Sons, Inc., 1956).

image is characterized by doubts, confusion, incompleteness, and oversimplification. In short, his image is characterized by a high degree of uncertainty. Psychologists would call his image a highly subjective one since the processes of perception and recall which produce it are almost always influenced by personal needs and desires. It may be that some of the subjective distortion of his conceptualization may be traced to a need for certainty and confidence in management decision making. Finally, what is turning out to be

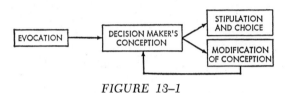

FIGURE 13–1

an increasingly important aspect of uncertainty may also characterize the manager's initial model of the choice problem, the lack of a clear idea as to what his own and his organization's objectives are.

The manager whose image is thus characterized by high uncertainty is unwilling and unable to make his choice. His response to the initial conceptualization may well be that something must be done to reduce uncertainty before he is ready to act. It is not difficult to suggest some hypotheses as to what his response might be to an image characterized by high uncertainty:

1. Evidence gathering.
2. Analysis, reasoning, or thinking.
3. Search for additional alternatives.
4. Delay the decision (maybe something will happen).
5. Absorption or denial of uncertainty (ignore it, and pretend certainty).
6. Goal clarification.
7. Seeking staff assistance.

These responses generally have the effect of modifying his model or image of the choice situation, hopefully in the direction of increasing certainty. Which responses will a manager elect and how long will this process go on before he finally makes a choice? It has already been hypothesized that managers are characterized by a level of uncertainty which they are willing to tolerate. When their responses have brought the uncertainty of their conception down below this level, they go ahead and make a choice. For the manager, however, this process does not go on forever. Eventually he develops a conceptualization of the decision which he is willing to stipulate. Concluding that a view of the decision problem has evolved which will serve as a basis for choice, he will act in a way consistent with his present conception of the problem rather than modify it further.

One would very much like to know how he will go about this process of developing his image of the decision. Which response will he elect? Does he evolve complex strategies using several of these responses? In particular, when will he resort to staff assistance? One might also ask the normative questions about whether his responses seem logical and consistent in the light of his objectives.

At present, a theory which provides interesting answers to such questions is some ways away. There is much work to be done; yet some promising hypotheses have been developed and tested. Most often, the tests have been made under controlled laboratory situations with decisions clearer and simpler than business decisions and with decision makers not primarily businessmen. But this, after all, is the way one must begin. Let us consider some of these hypotheses.[7]

1. The greater the uncertainty the greater the effort devoted to modifying the conception, and thus the greater the decision time.

2. The system of censures and rewards for successful and unsuccessful decisions which determine the decision maker's earnings and advancement will influence his response. If the system tends to insist on "results" and be intolerant of "mistakes," considerable effort will be devoted to evidence gathering and search in order to reduce uncertainty. If the system recognizes the necessity

---

[7] In what follows, a heavy debt must be acknowledged to March and Simon who have performed a considerable feat of bringing together and organizing the empirical and theoretical material on decision making. In addition to their book, a bibliography has been provided by Paul Wasserman and Fred S. Silander, *Decision Making—An Annotated Bibliography* (Ithaca: Cornell University Graduate School of Public Administration, 1958). Other studies especially useful include G. M. Becker, "Sequential Decision Making, Wald's Model and Estimates of Parameters," *Journal of Experimental Psychology*, Vol. 55 (1958); Richard M. Cyert, Herbert A. Simon, and Richard M. Trow, "Observation of a Business Decision," *The Journal of Business*, Vol. 29 (1956); Ward Edwards, "Utility, Subjective Probability, Their Interaction and Variance Preferences," *The Journal of Conflict Resolution*, Vol. 6, No. 1 (1962); W. K. Estes, "A Descriptive Approach to the Dynamics of Choice Behavior," *Behavioral Science*, Vol. 6 (1961); Marion B. Folsom, *Executive Decision Making* (New York: McGraw-Hill Book Co., 1962); Garlie A. Forehand and Harold Guetzkow, "Judgment and Decision-Making Activities of Government Executives as Described by Superiors and Co-Workers," *Management Science*, Vol. 8, No. 3 (1962); Alvin Scodel, Philburn Ratoosh, and Minas J. Sayer, "Some Personality Correlates of Decision Making Under Conditions of Risk," *Behavioral Science*, Vol. 4, No. 1 (1959); Charles E. Summer, Jr., "The Managerial Mind," *Harvard Business Review*, January–February, 1959; and Anders Sweetland and William W. Haythorn, "An Analysis of the Decision-Making Functions of a Simulated Air Defense Direction Center," *Behavioral Science*, Vol. 6, No. 2 (1961).

for choices based on limited information, the decision maker may be more ready to act in the face of risk and uncertainty.

3. If one of the evoked alternatives is clearly preferred and is also acceptable there will be a quick decision and no ex post facto rationalizations and re-evaluations.

4. The more complex a decision situation the more likely the response will be other than immediate choice. One measure of complexity of a decision is the number of alternatives being considered.

5. The greater the amount of past experience with the decision situation the more likely the response will be immediate choice.

6. In the face of technical uncertainty the first step will be evidence gathering to reduce uncertainty. If this fails, the search for additional alternatives will be undertaken. The decision process thus becomes a sequential process of studying a few alternatives and, if a choice does not result, of moving on to study others.

7. If several nearly equally acceptable alternatives are evoked, choice will be made quickly and will depend on the order in which the alternatives are examined and the cues which attract the decision maker's attention.

8. The tendency to resolve uncertainty before searching will be stronger in ordinary, familiar, repetitive situations than in unusual, unfamiliar, non-repetitive ones.

9. The search for new alternatives will increase in speed and effort inversely as the desirability of the best available alternative. The search rate also increases as time pressure increases.

10. The greater the felt need to make a carefully calculated, rational decision the greater the uncertainty, and the less likely a quick choice.

11. The greater the forward time perspective of a conception the greater the uncertainty and the greater the reliance on evidence gathering.

12. The greater the history of past decision-making success the greater the tendency toward certainty, and the more likely a quick decision.

13. As time pressure increases, the willingness to stipulate, the tolerance for risk and uncertainty, and the tolerance for lack of clear evaluations tend to increase.

14. A decision maker, confronted with two alternatives will:

a) Require a longer time for choice as the similarity between the two alternatives increases.

b) Devote more effort to evidence gathering, the greater the similarity.

c) Reduce the perceived difference between the alternatives which is necessary for choice as pressures are increased.[8]

15. As long as there exists a reasonably visible possibility of obtaining information relevant to refining the conception the decision will be postponed.

16. The existence of a well-developed set of policy categories with operational rules for application tends to produce conceptions of certainty and quick decisions.

17. The greater the necessity for a decision maker to persuade others to

---

[8] Postman and Zimmerman, *op. cit.*

accept his choice the greater the uncertainty and the greater the effort devoted to evidence gathering, search, and analysis.

18. The further into the future an event the greater the decision maker's tolerance for uncertainty about it.[9]

19. The planning horizon for most business decisions is relatively near. Heller, for example, in studying investment decisions found, "Firm capital investment plans are typically limited to a few months. Quick and unpredictable changes in such plans are the order of the day."[10]

20. Conceptualizations of repetitive decision situations are not modified often. When they are changed, the change is drastic and in response to some dramatic change in the environment.[11]

21. The greater the time pressure the greater the tendency to rely on intuition rather than analysis, data gathering, or search.

22. A quick intuitive decision, made and communicated in a steady, positive fashion, tends to convince others as to its correctness.[12]

23. The manager, in choosing an action, may bring to bear considerations of personal objectives, habits, and predictions which are not acknowledged as part of the explicit model of the decision. For example, the manager may:

   a) Choose an action which will be easy to implement.

   b) Continue the customary or conventional action, unless a new course of action is better than current practice by some significant amount.

   c) Choose an action which agrees with some predisposition on the part of superiors. It will be easy to sell.

   d) Choose an action which tends to justify his own past positions or tends to be consistent with his past actions.

   e) Choose an action which is easy to justify or explain if it is unsuccessful.

   f) Choose an action which has a small probability of great success for which the manager may claim credit and for which the responsibility for failure may shift to others (to advisers, for example).[13]

   g) Use a rule of thumb.

   h) Play a hunch.

   i) Choose an action which will be easy to recover from, make up for, or suppress, if something goes wrong.

24. After-the-fact analyses of decisions are seldom made, and when they are they tend to see the successful decision as one made under conditions of certainty. The agonies of uncertainty are suppressed and learning is thus impeded. Rewards and status given to the successful decision maker are explained in terms which suggest he acted quickly and without uncertainty.

---

[9] See Michael Gort, "The Planning of Investment," *The Journal of Business*, Vol. 24 (1951); and Norman H. Martin, "Differential Decisions in the Management of an Industrial Plant," *The Journal of Business*, Vol. 29 (1956).

[10] Walter H. Heller, "The Anatomy of Investment Decisions," *Harvard Business Review*, Vol. 29, No. 2 (1956).

[11] George Katona, *The Psychological Analysis of Economic Behavior* (New York: McGraw-Hill Book Co., 1951).

[12] E. P. Learned, D. N. Ulrich, and D. R. Booz, *Executive Action* (Boston: Harvard University Graduate School of Business Administration, 1951).

[13] William A. Reitzel, *Background to Decision Making* (Newport: The United States Naval War College, 1958).

The hypotheses already raised in the discussion of the need for certainty should be included here. In brief, these suggest that the need for achieving certainty in conceptualization is correlated with:

1. Demands for control and reliability from superiors.
2. Requirements for communicating the conception.
3. Preservation of self-image.
4. Custom and social sharing of conceptions.
5. Need for coordination with other decision makers.
6. Optimism.

Further, another series of hypotheses suggests that certain responses will be used increasingly as a function of the strength of the need for certainty. These responses include:

1. Utilization of resources for reducing uncertainty.
2. Utilization of categories and policies.
3. Denial, absorption, and overlooking of uncertainties.

In the case of a strong need for certainty, coupled with the frustration of attempts to satisfy this need, a conscious or unconscious remaking of the conception to exclude uncertainty is hypothesized.

If the sort of hypotheses sampled here are worth talking about, it may be because:

1. They are supported in many cases, by some carefully controlled evidence.
2. They may be interesting enough for one to hope eventually for extensive investigation of their validity.
3. They have been shown to be of immediate use to the man actively engaged in management science in industry because they suggest plausible explanations of some of the mysterious things which happen to him.

It may, however, bear repeating that these are simply hypotheses and their usefulness is of the sort suggested by the previous discussion of the hypothetical method. They do suggest, for example, a need for a somewhat larger view of the process of developing advice than is ordinarily given. Often the process is represented as entirely lacking in dynamics.

An important part of what has been said about the decision-making process in management science might be usefully thought of as statements of the following form: "If you have a given conception of a decision, here is a suggestion as to how your choice should be made." The process is one of going from a conception to a choice. Indeed, much that is written about, say, capital-investment decisions might be interpreted as telling one how to take a given set of numbers relative to the economic behavior of two machines and stick them into a formula which will lead to a suggestion for choice. Again, some inventory policy studies might be read as, "If your perception is one of fixing an inventory level in the face of probabilistic demand, here is a principle which will lead to a recommended alternative."

The point is not the disparagement of this kind of work but rather the suggestion it be enriched and built upon to reflect more nearly how managers make decisions. Nor is this a pious proposal based on a purely academic desire to make simple ideas complicated. Perhaps the only symptom of difficulty one need point out here is that managers do not always rush eagerly to do what is recommended. They are not willing to take the suggestion that a principle of choice be applied to the model developed by the staff and that the decision be made accordingly. This unwillingness finds dramatic expression sometimes, as everyone who has experience in presenting staff work to managers well knows. At this point one may entertain the hypotheses that the manager is foolish or that the conception-choice scheme needs development. A sound rule here appears to be to devote rather considerable study to the latter hypothesis before accepting the former.

It is a convention in much engineering teaching and writing to use the structure, "If you have this view of a problem, then here is a solution for it." The question of how one arrives at the particular view mentioned, whether one ought to have that view, or whether a more or less refined view would be better, is seldom raised. This gives the problem-solving process an unrealistic static quality.

Still thinking in terms of recommendations, one might ask what the manager's *best* response might be in the face of a given conception of a choice problem. *Should* he simply choose on the basis of the evidence at hand, or should he modify his conception, perhaps by evidence gathering, analysis, or the search for more alternatives? Perhaps, considering his objectives, he *ought* to elect some response other than stipulation and choice. The suggestion is that staff recommendations might ultimately include a greater variety of responses than is now usually the case.

If this were possible, then the normative theory which produces recommendations would begin to look more like the descriptive theory which hypothesizes the way in which the manager makes his choices. The result might be that the staff would become involved in a sort of evolutionary fashion in the decision process, rather than showing up at the end with a nicely formulated conception and the consistent recommendation. The importance of this is considerable and will be explored in Chapter 17.

To do this is not trivial. What is being asked, really, is a solution to what has been called here the fundamental problem of normative decision theory, "When should one stop modifying the model and proceed to make a recommendation?" In the process of raising these questions the original conception-choice scheme has been generalized to what might be called a conception-response scheme. One is now confronted by a new decision in which the alternatives are various responses to a conception. Two alternatives, evidence gathering and searching for new alternatives, will have the effect of modifying the original image of the decision. One is, in fact, studying decisions about how to respond to decisions. Schematically, the proposal is suggested by Figure 13–2.

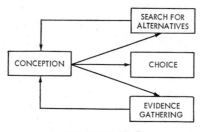

FIGURE 13–2

The answer to the question, "What response ought the decision maker elect?" is somewhat beyond general understanding at present. In certain cases of data gathering and analysis, statistical decision theory offers a complete logic for answering questions about when to cease observation and stipulate. In a statistical situation, one in which one knows a good deal about the probability distributions of the observations one might make, it is possible to calculate the effect of each observation on the decision model and decide when it is no longer worth while to make further observations. Certainly very few interesting business situations can be viewed as statistical in this rich sense, but if one does not insist on quantitative results the logic of statistical decision theory may well suggest the right way to think about the problem. More of this appears in Chapter 15.

One might also wish to introduce into the normative scheme the possibility of searching for new alternatives. That is, it might be that the alternatives presently available in one's perception are unsatisfactory and rather than choosing among them one might set out to find still others. The decisions then must be confronted as to when one ought to search for new alternatives, how this search should be conducted, and how long it should go on before a choice is made. Actually, this might be viewed as a special case of the evidence-gathering response.

In the case of the search for new alternatives, two general normative principles are available. The classical principle of search suggests the extent of search be based on the usual principles of marginal analysis. Continue the search for additional actions until the marginal benefit expected from the discovery of an additional action is just equal to the marginal cost of the search. While this is unquestionably an ideal basis for a recommendation, it is virtually impossible to apply because it requires the very difficult prediction of the benefits from an alternative as yet undiscovered, as well as the costs of conducting a search of highly uncertain extent. A weaker but far more realistic principle suggests the more descriptive notion that the extent of the search is determined by the achievement of a satisfactory course of action. This is again an aspiration-level concept which implies that as each alternative is discovered it is evaluated and the search is continued only if it is unsatisfactory. Here, as before, one may introduce some dynamic modifications of the aspiration levels. This principle is consistent, for example, with the notion of a minimum satisfactory rate of return in capital-investment analysis. But, of course, this confronts one with the question of how standards for satisfactory actions ought to be chosen and how they ought to be modified as time passes and information accumulates.[14]

Finally, let us consider some descriptive hypotheses about one particular response, that of seeking advice. Staff assistance is called for under conditions which generally indicate a routine decision-making process has broken down. Insofar as management science is concerned, it is supposed that the adviser develops an explicit conceptualization of the decision process, both by taking what he can of the chooser's conception and by making his own study of the stimulus situation. Advice giving is a process which aims at having some impact on the decision maker's conceptualization.

One might then suspect that a decision on which staff advice would be sought might be one in which the manager's estimate was characterized by:

---

14 For initial formulations of these problems see Morris, *op. cit.*, Chapters 16, 22.

1. Lack of clear relation between outcomes and goals.
2. Lack of operational goals.
3. Outcomes which promise losses and gains that are difficult to combine into a simple evaluation of the action.
4. An attitude of neither strong pessimism nor strong optimism.
5. A belief that a way out can be found but no acceptable action is presently available.
6. Complexity.
7. Unfamiliarity, lack of past experience.
8. Failure to fit clearly into an established policy category.
9. Nonrepetitive, without a history of past success, cannot be pooled with a larger class of decisions.
10. Time pressure not severe.

The decision, it would be further hypothesized, is likely to be one:

1. Which the manager must initiate rather than simply approve.[15]
2. In which the results are an important part of the evaluation of his performance made by his superiors.
3. For which he cannot shift the blame for failure to others.
4. In which failures are difficult to defend and compensate for.

The manager will seek advice when his criteria for the acceptability of an action are changed by some outside event, and when his rules of thumb, habits, and established policy categories are challenged. He will look to the staff on decisions for which he lacks boldness, feelings of power, confidence and willingness to take responsibility.

He will, it is hypothesized, seek staff support when

1. He cannot distinguish a preference among the alternatives.
2. He can find no other decision maker to imitate.
3. Those he imitates are using staff assistance.
4. His past decisions have been subjected to ex post facto evaluations and criticisms.
5. He is forced by the pressure of near-term events to turn away from long-range planning.

Many of these hypotheses are vague, many seem to lack obvious operational interpretations, yet perhaps they are suggestive and will perform the functions required of them in Chapter 8. We turn now from the problem of how managers seek advice to the problem of how they react to it.

---

[15] Robert A. Gordon, *Business Leadership in the Large Corporation* (Washington, D.C.: The Brookings Institution, 1945), p. 81.

Chapter 14:

THE USES

OF ADVICE

"The work of the philosopher is to make ideas available, not to force them upon anyone."

The literature of management science, casually examined, presents in some instances a curious lack of concern with what use was actually made of the advice produced. Did management act on the resulting recommendations? Certainly in many cases the advice resulted in action, and these are presented and interpreted as clear achievements for management science. Yet in other instances recommendations were not acted upon, or if they were no mention is made of this fact in reporting the work. This latter kind of study continues to be produced and, in some sense, consumed. It is bought and paid for by men who are hardly renowned for the idle spending of money without getting something of value in return.

There can be no argument but that the stated objective of advice giving is to provide a basis for acting. Good advice is most easily recognized by the improvements it brings in the conduct of affairs when it is acted on. No one contests the kind of demonstration of the power of scientifically based advice which concludes with a neat tabulation of the increases in profit or reductions in cost which can be traced directly to the fact that managers followed the recommendations they were given. It is to this end that the efforts of management science are directed and for this reason it presses hard to bring about implementation of its conclusions. It is not always possible, however, to attribute even good results directly to the recommendations of the staff. Nor indeed is it always possible to argue that if management decisions are consistent with staff advice management acted as it did because of the advice. Finally, of course, there are those particularly discouraging instances where recommendations seem to provoke no action at all or action quite different from that suggested by the staff. All this may be intensely disappointing to staff people, but hardly surprising. After all, even well-established sciences such as economics seem to have noticed over the years that they cannot expect to have their advice accepted in every case without reservation. Indeed, the remarkable thing is perhaps the continued existence of staff groups for extended periods without any opportunity or attempt to identify observable consequences of their output. All this suggests staff advice has other functions and uses for which it is valued beyond the obvious one of attempting to provide a rational basis for decisions. Before pursuing these other uses, a brief recapitulation of the situation up to this point is in order.

The function of guiding action is necessarily the end toward which data gathering, analysis, prediction, and the search for new courses of action are directed. The argument so far has been aimed at pointing out that advice which requires of itself some attributes of science brings certain formal capabilities and limitations to this task. Further, its impact must be understood in terms of the thinking processes of its consumers.

From a formal point of view, it seemed reasonable to suggest that scientific advice was in many ways an incomplete guide to action. Toughmindedness tended to focus its attention on verifiable terms and propositions. An insistence on discussing its own validity tended to keep management science out of the realm of the non-repeatable decision situation, where indeed most business decisions of consequence and high uncertainty seem to fall. On balance, however, it was argued that even the simplifications of science have potential and demonstrated contributions to make to increasing the explicitness, consistency, and validity with which decisions are conceived.

The conclusion was that the function of advice was to construe the actions of management as experiments. Its work was that of producing hypotheses which, on logical and previous experimental grounds, seemed good ones. In the judgment of the adviser they appeared "most likely to succeed." The role of science thus became that of suggesting well-designed experiments and securing progress in the evolution of managerial effectiveness through analysis of the "experimental results."

Management science does not propose to teach managers how to make decisions in general, nor does it propose to replace what managers regard as good judgment. If it set out to do these things, managers would be justly resentful, for it would take on more than it can manifestly accomplish. It does hope, however, to provide some assistance, supplement, and extension for the manager, mainly to permit him more freedom to exercise his very particular skills as a decision maker.

The effect of advice on the advisee, as was suggested through an array of hypotheses, is not simply that of provoking action or inaction. A start was made at hypothesizing some useful explanations of the reactions of a decision maker to the suggestions of his advisers.

The attempt now is to catalog some of the uses of staff advice, which, while they do not rule out its use as a basis for action, do not necessarily include the direct and obvious response of implementing the recommendations. These hypotheses may not seem surprising to many who place similar interpretations on the evidence available as to the uses of advice by management. They have not been set down together in one place, nor in some cases have they been made explicit in the literature. Indeed, it may well be they have been suppressed by some who rightly hope to settle for nothing less than action as a consequence of staff recommendations.

It will appear that a number of these hypotheses say the same thing in different ways. This redundancy is intentional, for there is always the problem that a given pattern of behavior may be interpreted in more than one way.

It will be clear to advisers that some of these uses of their talents and outputs are intended uses. They constitute the employment of advice and advisers for purposes staff people will tend to see as legitimate and in accord with their professional purposes. Others will appear as misuses and prostitutions of scientific talent and results. This question of legitimacy and the problems it introduces in staff-management relations will be taken up in a subsequent chapter, and any such classification will be avoided at this point.

Although the role of advice in reducing uncertainty in the decision maker's conception of the choice situation has been emphasized, it has also been hypothesized that at the same time it may result in quite the opposite tendency. A part of the consequences of advice may actually be an increase in uncertainty, confusion, and doubt. This is particularly true when the details of the data and reasoning involved in a study are presented without suggesting to the manager how the study can be used to reach a specific recommended course of action. The mechanisms by which scientifically based advice may actually tend to increase uncertainty include:

1. Making the decision problem more complex, introducing new elements, and eliminating the simplifications usually made by the decision maker.

2. Destroying illusions of certainty, raising and making explicit doubts suppressed by the decision maker.

3. Requiring, as was suggested at some length, that management decision and action be viewed as primarily an experimental process rather than a process of resolute and confident progress toward action.

4. Confronting the manager with examinations of conditions and reservations which might invalidate the advice, leading to a generally indeterminate recommendation.

5. Requiring the manager to judge validity in a more complicated fashion, when he may be used to simply accepting advice as valid or rejecting it as false.

6. Challenging habits.

7. Making clear what is known and what is unknown in a situation.

8. Making risk explicit by the introduction of probabilities. (The introduction of probabilistic weather forecasts has had the same effect on parts of the public.)

9. Encouraging the manager to make his goals and objectives explicit, perhaps thus bringing to light the rather considerable uncertainty as to what these are.

All this is coupled with the fact that the more objective an adviser is the more he observes the cautions of science in drawing conclusions and the more his reports are filled with doubts, assumptions, reservations, and conditional statements. Harold Laski, speaking of the manager's problem with his advisers, said, ". . . he must quicken their doubts into certainties."[1]

This sort of dysfunctional consequence has long operated to the disadvantage of scientific advice so far as popular acceptance by managers is concerned. Furthermore, it has not gone unnoticed by others who sell advice for a living. This has produced a great deal of advice which claims to be scientific, thus taking advantage of popular impressions of scientific incontestability, but which, at the same time, avoids all the requirements of *being* scientific. Work of this sort is deliberately calculated to increase certainty. It consists of a recommendation, perhaps vaguely stated to allow the manager considerable freedom of interpretation, together with evidence exclusively in favor of the recommendation. No examination of validity or assumptions appears, of course.

In the discussion of the quest for certainty some things were said about the use of advice to resolve conflicts over choice on the part of an individual decision maker. Advice, as it was seen there, had

---

[1] Harold Laski, *The Limitations of the Expert* (Fabian Tracts No. 135) (London: The Fabian Society, 1931).

among its functions the removal of conflict in decision making by helping the chooser work toward a satisfactory conception of the choice situation to which he was willing to stipulate and thus act. This view of the role of advice is usually implicit in the definitions and analyses of operations research and management science. Like almost all advocates of a particular staff technique or staff function, management science's advocates have repeatedly urged that it express itself directly to "top management." By being responsible only to the most powerful decision makers in the organization, the staff could first of all have access to full information about goings on throughout the firm; but more importantly, having overcome or resolved the deciding difficulties of the really powerful decision makers, it would be clear sailing from there on. The head man need only order that what the staff recommends is what is to be done and the problem of implementation is solved. There are certainly opportunities for greater effectiveness if advice is given at the top, but things seldom work out this way. In fact, after having secured the agreement of one decision maker, the staff may find that the process of bringing action out of the complex organizational process has just begun.

Just as the individual may experience conflict arising out of an unsatisfactory conception of the choice problem, so also one may imagine organizational conflict which arises when the members of an organization are unable to act routinely as an organization.[2] If all members of an organization share the same or effectively the same conception of a decision situation, they will be able to act whatever the power and influence relations that may exist between them. If, at the other extreme, all members of the organization hold differing conceptions of the situation, and these conceptions differ in the responses they suggest, then a dictatorial power structure is needed for action. In the great middle ground between these two extremes lie all the possibilities for the varying degrees to which conceptions may be shared and the endless possibilities for the distribution of power and influence among the members of the organization. No attempt will be made to analyze these situations, but the fact should be noted that organizations tend to work toward consensus in deciding and even those in management who might, if they wished, assume dictatorial powers are wisely reluctant to do so.

Thus, in organizations the dynamics of choosing involve very

---

[2] James G. March and Herbert A. Simon, *Organizations* (New York: John Wiley & Sons, Inc., 1958), pp. 113–36.

often the resolution of conflict by one decision maker persuading others as to the desirability or acceptability of a particular conceptualization of a decision problem. In this persuasion, scientific advice is well known to be, and widely used as, a powerful ally. Every staff person finds himself sooner or later involved in this organizational conflict-resolving process. He is subjected to pressures to produce results which can be sold to others and to spend his time making numerous presentations and "pitches" to groups of decision makers. He is inevitably a party not only to presenting the recommendations to one powerful decider but also to helping one manager convince others. Here the use of scientific advice should be emphasized not only for its recommendations for action but also for its utility as a "persuader" in committee meetings.

March and Simon have carefully summarized the conditions which lead to conflict among decision makers in an organization.[3] They have gone on to suggest that the reactions to conflict observed in organizations may be classified as:

1. Problem solving. Here it is assumed the decision makers agree as to the objectives and how outcomes are to be evaluated. The need is to search for alternative actions, to predict the outcomes, and to evaluate these outcomes in the agreed terms until an agreeable course of action is discovered.

2. Persuasion. In this case there is some disagreement as to goals and objectives but there appears to be the possibility of attaining agreement. This is done by trying to show that the outcomes of various action alternatives will indeed serve the differing objectives of various decision makers.

3. Bargaining. This process begins with an acknowledged conflict of interest among the decision makers and tries to reach agreement without persuasion or problem solving.

4. Politics. Here the term refers to the same basic situation as bargaining but the implication is that the bargain is not limited to the particular decision at hand.

The role of advice in problem solving and persuasion is clear. It also may play various roles in bargaining and in politics, as in wage negotiations, by the attempt to establish certain objective facts about job performance to which both parties will stipulate because they are confirmed by "science." In addition, work is under way which may eventually produce normative recommendations as to how to bargain effectively. In politics, the very simplest role of advice is that of being asked to support not only recommendations on a given decision but a larger, more comprehensive program of

---

[3] *Ibid.*, p. 128.

action as well. Later some of the specific ways in which advice finds its way into bargaining and politics will be mentioned.

Some useful insights may be suggested into the role of advice in organizational conflict by paraphrasing some hypotheses advanced by March and Simon as to which processes will be used by organizations. If the difficulty in reaching a group decision stems from the fact that individual decision makers are themselves unable to come to individual choices, then problem solving and persuasion will tend to be the responses of the organization. Thus this is one situation in which one would expect advice to play a part.

Bargaining and politics place new strains on the power and influence system of the organization. If top management wins in these processes it tends to tear down the illusions of democratic procedure and delegation of authority which most managements strive for. If top management loses, their position may be weakened and their effectiveness impaired. In addition, bargaining and politics tend to recognize and thus sanction differences in objectives among decision makers. This works against the sometimes elaborate techniques management uses to operate and control the organization by motivating all decision makers to work toward the common goals of the firm. Thus, bargaining and politics have undesirable consequences and management may well seek to avoid them as responses to organizational conflict.

It is hypothesized that management will tend to view organizational conflict, whatever its source, as resolvable by means of problem solving and persuasion. These responses, involving sometimes the utilization of staff advice, will continue to be insisted upon, even when they appear inconsistent with the nature of the conflict. Further, it is suggested that when bargaining and politics do take place they will be clothed in the language and logic of problem solving and persuasion. Again postulating the role of advice in problem solving and persuasion, at least the outline of its uses in organizational processes of choice emerges.

A further major use of advice is testing and confirming a course of action currently in use or toward which management has a strong predisposition. The tendency of the results of advice to resemble well-developed practice has been explained in the form of the "flat-top hypothesis." The tendency for management to require confirmation of an adopted or predisposed course of action is explainable simply in terms of the quest for certainty. The credit which may be ascribed to advice in this type of instance is limited because no basis for sole claim to responsibility for the action taken may be made by advisers. The disheartening evaluation, "We are already doing that," or "We plan to do that anyway," seems to devalue the contribution of advice to a great extent.

The reverse role for advice is that of a challenger of custom, routine, dogma, habit, and predisposition. The unpopularity of the adviser who continually asks, "Why is it done that way?" when the only answer available seems to be, "We've always done it that way" is well known. Here we must recall the "sunk cost," or resistance-to-change aspects of a decision to change an entrenched course of action. It is hypothesized that the challenging recommendation must make claims to being more than just a little better than the current alternative in order to warrant a change in the eyes of the decision maker. These two uses of advice find it in the role of analyzing alternate ways of doing something, rather than in the more enviable role of showing how something may be done which could not otherwise be accomplished.

As has been argued at length, there seems to be little reason to suppose a full and explicit means of making evaluations of outcomes will be readily available in organizations. Thus, a central role for advice is value clarification. While the position has been taken here that the role of actually choosing objectives and thus of specifying values is reserved to management, there is a useful service advice may perform in helping to carry out this process and making the results explicit. Still further, it may well be that any statement of goals and objectives must be ultimately viewed as an experimental hypothesis, thus opening the possibility that advice may play a role in the testing and revision of such hypotheses. The ways in which advice participates in value clarification would appear to include:

1. Attempting to make explicit and perhaps "measure" the preferences of decision makers.

2. Giving decision makers a fuller and more adequate understanding of the kinds of outcomes which must be evaluated or about which they must develop some preferences.

3. Exploring the relationship among goals, showing which are in conflict and which are simultaneously possible of attainment.

4. Forcing the decision maker to deal with value judgment at an explicit and conscious level.

5. Factoring the problem of evaluation into operational and nonoperational aspects, thus making it clear in just what areas management must make its judgments.

The role of advice as objective arbitrator of interdepartmental conflict has received considerable emphasis in management science. In recent years scientific studies are being made which are, for the first time, of sufficient scope to encompass management problems cutting across departmental lines. The traditional decision-making conflicts among the production, sales, and finance functions have been examined through studies which have attempted to relate the actions of all three to the goals of the firm as a whole, emphasizing the problem of the relationship between organizational objectives and those of subunits.

Wilensky has shown, in the case of labor unions, that there is evidence for another use of the advisory staff: "taking the heat."[4] It appears inevitable that advisers must take some of the responsibility and indeed some of the blame if their recommendations lead to programs which are not successful. They must carry some of the burden of the organizational pressure which bears upon the decision maker whom they advise in the conflict situations generated by their work. In spite of the notion that a manager must himself assume full responsibility for his decisions and their results, it is difficult to imagine that advisors could avoid having some of the responsibility shifted to them. This may range from the manager's apology to his displaced subordinates, "I hate to do this, but the staff report requires it" to the complete sidestepping of responsibility for an unsuccessful program, "I made that decision strictly on the basis of the staff recommendation, and they are going to hear about it." It is hypothesized that this effect may often be unbalanced in that the manager may neglect to give the staff any credit for good advice while transferring to it the pressure resulting from failures.

There are three special cases of interest in which the advisory staff finds itself in the role of scapegoat.

1. In the case where a program is unsuccessful or has a result importantly different from that expected, and further, where this can be explained in terms of some event specifically assumed away in the staff study on which the decision was based.

Every study is finite, explicitly assuming some things away and dealing with a particular set of conditions. The adviser may very well feel that if things turn out differently than he had predicted—and if this can be explained in terms of some specific assumption he has made—then his advice has not been

---

[4] Harold L. Wilensky, *Intellectuals in Labor Unions* (Glencoe, Ill.: The Free Press, 1961).

shown to be invalid. His specifically stated assumptions relieve him from responsibility if things are not as predicted, as long as he can show this is due to the fact that his assumptions were not, in fact, met. Indeed, in the usual context of scientific verification, this is not an unreasonable attitude. The manager, however, is unlikely to see things this way, especially if he is not intimately acquainted with the details of the study. This sort of event will be variously regarded as "an error in judgment" or "a mistake anybody could make," but the manager's conclusion is likely to be the natural one: he received bad advice.

This, of course, is one meaning of the distinction between theory and practice. In nonaction research, the failure of a prediction, when traced back to an assumption which was not met, does not invalidate the work involved. In action research, however, those who must act cannot take such a position. The indeterminacy that nonaction researchers find natural and necessary is not so easily tolerated in the world of action.

2. In the case where the decision maker is subjected to strong pressures for prompt and immediate action. Here the advisory staff provides a natural and convenient explanation of delay. It is quite legitimate in the view of managers to shift to the staff the burden of these pressures. "I'm waiting for the study the staff is doing right now on this problem" is almost a stock answer to demands for immediate action.

3. In the case where an adviser who is admittedly responsible for a recommendation leading to an unsuccessful course of action will take the blame as a service to the manager. Wilensky found that in labor unions many advisers accepted this as a natural and tolerable use of their services. The adviser willing to do this feels his position is relatively secure against the pressures generated by failure. Further, there may be a tacit understanding between adviser and manager that the adviser will be repaid, perhaps in the form of additional job security, for this service. One special instance of this is the consultant who comes into an organization and performs the function of taking the heat for whatever unpopular recommendations he may present to management.

Attempts to transfer blame by managers would probably be resisted by the more scientifically trained staff members who have limited skills in "getting along" in the organization. They may also view it as a threat to their professional reputations and their insistence on objectivity.

This transfer of responsibility to the staff is related to the difficult problem of the extent to which managers should rely on scientifically based staff advice. In general, any given decision will be based partly on managerial judgment and partly on analysis. The whole point of management science is to relieve management from the necessity of relying entirely on judgment. There has, however, been some comment on going to the other extreme, that is, on managers who abdicated what in some sense were their legitimate decision-making responsibilities in favor of a complete and slavish reliance on scientific advice. There has been some suggestion that one use of advice is to permit managers to abdicate their responsibilities to a point not warranted by the competence of the scientific advice on which they have chosen to rely.

Scientific advice, especially when the adjective "scientific" is prominent, has long been regarded in politics as a highly useful argumentative device. Elliot L. Richardson, speaking of politics in Massachusetts, has said, "In a state, meanwhile endowed through its colleges and universities with unparalleled riches in expert judgment, the expert's opinion is all too frequently sought and used merely as a stick with which to beat the opposition."[5] The same attitude has been ascribed to some "realists" in management who suggest scientific advice finds its major use as a rhetorical device. In the development of "scientific management" this sort of thing has a long history and has been called by Adam Abruzzi "proof by proclamation."[6]

What is being referred to here is, essentially, the appeal to the false images of science which seem widely held by nonscientists. Any conclusion or recommendation labeled "scientific" can be advocated by playing upon the prejudices people have about science. The view that science is capable of almost anything, is incontestable, and produces conclusions of unimpeachable validity, suggests that any policy billed as scientific should be accepted by all reasonable and right-thinking men. The very effectiveness of this method of persuasion has led the term "scientific" to be attached to all manner of statements which simply served the interests of particular persons. Who, after all, can argue with the mystique of science?

One function of management science is to make decision processes explicit, without contributing directly to the validity or factual content of the process. At the level of an individual decision maker, the benefits of making the choice process explicit include the opportunity to check the decision, test for consistency, and communicate the process to others. Even beyond these benefits others were hypothesized of an almost therapeutic nature. Facing the situation explicitly, in the sense of stating the vague doubts and fears which attend the decision, may indeed have the effect of relieving the manager's mind of some of the burdens of his duties. Even if the staff does little else other than translate vague problems into explicit ones, this may itself be useful to managers in the same gen-

---

[5] Elliot L. Richardson, "Poisoned Politics," *Atlantic Monthly,* October, 1961.

[6] Adam Abruzzi, *Work, Workers, and Work Measurement* (New York: Columbia University Press, 1956).

eral sense as there are therapeutic benefits associated with making the unconscious conscious.

At the organizational level decisions are often reached by bringing together complex judgments made by a number of different persons. This process sometimes tends to appear somewhat chaotic and unexplainable. For example, one organization was concerned with the very difficult task of allocating funds among various research projects.[7] A number of people in the organization participated in this decision by making judgments in their own specific areas of competence, giving recommendations on the basis of their own opinions, and arguing over proposed solutions to the problem. A study was done which quite simply factored the judgments involved into specific statements, gave those who had to judge scales on which they could express their estimates in the form of numbers, and then suggested a specific way in which these numbers could be combined to produce an allocation of funds consistent with the judgments. No factual contribution was made by the study, which simply attempted to make explicit the process already in use. No one would suppose the results would be accepted blindly and mechanically. They were, of course, subjected to review and consideration from many points of view. Nor can one claim the allocation process has been made more objective by the addition of new data. All that really happened was that the decision process of the organization had been given some semblance of order in place of somewhat unexplainable confusion. The fact that the results were quite eagerly adopted by the organization is something of a demonstration that it met some organizational needs. Perhaps its usefulness lay in the fact that it:

1. Made the decision process more orderly and clarified the steps involved.
2. Made the judgments considerably simpler to arrive at by factoring them from complex ones into simpler ones.
3. Made formerly vague opinions, rules of thumb, and policies considerably sharper.[8]

A part of the function of the staff may be to act as an additional means by which management finds out what is going on in the organization. In addition to the data collected in the process of conducting studies aimed at particular decision problems, the staff

---

[7] Howard A. Wells, "The Allocation of Research and Development Resources" (M.S. thesis, Ohio State University, 1958).

[8] The project evaluation and review technique (PERT) is a currently popular example of this.

may have the effect of revealing conditions in the organization quite aside from those it set out to study. Casual remarks made by the staff after investigations may reveal to management conditions they might not have noticed otherwise. In the process of pursuing other ends, the staff may make explicit for management conditions of considerable importance, and this effect may have greater impact than the results of the study itself.

Alternatively, it could be hypothesized that the failure of the staff to mention undesirable practices after doing a study in a particular department may well be interpreted by management as an additional indication things are going well in that department.

It may even be that the staff is valued quite apart from its recommendations as a routine information-flow channel which supplements rather effectively those otherwise available to management. Such a hypothesis is consistent with the rather common attitude shared by those who fall within the purview of the staff. These groups tend to regard the staff not as objective investigators pursuing some announced management problem but as generalized spies for top management. As spies, they are suspected of seeking out and reporting all sorts of conditions to management, particularly instances in which announced policy is not followed. In the extreme, the staff may be regarded as operating under the cover of a strictly sham investigative problem.[9]

This effect places the staff in a particularly difficult dilemma. Management may expect and demand the staff perform this sort of communication function. The staff may thus find it extremely difficult to object, even though the members view it as inconsistent with their legitimate and announced functions. If they agree to operate as such a source of information, the other members of the organization, whose confidence and cooperation the staff must have to pursue its legitimate ends, find direct confirmation for their spying hypothesis. It then becomes exceedingly difficult for staff people to find out what is going on in the organization and to obtain the data they need, and the difficulties of assuring implementation of their recommendations mount considerably. Again in extreme cases, there is evidence that employee groups have deliberately sabotaged the recommendations of the staff in order to discredit them in the eyes of management. Ultimately the staff may find itself in a delicate and uncomfortable middle position.

---

[9] This is carefully documented by Melville Dalton, *Men Who Manage* (New York: John Wiley & Sons, Inc., 1959), pp. 73, 100, 201.

A service management sometimes expects the staff to provide is the furnishing of quick answers to questions asked out of context— that is, questions which do not arise in the context of any particular study the staff is undertaking, questions on which management does not expect an investigation but only a quick opinion, and questions which have arisen within a context management may not fully reveal. Many types of staff people are valued specifically for their ability to render this type of quick opinion. They consult with management, not because they are equipped to undertake scientific studies of management problems but because they can draw immediately from past experiences opinions which management elects to use. Management scientists tend to see themselves, in their professional roles at least, as scientific investigators who will produce carefully supported and well-reasoned recommendations that will stand the tests of objectivity. In the face of impatience on the part of management they may find themselves giving "off-the-cuff" answers, but in doing so they may feel their behavior is inconsistent with their professional criteria. They tend to be especially concerned that management may attach the same sort of validity to both kinds of answers. They may even see themselves in two rather distinct roles, speaking at some times as consultants or experts basing their opinions on experience, at others, as scientists reporting on the results of their research.

The staff may also be used by management as a tool for organizational manipulation. There may be confusion on the part of the staff as well as on the part of other members of the organization over the amount of authority actually possessed by staff people. Although in the language of the organization chart the staff is supposed to be without authority, its purely advisory position may become less clear in fact. One would hypothesize:

1. That staff people, taking advantage of the tendency of employees to ascribe to them the authority of the managers to whom they report, may assume and exercise some authority. Management may condone this assumption as long as the staff acts consistently with management purposes.

2. That the staff may be used by management as a channel for issuing directives to the organization. This frequently happens when the staff is asked to carry out programs implementing the recommendations it has produced. In other cases the staff may simply be told to "tell those people to do so-and-so."

The staff may, of course, be asked to produce evidence supporting the enlargement or elimination of particular subunits of the organization, the advancement or elimination of particular persons in the organization, or the furthering of particular programs. The very presence of the staff and the announcement of the problems on which it is working may be used to stimulate organizational changes. For example, in one case it was announced that the staff was undertaking the design of a statistical quality control program for the plant. This very announcement apparently made it clear to employees that management was placing a new emphasis on quality, and even before any recommendations were made by the staff a noticeable improvement in quality was seen. When a subunit of the organization discovers it is to receive the attentions of the staff, a general improvement in performance may result, quite independent of the particular problem the staff may be studying.[10]

In other ways, the presence of the staff may be used by a manager to enhance his own position in the organization. The development of the staff advisory group is one means by which managers "build their empires" thus increasing their power, responsibility, and perhaps even the security of their own positions. Similarly, the staff increases the decision-making capabilities of the manager, permitting him to delegate less, consult fewer associates, and use large amounts of information not available to others. All this, of course, increases his own personal power in the organization and gives others less opportunity to participate in his decisions or even to question them.

It is hypothesized that the management science staff may be used by a manager as a mechanism for enhancing his own status in the organization.[11] He may derive status from:

1. Being able to speak with the authority and support of scientific studies.
2. Having staff advisers, since they are one of the badges of rank.
3. Supervising more people.
4. Having available modern scientific techniques, being up with the very latest ideas in management.
5. Having an automatic computer.
6. Making better decisions.
7. Having his organization "under control."
8. Having more time for nonroutine work.

---

[10] For another example see Acheson J. Duncan, *Quality Control and Industrial Statistics* (rev. ed. Homewood, Ill.: Richard D. Irwin, Inc., 1959), p. 132.

[11] Alfred Politz remarked in connection with market research: "Market research as a status symbol need not perform, it need only exist. It is not expected to solve problems, nor does it lead to marketing actions. It will merely revel in the glitter of words." *New York Times*, May 20, 1962.

9. Speaking patronizingly of the staff, thus giving the impression he is perfectly capable of making decisions unassisted but is tolerant of the staff and their pedestrian scientific ideas.

Merton has emphasized the frequency with which social scientists who have gone into advisory positions in government have discovered that they were not expected to participate in the making of decisions nor even to offer scientifically based advice before the fact. They found themselves simply called upon to provide justifications and explanations for decisions made by those in positions of authority. This fact and its importance were discussed by Thurman Arnold in *The Folklore of Capitalism;* the function of learning, he said, was to satisfy a demand "for rounded explanations of institutions, for ideals, and for principles which would extend the culture of the present into the future." He further remarked, "Scholars like to think of the legal and economic principles which they so laboriously formulate as a practical guide. It is difficult to convince most of them that they are not practical advisers because when their guesses go wrong they can always ascribe the blame to factors such as human nature or politics, which lie outside their sciences."[12]

More recently, Paul Henri Spaak has said, "The major trouble with political conferences is that when politicians can't agree on something they create a committee and refer the problem to experts. Whenever you see this announced in a communique be wary, it means that the difficulties are really very great. Such cases attest to inexcusable shifting of responsibilities, for experts are not made to resolve difficulties, they are made to find technical solutions to political decisions already taken by heads of governments. My own experience allows me to state that when there is a political will there is no technical difficulty which cannot be overcome."[13]

One would suspect there is a direct parallel in management science in which the staff finds its functions to be limited to justifying and finding the means for executing decisions previously made. Further, this seems particularly likely to happen when the manager is under pressure to make a decision quickly or is without the resources for any investigation. It will also occur when the manager takes the attitude that a given decision is "too important" to be left to the staff. Here it may not be clear to the manager that any staff

---

[12] Thurman Arnold, *The Folklore of Capitalism* (New Haven: Yale University Press, 1937), p. 85.

[13] Quoted by W. L. Whitson, "The Growth of the Operations Research Office in the U. S. Army," *Operations Research,* Vol. 8, No. 6 (1960).

assistance could be useful, for he may feel himself fully competent and traditionally bound to make the big decisions himself.

One of the more cynical anecdotes of this kind deals with a manager who was convinced that since many other organizations were being decentralized his should be also. A staff study of the advantages of decentralization recommended no such change be made. The manager quietly filed the study and some time later had another study done by a different group. This process was continued until he finally received a study which did indeed recommend decentralization and, of course, he then chose to act on the basis of these recommendations.

Advice may be said to have some effect on the decision maker if he acts differently as a result of having received it. Unfortunately, this is not altogether a clear and objective criterion since advice may simply give clarity and certainty to an action which might have been chosen in any case. It is even more difficult to show whether or not a particular decision was a good one, given that it must be based on a limited conception. It is not easy to demonstrate that advice was influential in a decision nor that it was good advice in the short run. It is hypothesized that the observable effects and perhaps the more important benefits of advice become apparent only in the long run. Even then, of course, it remains difficult to ascribe an improvement in the state of affairs to the staff, for multiple causes are certain to be present.

Continued existence of the advisory staff may depend on short-run demonstrable results. This is so not only because managers may apply the same evaluation criteria to advice that they apply to the other resources they buy but also because some demonstrable impact may be a prime requisite in determining the job satisfaction of the adviser himself.

However, advice does, when allowed to continue, appear to play a gradual but important long-run role in the improvement of affairs. This is confirmed by experienced advisers, who indicate that the manager himself may not even realize he is being influenced. John Maynard Keynes realized this and remarked at the end of his *General Theory of Employment Interest and Money*, ". . . the ideas of economists and political philosophers, both when they are right and when they are wrong, are more powerful than is commonly understood. Indeed the world is ruled by little else. Practical men, who believe themselves to be quite exempt from any intellectual influences, are usually the slaves of some defunct economist.

Madmen in authority, who hear voices in the air, are distilling their frenzy from some academic scribbler of a few years back."[14]

It is difficult, even for the manager who realizes this, to justify the continued existence of his advisory staff without some demonstrable short-run payoff. It is perhaps even more difficult for the adviser to content himself with the hope that if he perseveres eventually there will be a gradual improvement in management decision making, although he may be unable to obtain recognition publicly for his part in this.

Yet this is often thought to be among the more important functions of advice giving. The gradual increasing of the manager's understanding of the affairs he manages, the evolution from vague and confused deciding to sharp and explicit policy, and the increasing clarity with which decision situations are conceived and studied may represent the most effective product of management science.

Certain other hypotheses concerning the uses of advice should be mentioned:

1. To keep up with the competition, both among companies and among plants within the same company.

2. To postpone, sidetrack, and give the impression of doing something about difficult decision problems.

3. To evaluate, criticize, and supplement the inadequacies of subordinate decision makers. Here the recommendations of the staff for the conduct of affairs within the responsibility of lower-level managers may be used by top management as indicators of shortcomings. "Why aren't you doing this? How come the staff had to figure this out when it's really your job?"

To the extent these hypotheses concerning the uses of advice might be confirmed, some general conclusions would be possible. Advice appears to have a variety of uses, only some of which have operational consequences. There is a basic conflict between the long-run results of management science and the necessity for demonstrating short-term payoffs. It will be difficult for the staff to demonstrate that results are attributable to their work. Finally, many of the uses of advice appear to produce conflicts between line and staff.

---

[14] John Maynard Keynes, *The General Theory of Employment, Interest and Money* (London: Macmillan & Co., Ltd., 1936), p. 383.

Chapter 15:

HOW MANAGERS

EVALUATE

ADVICE

"One sure mark of the man of action is the use of intuitions in place of abstractions . . ."

—LYMAN BRYSON

One encounters two rather vague impressions of what is supposed to happen when advice is given to managers. One view has it that the advice must consist not merely of a scientific treatise but should contain a recommendation in favor of a specific course of action. The manager is then supposed to either accept or reject the recommendation—whether on the evidence offered in support of the recommendation, or not, is unclear. This is the military doctrine of decision in which the commander is pictured as either signing the staff report or throwing it out with dispatch. The other view pictures the staff adviser with a firm conviction that his recommendation is the true and complete solution to the *manager's* decision problem. The adviser's personal involvement with the recommendation together with some sense of responsibility for its implementation leads him to attempt to *sell* the results to management. Here again it is not clear how much this persuasion emphasizes understanding of the recommendation and its supporting evidence, and how much it depends on the "art of salesmanship." This chapter's central hypothesis is that neither stereotype suggests an adequate description of the manager's response to a recommendation. Further, it appears there is sufficient evidence (of a casual sort) to indicate that neither approach, adopted as a norm for behavior, will enhance the effectiveness of the adviser. Now a few hypotheses can be offered on the manager's decision about a recommendation, which follow from the analysis so far set out. Three kinds of hypotheses are listed here in roughly increasing order of complexity.

1. Hypotheses about the tests or criteria managers use in deciding how to react to a recommendation.

2. Hypotheses which suggest relations between the characteristics of managers and the criteria they might use.

3. Hypotheses about the processes of communication and persuasion that take place between advisers and managers. This is coming as close as seems wise to "kitchen recipes" for bringing about the acceptance of recommendations.

A variety of uses for advice, not limiting its function to that of providing a basis for action, have already been considered. It seems reasonable to suppose that the test a manager uses in evaluating staff advice may depend on the uses he has in mind. It may also be that only after the advice has been evaluated do the uses he will make of it become clear to the manager. Implementation, in the sense of action based upon the recommendation, is the primary purpose of advice for the present analysis. Implementation is, however, neither a simple nor an entirely satisfactory concept. It leads to operational difficulties because often one cannot correlate a clear, resolute decision with a definite recommendation nor correlate a given action with a particular decision. There are always factors quite apart from the recommendation which lead to a decision, and these factors may vary in importance so as to make it quite difficult to say what is meant by implementing a recommendation. Management decisions are so complex that it is sometimes difficult to know what action has been taken or what policy adopted.

Still other difficulties arise out of advisers' natural equation of implementation with success. Implementation and thus success may be observable only in the long run. Action may be frustrated by influences quite beyond anything the adviser is able, or is permitted, to study. There may also be difficult conflicts between the traditional criteria of scientific success and those of managerial success of implementation. All these complexities notwithstanding, here only the manager's decision to implement or not to implement a recommendation will be considered, saying little or nothing about the other purposes he may have in mind. This is, after all, the avowed purpose of the staff. It tends to bring to bear tests more stringent than might otherwise be made of advice.

Perhaps three fundamental characteristics of the adviser-manager relationship pervade the whole problem of evaluation.

1. Advice's validity is usually far easier to establish in the physical sciences without requiring any particular depth of understanding on the part of the

decision maker.[1] All one has to know about a machine is that it will perform more effectively and at lower cost than another machine. Often an experiment may be used to demonstrate this. The results of research can be built into a device which can be used with little understanding of the basic ideas involved. In management science the situation is more complex and seldom parallels that in physical science.

2. Advice is designed to *supplement* and *reformulate* the manager's conceptualization of his decision problem.

3. Advice on management policy almost always has among the consequences of its implementation the changing of human behavior. The usual situation is that the recommendation suggests how to do better something already being done. This is a fundamentally different situation from advice that suggests how to do something which has not yet been done or cannot otherwise be done. Advice on questions of feasibility is always better received than advice on questions of efficiency.

The question of how managers evaluate the advice which comes to them from their staff management scientists could be vastly simplified if it were always possible to give an experimental demonstration of the validity of a recommendation. Confirmation with prima facie evidence from the real world is the ultimate method of laying to rest all doubts and objections. That this is seldom possible in management science without the active support of management has been continually emphasized. Thus the principal problem of the management scientist is often to bring the manager to stipulate a recommendation in order that the real-world experiment may be undertaken. What criteria do managers thus apply to staff results? Once again some hypotheses will be undertaken in this regard.

Objectivity and careful reasoning are certainly not the exclusive province of scientifically trained analysts, and it is clear that many managers, whatever their training, will apply to some degree the same criteria to scientific advice as would scientists.[2] Perhaps the hope of every adviser and the aim of presentations to management are to have staff work evaluated according to scientific criteria. For this, the manager must have some understanding of the reasoning employed, the hypotheses tested, and the kind of demonstrations of validity it is possible to make. This implies a rather full understanding of what variables are included in the analysis, how the data were obtained, and the techniques of inference applied. The manager should have some appreciation for the repetitiveness of the

---

[1] One should not oversimplify the problem, however. See Albert H. Rubenstein, "Setting Criteria for R and D," *Harvard Business Review*, January–February, 1957.

[2] I. J. Good, "How Rational Should a Manager Be?" *Management Science*, Vol. 8, No. 4 (1962).

situation with which the study deals, the assumptions incorporated, and the nature of the stipulations made by his advisers. Ideally, of course, this would require the manager to be scientifically trained, but it is certainly possible for useful scientific tests of advice to be made without such specialized background. Basically, the manager can make a useful evaluation of the recommendations if it is clear to him to what extent the result is

1. Consistent with the assumptions stipulated by the staff.
2. Consistent with the beliefs and values to which he himself stipulates.
3. Consistent with objective evidence.

Even if he does judge the adequacy of the recommendation by the same grounds as a scientist might, he need not come immediately to a final conclusion. Rather, the manager must consider whether an experimental test is warranted. He must ponder not only the internal objectivity and consistency of the work but consider the assumptions it has made, what it has left out, and the ways in which the research problem differs from his own problem. This is, of course, expecting a very great deal.

Time, training, and inclination suggest that managers will seldom meet scientists on scientific grounds and that further hypotheses are necessary. The main purpose of Part II has been, however, to contribute to the effort toward objective evaluations by management.

Recommendations must agree with the manager's own insights and intuitive analysis of the decision problem. If they do not, an adequate explanation must be made and understood. Counterintuitive and seemingly paradoxical results are unlikely to gain any sort of credence until they are given face validity. There are many examples of common sense or insight based on considerable experience which is extremely effective, often more so than detailed scientific studies. This test indeed represents the manager's most prominent skill. On the other hand, this does not imply a priori acceptance of the dictates of intuition. One might almost say that the policies which have the clearest and strongest intuitive support are exactly those which require the most careful analysis.

A manager must "understand" a recommendation in order to adopt it. In one sense this means he must be able to integrate the results of staff work with his own conception of the decision problem. The point of Chapter 13 was that advice seeks to modify and improve, and not simply to contradict, his intuitive response to choice situations. The manager is, after all, committed to intuition as the basis for his livelihood—his skill as a decision maker.

While common sense and scientific validity represent in some sense the best criteria, there is evidence that managers resort to further tests in addition to and sometimes instead of these. For example:

1. Is the recommendation acceptable to a manager's superiors? It is common to find that a decision maker is highly sensitized to the kind of decision which his superiors find acceptable and the courses of action toward which they are predisposed. Even though a manager has full authority to decide and act, there is inevitably a time when his choices are reviewed at higher levels and he must often defend them.[3]

2. Is the recommendation consistent with what others, particularly competitors, are doing? The tendency to focus on competitive position in terms of share of the market as a primary objective results often in the testing of recommendations in terms of what others are doing. Typically, a manager wishes to be neither the first nor the last to try something new.[4]

3. How much mathematics was used in the analysis? How much data were collected? Was a computer used in the study? These kinds of tests have an importance which should not be minimized. The amount of money, time, and data; the number of people; and the number of computer hours are considered. A BIG study may carry more weight than a moderate one simply because everyone knows you get what you pay for.[5]

4. Is it possible for the manager to readily assimilate the staff study into his own conceptualization of the decision problem? If one accepts the conclusion that scientific advice is necessarily incomplete as a guide to action, it follows that the staff conception of the decision must be communicated to the manager in such a way that he can make it a part of his own thinking and reasoning. In a sense, the most important attribute of advice is its assimilability.

5. Is the recommendation "appropriate" for the firm? Sometimes a recommendation which is persuasively supported in terms of the values made operational by the staff study, and to which the manager may be willing to stipulate verbally, is still not acted upon. The explanation is that the recommendation is fine but it simply does not represent the kind of thing which the firm "does." It is easy to call this an unresolved value conflict on the part of the decision maker but difficult to do very much about it.

The very insistence of scientific advisers on the objectivity of their work may be responsible for a tendency to depersonalize the

---

[3] The editors of Fortune, The Executive Life (Garden City, N.Y.: Dolphin Books, 1956).

[4] James G. March and Herbert A. Simon, Organizations (New York: John Wiley & Sons, Inc., 1958), p. 188.

[5] Walter J. Strauss (Institute for Air Weapon Research, Laboratories for Applied Sciences, University of Chicago), "The Validity of Operations Research Studies with Emphasis on Those Pertaining to Force Composition Studies," WADD TR 60–336, IAWR Report 60R3, Contract No. AF33(616)–6824, February 1960.

process of giving advice. While objectivity in testing the validity of recommendations is much to be hoped for, it is widely observed that though management may not know science it is usually an excellent judge of character. Managers know people, and thus the adviser tends in their view to personify his results.[6] There is no known substitute for the confidence of management as a basis for gaining acceptance of even the most objective of studies. Confidence must be won, and demonstration is the way in the long run.

Many firms, however, in the process of introducing management science, are forced to search for indications which call for confidence before it can be based on performance. In fact, it is hypothesized that during the initial stages of the employment of management science in a firm the majority of the difficulties between manager and adviser stem from matters of lack of confidence in the staff person himself, rather than from questions of fact or value concerning the substance of the study. Just as the doctor, realizing the basis on which patients must evaluate his first advice, is conscious of his personal relations with his patient, so the staff man must recognize that the decision maker relies heavily on character judgments in his evaluations. The adviser and his advice can be separated in the eyes of management only with the greatest difficulty. Three rather common observations testify to this.

1. Managers to some extent value advice for its cost. If the recommendations cost little or nothing they are usually taken to be worth little or nothing. This is reputedly the basis upon which some consultants determine the size of their fees to management.

2. The prestige of the staff person is more important than his results. This is supported by the use of Ph.D.'s and university professors to lend credence to many undertakings in science. In any case, it is very helpful if the person who presents the results to management has a few gray hairs.

3. In employing advisers, whether as temporary or permanent staff members, the greatest stock is placed on recommendations of peers, especially businessmen who are successful and respected themselves.

In the case of relatively young management scientists, working in newly formed staff groups, managerial evaluations apparently tend to be heavily influenced by the age and experience of the staff.[7] Managers, wondering how the staff can in any way supple-

---

[6] Melville Dalton, "Conflicts Between Line and Staff Managerial Officers," *American Sociological Review*, Vol. 15 (1950); and I. Gerver and J. Bensman, "Towards a Sociology of Expertness," *Social Forces*, Vol. 32 (1954).

[7] Melville Dalton, *Men Who Manage* (New York: John Wiley & Sons, Inc., 1959), p. 75.

ment their own long experience, ponder such questions as, "How do you know?" "Were you there?" "Have you ever worked in a shop like ours?" "Not that again. We tried that once years ago and it didn't work."

These same staff groups, feeling themselves very much on trial in the eyes of management, press hard to prove their worth and justify their existence. The result may well be simply to reinforce management's ad hominem rejection. Managers, like anyone else, will not accept advice which is forced upon them, especially when it comes from younger men who seem ambitious, bright, and aggressive and when the actions of these young men can easily be interpreted as threatening their reputations and powers of decision. Obviously, the tendency toward ad hominem evaluations can be used to gain acceptance of advice as well. While deliberate employment of this tactic may seem distasteful to scientists who hope for more objective evaluations, it is certainly an important method for nonscientific advisers of all sorts.

The history of attempts to gain acceptance for nonscientific advice by false claims of scientific objectivity is evidence for the fact that the name and reputation of science is a powerful basis for acceptance.[8] Undoubtedly, the success of the physical sciences, which is obvious enough to the laymen who enjoys the end products, creates something of a halo effect for all sciences. Management science appeals to some, it would appear, both as an opportunity to associate management with this highly respected body of scientific activity and as a potential source of "supersolutions" to troublesome management problems. As Tacitus remarked, "Whatever is unknown is held to be unusually great."

At a slightly more specialized level, one would expect a manager's evaluation to depend in part on the reputation enjoyed by particular techniques or tools used in the study. Computers have always lent great weight by their presence. Linear programming and PERT[9] are widely discussed and carry with them some image of potentiality. Negatively, one hears managers speak of techniques which "everybody has tried and it doesn't work." Or, "We were sure sold a bill of goods on that one."

Management science, operations research, and industrial en-

---

[8] A. Hunter Dupree, "Public Education for Science and Technology," *Science,* Vol. 134 (1961), pp. 716–18.

[9] Project Evaluation and Review Technique. Linear programming was recently the subject of a full-page newspaper advertisement by a major advertising agency which is using it for media selection. See *New York Times,* Oct. 8, 1962.

gineering enjoy reputations of various sorts in the eyes of managers. It may indeed make some difference whether a particular staff calls what it does operations research or industrial engineering. Examples of what these activities have accomplished in other companies would appear a convincing aid to evaluation, at least at the start of a study. Managers, however, share the general proposition that what works in one company will not work in others. "That's fine, but of course our business is different." "In our line you just can't predict."

Like the decision to buy any other input to the firm, the decision to buy advice is traditionally examined and defended in economic terms. Like the purchase of a machine, the purchase of advice must sooner or later meet the test of subtracting expense from income. Unlike the machine, however, it is exceedingly difficult to do this in many instances of staff recommendations. A manager's evaluation of past advice acted upon is surely enhanced by a computation of how much better off the firm is as a result. Increasing the profit is a persuasive test. This is made difficult by the inability to associate results directly with advice. The uses and benefits of advice are difficult to measure. This is compounded by the fact, soon to be examined, that implementation and claiming the credit for these accomplishments are not always compatible. Considering the various opportunities the firm may have for investment, it is no easy task to decide and to convince others that money invested in staff work is well invested.

The task of economic evaluation of staff efforts is complicated in several ways. It is often impossible to tell what the impact of this effort has been. Is it true that what management did, it did because of the staff study, or did the staff merely confirm what was already its intention? Especially if one looks to the long run for a realization of the ultimate benefits of staff services, economic evaluation is hopeless. If one promises a manager that a certain staff program will save him $100,000, the manager is in a difficult position. His failure to take up the opportunity must be justified by directly attacking this claim. Since there is little a priori basis for such predictions, the result is simply an argument about guesses. If he does undertake the investment in analysis, his expectations are rather well formulated. If these expectations are not realized he must either explain to others why he made such a bad investment or find some means of shifting the responsibility. Conservative management scientists, knowing such claims in advance are usually rank speculation, are wisely reluctant to promise dramatic results—or even any results at all. One can agree to do research but one can hardly promise what the results of the research will be, while maintaining any semblance of objectivity. The manager may thus find that the kind of evaluation he is most confident in making is not available to him.

Some managers have a suspicion that staff work will "stir up trouble, disrupt normal operations, and bother a lot of people." This apparently suggests to them that the indirect costs involved are likely to be large, perhaps out of proportion to any possible benefits.

The problems of the economic evaluation of management science are much akin to those of evaluating research and development efforts of other kinds. Much remains to be done on this problem, and managers have often failed to work out even rough empirical solutions. In a recent study, only about 25 per cent of the managers interviewed in some 200 companies had any formal method of estimating the financial return on research expenditures. Some indicated they had made no attempt at all to appraise the results of research and development.[10]

Questions of the economic justification for advice lead often to the "make-or-buy" problem. Should an internal staff group be developed on a permanent basis, or should an outside consulting firm be engaged for a particular problem? In principle, the problem is like the "make-or-buy" question in the case of anything else. As was suggested in Chapter 3, it is a function of the size of the firm and the resultant opportunities it has to take advantage of specialization in decision making. The answer resists generalization, however.[11] Consultants can be used to produce recommendations on a particular decision, to develop management science competence on the part of the company's existing staff, or—as is usual—to do some of both. The question of economics is immediately complicated by other arguments commonly advanced in favor of outside staff groups. They are said to:

---

[10] National Science Foundation, *Science and Engineering in American Industry: Final Report on a 1953–1954 Survey* (Washington, D.C.: U.S. Government Printing Office, 1956), p. 49.

[11] Thomas W. Ware, "An Executive's Viewpoint," *Operations Research,* Vol. 7, No. 1 (1959); and Rensis Likert and Ronald Lippitt, "The Utilization of Social Science," in Leon Festinger and Daniel Katz (eds.), *Research Methods in the Behavioral Sciences* (New York: The Dryden Press, 1953).

1. Possess greater objectivity.
2. Have the ability to see beyond the symptoms to fundamental problems.
3. Bring with them "experience" from other companies.
4. Be able to provide a variety of highly specialized people economically.
5. Be more effective at getting cooperation leading to implementation.
6. Have greater ability to enlist the support of top management and utilize their power and influence.
7. Have a useful freedom from the informal organization of the firm, with its cliques, jealousies, power struggles, and compromises.
8. Benefit from greater ad hominem reputations.
9. Be free of many of the frustrations which beset staff people (which will be examined in Chapter 17).

Again, these are more or less interesting hypotheses which may bear examination but for which there is little more than anecdotal support at present.

A further useful dimension in understanding how a recommendation is evaluated is the extent to which the staff will be responsible for implementation.[12] A recommendation to install a statistical quality control system may carry with it the implication that, if management agrees, the staff will undertake all that is necessary to put the idea into practice. The staff may undertake responsibility not only for the technical details of the plan but also for convincing all those who must be convinced. The staff, and not the manager, may bear the burden of all the human relations problems associated with action. The manager's role will be limited to lending his approval and authority to the program. At the other extreme, recommendations as to the size of the work force or the levels of inventory may find the manager taking the major responsibility for putting the program into practice while the staff is limited quite literally to making recommendations.

Obviously enough, one might hypothesize that in the former case the adviser's model, his definition of the research problem, will be more complete with respect to the difficulties of implementation than in the latter. Indeed, when the staff expects a minor role in implementation, its conceptualization of the problem may be seriously deficient in the degree to which it captures the troubles involved in taking action.[13] This is the root of one important meaning which managers attach to their distinctions between theory and practice. In such a case, managers find their central role is like

---

[12] The process of implementation is described by March and Simon, *op. cit.*, pp. 172–210.

[13] These difficulties are well documented in Dalton, *Men Who Manage, op. cit.*

that of the politician who must deal with what *can* be done, the art of the "possible." While advice on what to do is inevitably bound up with how to do it, there is a natural tendency, in simplifying a real problem in order to make it a research problem, to leave aside some of the troublesome aspects of execution. Many elaborate recommendations on equipment-replacement policy overlook the small detail of where the money is to come from. In other cases, it may be the resistance of those whose behavior must be changed that is glossed over. The resistance of lower line personnel and the frictions which arise between them and the staff are discussed in Chapter 17. They are interestingly illustrated in Dalton's study involving close observation of a plant situation.[14]

Thus an important test used by a manager would be to ask to what degree the actions recommended fall within his responsibility, skill, power, and resources to act. He is wary of the consultant, spending a brief time with the firm and quickly departing, who recommends radical changes in the organization and operation of affairs.

One interesting special case of this is the sort of study which is potentially suggestive of changes in the behavior of the manager to whom the staff reports. Experience indicates that the manager who foresees such a result will attempt to prevent the recommendations from ever being produced. This, of course, is the basic reason why the staff should report to an organizational level higher than those at which changes are anticipated.

The need for certainty in decision making has been thoroughly discussed and now it should simply be noted that this implies a criterion for evaluating advice. The manager certainly expects the staff will succeed, perhaps dramatically, in reducing his uncertainty. If this expectation is realized, one would assume a greater tendency to accept the advice. But it has already been suggested that the results may be quite the opposite, actually producing an increase in uncertainty. Advice is more likely to be accepted if the manager is insulated from the residue of uncertainty which inevitably accompanies scientific results. One may attempt to press for acceptance by failing to make explicit all the simplifying assumptions, judgments, and stipulations inherent in the recommendation. Only arguments in favor of the conclusions might be presented. This is, of course, characteristic of the "hard-sell" approach. Scientifically

---

[14] *Ibid.*

based advice may be something of a surprise and a disillusionment to the manager who expected to find unconditional assurance of successful action. Instead he finds his problems of stipulation are multiplied and hardly rejoices in the suggestion that management ought to be viewed as a continuing experiment.

Thus another key to understanding a manager's response is the way in which the recommendations measure up against his expectations. He has expectations of varying strength and kind, both about management science in general and about the decision problem at hand in particular. If he initiated the study himself he may have a strong felt need for a carefully calculated choice and rather specific expectations about what the staff will produce. If someone else initiated the work his anticipations may be considerably more vague. Indeed, some studies are initiated by the staff in order to sensitize the manager to a decision problem and lead him to develop some expectations as to what the staff may accomplish.

Obviously, the study may cost more, take longer, and produce results less easily integrated into his own thinking than he had supposed. The study may show that what he had considered a relatively simple problem is nothing of the sort. It may uncover deficiencies he would prefer to ignore and suggest he has not solved some of the problems he thought he had solved. In part this comes about, as has been indicated, through the necessity for transforming the manager's problem into a research problem. How extensive this transformation must be is, of course, the critical aspect of realism in management science. It may lead to results the manager finds immediately useful, or it may seem to him that he has been given the solution to a problem which is quite different from his own. Science simply cannot solve all management problems, and it must redefine and reformulate them to bring them within its competence. One hopes that the problem solved has an understandable relation to the problem which exists. It has been said, perhaps a little too neatly, that, "Science is the process of substituting unimportant questions which can be answered for important questions which cannot be answered."[15]

Some managers will have nothing to do with analysis, some seem to have an almost blind faith in it, and between are those who appraise it with various degrees of reason and prejudice. It would be exceedingly useful to know what characteristics of man-

---

[15] This remark was made by Kenneth Boulding, I believe.

agers are predictors of the tests they will apply in evaluating the results of staff work. What values, attitudes, and experiences are related to the way in which managers use their staffs? How does a manager's self-image relate to his response to a recommendation? There is even less evidence available on these points than on some previously discussed; however, it may be interesting to try a few hypotheses, some of which are quite obvious.

Out of the available studies of the characteristics of managers, some traits might be extracted which seem relevant.[16] Among many other things, managers have been described as:

1. Having a strong need for achievement. Desiring money and power as symbols of their success. Apprehensive of failure.

2. Having a great aversion for "theory." Oriented toward "reality." Pragmatic. Not given to introspection.

3. Being accustomed to, and tolerant of, ambiguity in decision-making situations. Able to make up their minds on the basis of limited evidence.

4. Having self-confidence; optimistic about the success of their decisions. Positive in their attitudes.

5. Being tolerant of pressure in decision making.

Some hypotheses connected with these stereotyped management traits are now proposed.

Of the 900 top executives studied recently by *Fortune*, only three were under forty years old, and only one hundred were between forty and fifty.[17] It is generally true that management scientists are younger than the managers they advise. Dalton found this true of staff people in the plant he examined.[18] It is difficult for management to react favorably to the implication it needs guidance from younger, less experienced men than themselves. This ad hominem reaction is well known to staff people. Consulting firms have long recognized the need for "a few gray hairs" to give the necessary face validity to their recommendations.

Nor can the manager be expected to understand and apply ob-

---

[16] Ephriam Rosen, "The Executive Personality," *Personnel*, January–February, 1959; Francis X. Sutton, Seymore E. Harris, Carl Kaysen, and James Tabin, *The American Business Creed* (Cambridge: Harvard University Press, 1956); William E. Henry, "The Business Executive; Psychodynamics of a Social Role," *American Journal of Sociology*, Vol. 54, No. 4 (1949); Garlie A. Forehand and Harold Guetzkow, "Judgment and Decision Making Activities of Government Executives as Described by Superiors and Co-workers," *Management Science*, Vol. 8, No. 3 (1952). For some interesting insights see also Dean Acheson, "Thoughts About Thought in High Places," *New York Times*, Oct. 11, 1959.

[17] The editors of *Fortune, op. cit.*

[18] Dalton, *Men Who Manage, op. cit.*, p. 89.

jective criteria as a result of his previous job experience in the firm. The studies by *Fortune,* Dalton, and Newcomer show that executives have usually come up to their positions by way of jobs other than staff positions.[19] Dalton has also documented the difficulty of transfers from staff assignment to line management.

It would seem obvious enough that the tendency of a manager to use objective criteria in evaluating advice would be an increasing function of the extent of his education and the degree to which that education is scientific. Drawing from studies of large numbers of managers, some interesting hypotheses may be formulated.

1. Young executives have more education than their older associates. Newcomer found in a 1950 study that of those executives in office less than ten years, 45.8 per cent had attained a first college degree while an additional 20.1 per cent had done graduate work. These figures compare with 44.8 per cent and 12.6 per cent for managers in office more than ten years. Warner and Abegglen found that 1952 executives had considerably more education than those of 1928.

2. While executives are getting more education, it may be that less of it is scientific. There is some evidence of a shift away from science and engineering among top managers.

3. The rapidly increasing emphasis being given to management science by schools of business and engineering, and the gradual movement of management scientists into management positions, should react eventually in favor of more rational evaluation of staff work.[20]

4. As management science becomes more widely utilized managers will assimilate an understanding of it as a part of their work experience. They will, often without realizing it, begin to make decisions consistent with scientific analysis.[21]

5. Staff advisers, generally having more education than managers, may find this a source of friction. Management may regard staff education as assurance of theoretical, longhaired impracticality.[22]

6. Probability theory and statistics (which will be looked at in the next

---

[19] Mabel Newcomer, *The Big Business Executive; The Factors That Made Him, 1900–1950* (New York: Columbia University Press, 1955). A survey made by *Dun's Review* of the top 250 American firms showed the following: "Specialization or not, and technological progress notwithstanding, the survey finds that the man who has the best chance of making the penultimate top is one whose specialty is general management. No less than 18.5 per cent of the men who rule the 250 largest companies in America came up by that route. If he is not in general management, the executive succeeds best if he holds an engineering degree (17.5 per cent)." See Melvin Mendell, "How to Make the Top," *Dun's Review and Modern Industry,* Vol. 78, No. 4 (1961).

[20] Frank C. Pierson, and others, *The Education of American Businessmen* (New York: McGraw-Hill Publishing Co., 1959).

[21] See comments by Herbert Simon in George P. Shultz, and Thomas L. Whisler (eds.), *Management Organization and the Computer* (Glencoe, Ill.: The Free Press, 1960), p. 90.

[22] Dalton, *Men Who Manage, op. cit.,* p. 87.

chapter) are topics of the utmost importance in management science. Educational neglect of these ideas and the attendant misunderstandings are a serious difficulty not only for managers but for the majority of scientists and engineers whose academic programs have so far avoided this branch of mathematics.

Porter and Ghiselli have reported a revealing study of the self-perceptions of top and middle management.[23] Among a variety of characteristics embodied in the self-image of middle managers appeared the following:

Middle managers regarded themselves as:
1. Giving stability to the firm's decision making by reliance on careful analysis and investigation.
2. Not making quick, ill-considered, or rash decisions.
3. Less self-confident than their superiors in top management.
4. Relying on established policy rather than innovation in making decisions.

Some relevant features of the view top managers held of themselves include:

1. Not relying entirely on objective evidence in making decisions.
2. Confident in taking risks when decisions involved their judgment.
3. Confident their decisions would lead to success.

From these findings it would seem that perhaps middle management would be more receptive to advice than top management and might tend to use more objective criteria in evaluating it.

A study done at the Harvard Business School suggests an important test of a manager's ability is the way in which he utilizes staff assistance.[24] Some executives, this study learned, were simply not capable of having somebody else do part of their thinking for them. Others seemed to find staff advice a source of conflict in their drive for achievement.[25] The very existence of staff management scientists might be interpreted as a mild slur on management competence. Some executives seemed consistently to make changes in staff recommendations just to give them their own personal touch. To approve a staff report without change would be to become simply a rubber stamp. Discussions of the technological unemployment

---

[23] Lyman W. Porter and Edwin E. Ghiselli, "The Self Perceptions of Top and Middle Management Personnel," *Personnel Psychology*, Winter, 1957.

[24] E. P. Learned, D. N. Ulrich, and D. R. Booz, *Executive Action* (Boston: Harvard University Graduate School of Business Administration, 1951).

[25] Morris Rosenberg, *Occupations and Values* (Glencoe, Ill.: The Free Press, 1957).

of middle management by computing machines are not exactly reassuring.[26]

Staff assistance interferes with management's striving to demonstrate achievement in other ways as well.

1. There is always the chance that staff will "show him up," expose some malpractice or inefficiency, bring about unwanted personnel changes, or perhaps even cause a reduction in the scope of his authority.

2. A staff study nearly always means changes. In many cases, the measures by which managerial achievement is judged can be maximized in the short run only if the manager can preserve stability in his operations so as to concentrate on producing or selling.

3. If the staff recommendation turns out to be successful, the manager would like very much to create the impression that the important ideas involved were his own, and to him belongs the real credit for whatever has been accomplished. The staff often finds it necessary not to oppose this as a condition for having their results implemented. If the recommendations fail, the manager would very much like to transfer the blame entirely to the staff. Thus, at best, the manager's relations with the staff have a tendency to be sticky.

4. On the other hand, the manager may find it useful to have a management science staff and perhaps use a computer to show that he is "scientific" and progressive. His problem may then be to keep the staff from upsetting his operations or getting too much credit.

Management's drive for achievement is a rather generally accepted characteristic. What criteria for the evaluation of advice might be related to this need?

1. Acceptability to superiors, ease of selling in the organization.
2. Tending to reflect credit on the manager and justify his past decisions.
3. Avoiding criticism, change, or instability.
4. Increasing his authority, prestige, number of subordinates and assistants.
5. Giving him a way out in case of failure.
6. Agreeing with positions he has taken in the past and furthering programs he has supported.
7. Arising as a result of his own initiation and direction.

---

[26] Computers, though only tools of the management scientist, seem to represent the focal point of middle-management concern over the declining importance of their traditional decision-making activities. For an excellent discussion and examples see: "How Will Computers Affect Management?" *Technology Review*, May, 1961; "Advertising: Electronic 'Buyers' of Media," *New York Times*, July 15, 1962; and "Computers' Use in Arms Plans Splits Pentagon," *New York Times*, August 14, 1961. Carl F. Stover told a group of businessmen, "The control of the industrial economy is rapidly passing to scientists and technicians. Only men who understand operations research, systems engineering, and the sciences on which their corporations' work depends will find a place in that system. The others will join the ranks of the technologically unemployed." *New York Times*, July 7, 1962. He is director of studies in science and technology at the Center for the Study of Democratic Institutions, Santa Barbara, Calif.

Further, we would expect the manager would tend to:

1. Limit the role of the staff to finding justifications and methods of execution for decisions he has already made.

2. Utilize advice for purposes other than as a basis for action.

3. Look for solutions which tend to improve his score on the yardsticks used by his superiors.

4. Favor advice which helps to solve problems of great concern to his superiors, especially if others have failed to solve them.

5. Favor staff activities which free him from routine duties so that he may develop more fully his position in the informal organization of the firm.

One of the most frequent manifestations of the viewpoint of the executive is the depreciation of "theory." "That may be all right in theory, but it won't work in practice." One executive rendered his estimate of staff people this way, "They stir up too much trouble and are too theoretical."[27] Churchman and Ratoosh, in their experiments simulating attempts to implement an optimal solution, elicited the same remark from student participants in the laboratory.[28] Anyone who has attempted to give scientific advice to managers has certainly encountered this reaction. Part of it is explainable in terms of the technical jargon in which "theory" is sometimes expressed, for this is largely a closed book to the manager. However, this does not end the matter. The fact is that managers are heavily committed to action based on their own experience. They set great store by "getting things done" rather than reflecting about why or how. Perhaps the distinction goes back to the ancient question of which is the good life, the life of contemplation or the life of action. Let us, however, explore this further.

It is certainly true, as this book has been at pains to emphasize, that models and thus theories are incomplete representations of the manager's decision problems. Theories do not include all the known factors nor consider all possible contingencies and, furthermore, those who produce them say so explicitly. There is thus an admitted difference between research and policy, a residue of uncertainty which may undermine the manager's confidence.

On the other hand, there is no interesting sense in which an idea can be all right in theory but not in practice. If the model illuminates to some degree the manager's difficulties then it is prac-

---

[27] Melville Dalton, "Conflicts Between Line and Staff Managerial Officers," op. cit., p. 343.

[28] C. West Churchman, and Philburn Ratoosh, "Innovation in Group Behavior," in J. Banbury and J. Maitland (eds.), Proceedings of the Second International Conference on Operations Research (New York: John Wiley & Sons, Inc., 1961).

tical; if it does not then it is simply not useful. Recall Kurt Lewin's remark, "Nothing is so practical as a good theory."[29] Other conventions may be included in this distinction as well.[30]

1. The effort to reduce a complex management situation to exact terms in the statement of the model renders the model far more complex than the vague description of the situation in everyday language. The language of conversation is rich with meaning and correspondingly vague, thus a few words seem to suffice. The manager may find models more complex ways of thought than those to which he is accustomed. Yet clearly the model simplifies the world, suggesting to him that it leaves out things which he does not omit in his own considerations. "Theory" is at once too simple and too complex.

2. "The operation was a success, but unfortunately the patient died." There is a tendency for scientists to write off the failure of a theory in practice by noting that the theory only went wrong because something happened which had been explicitly assumed away in the construction of the model. Thus the work has met the scientist's criteria, but not the manager's. This attitude is, it is hypothesized, not prevalent among management scientists.

3. The tradition of science has been to restrict itself to the consideration of problems, the solution to which had no obvious use to practical men. Scientists were in no way to be held responsible for whatever use was made of the knowledge they produced. Management science and indeed the "policy sciences" run, for the first time, counter to this tradition.

4. Some theories, especially those from the older management literature, are largely lacking in operational content. They give the manager no clear idea of what they are recommending. Managers may thus have come to the point of finding little in "textbook theory" of any consequence for their business affairs.

5. There is the convention that "scientists and engineers neglect the human side of things." The implication is that scientific results leave out the "human element" and thus void the recommendations. While management science cannot pretend to have completely overcome this objection it is making every attempt to remedy the situation.

6. Since theory is, in science at least, supported by data, the manager must judge its adequacy in part by becoming involved with statistics. This is a source of pessimism which will be examined in the next chapter in some detail.

7. There is a long-standing convention that one can hardly give advice about something in which one does not have demonstrated competence and a

---

[29] Quoted by Likert and Lippitt, *op. cit.*

[30] For comments on this important problem see Paul A. Samuelson, *Economics* (New York: McGraw-Hill Book Co., 1958), p. 9; Churchman and Ratoosh, *op. cit.;* C. West Churchman, *Prediction and Optimal Decision* (Englewood Cliffs, N.J.: Prentice-Hall, Inc., 1961), p. 79; J. Sayer Minas, "Science and Operations Research," in J. Banbury and J. Maitland (eds.), *Proceedings of the Second International Conference on Operations Research* (New York: John Wiley & Sons, Inc., 1961); L. F. Urwick, *The Pattern of Management* (London: Sir Isaac Pitman & Sons, Ltd., 1956), Chap. 2; and Nehemiah Jordan, "The Application of Human Relations Research to Administration," *Management Technology,* Vol. 1, No. 3 (1961).

record of achievement. As some question the celibate priest's advice on marriage, line people resent advice from those who have never worked in line management. Any other qualifications than those of direct, responsible experience are regarded as producing only "theory." Thus the businessman's desperation attack, "Have you ever met a payroll?"[31]

8. The manager who has once witnessed the failure of a staff recommendation feels justified in generalizing this experience.[32] It is hard for him to see that one could have any use for a "theory" which is not even supposed to be right all of the time. The scientist's tendency to work with error contrasts markedly to the manager's philosophy which cannot, from an a priori viewpoint, easily contemplate the possibility of being wrong. This is perhaps a major impediment to wide acceptance of the notion of management as experiment. This attitude, on the other hand, may produce in the staff a rather unscientific striving for infallibility.

9. It is a popular convention that anyone with a particular specialized training has a narrow view of things. The "expert" is supposed to see affairs rather strictly from the vantage point of his own specialty and this narrow bias renders his theories impractical. Granting that a scientific study has bounds, there is little evidence to support this as a generalization.[33]

Chapter 12 emphasized the universality of the quest for certainty. As a manager moves up the ladder perhaps the central feature of his work is the increasing uncertainty, the increasing ambiguity, with which he is confronted. Responsibility, freedom, and the power to make decisions mean he must act in cases where policy and experience do not give clear guides. He must formulate conceptions of new choice situations and deal with them on the basis of increasingly scarce evidence. The resort to well-established policy is, after all, the easy way to reduce uncertainty, and it is not what top management is paid to do. Thus one would hypothesize that uncertainty and ambiguity increase as the manager's power, responsibility, and rewards increase.

This is accompanied by a second-order effect of the following sort. Those who succeed in achieving upper management positions develop a tolerance for uncertainty and ambiguity.[34] They suppress and accommodate the need for certainty, working out for themselves ways of responding to the underdefined problems with which they deal. One does not need to ponder long over which came first, the tolerance for uncertainty or the achievement of a

---

[31] Melville Dalton, *Men Who Manage, op. cit.*, p. 75.

[32] *Ibid.*, p. 88.

[33] Jaleel Ahmad, *The Expert and the Administrator* (Pittsburgh: University of Pittsburgh Press, 1959).

[34] For a development of this idea see Dalton, *Men Who Manage, op. cit.*, pp. 241–59; March and Simon, *op. cit.*, pp. 112–35.

top-management position. Which is the result of the other is not so important here as the hypothesis that they occur together.

Those who achieve substantial managerial responsibility might be characterized as:

1. Tolerant of dilemmas.
2. Making policy, rather than following it.
3. Creating rules, rather than obeying them.
4. Working toward goals, not bound by conventional methods.
5. Creating their own interpretation of policy, rather than seeking its protection in decisions.
6. Not hesitant to act without consulting superiors.
7. Adjusting quickly to failures.
8. Able to improvise in unstable situations.
9. Able to live with confusion.
10. Not resistant to change or experiment.
11. Reducing uncertainty for themselves, rather than looking to the organization to do it for them.
12. Able to use ambiguity for their own ends.

All these characteristics seem to say that such men have less need for the reduction in uncertainty which the staff can provide. They do not lean heavily on explicit problem formulation, explicit data collection and analysis, or explicit policy statements. They do not rely on policy categories as a decision-making tool to the extent that their subordinates must. In short, they feel less need for exactly what the staff has to offer. Paradoxically, however, they tend to be more sympathetic to the view that management science leads to experiments.

All this is closely related to the executive's self-image of the calm, confident decision maker, acting wisely in the face of uncertainty, under great time pressure. Success breeds confidence, and confidence breeds success, for good judgments and good decisions require some measure of self-confidence. In this connection one might consider the following hypotheses:

1. The greater the confidence the greater the tendency toward ad hominem evaluations of advice.
2. Lack of confidence may produce an unwillingness to admit the usefulness of advice or a complete reliance upon it.
3. The greater the confidence and time pressure the less willing the executive to invest the time to create a staff group, to become involved in its work, and to read its reports so that objective criteria may be applied.

What is the staff adviser to learn from all this? What hypotheses should he formulate and test concerning his own behavior and his relations with management? Most of the lessons are obvious enough; however, it may be useful to set down some which seem especially demanding of his attention. Much of what has been said on the subject of how advisers ought to get managers to implement their recommendations seems to make the following points:

1. Salesmanship is required, but selling is difficult to define operationally.
2. Simplicity of thought and language is required in presentations. Mathematics quickly alienates the audience, as does technical jargon.[35]
3. Visual presentations and short, easy to read reports are essential.[36]
4. One must "know one's management" and operate accordingly.

Each of these ideas, representing the distillation of considerable experience, contains its germ of truth. The problem, as this entire discussion has aimed at pointing out, is not well understood in such simplicity. There is a distinction between the knowledge a particular adviser may, after long experience, develop about a particular manager and the beginnings of somewhat more general knowledge of this communication problem. The first sort of knowledge must eventually prevail, and success depends heavily upon it. The second kind of knowledge will speed up the process of attaining it, however. This is another way of saying that we are in the business of suggesting hypotheses which must be tested in particular situations.[37]

------

[35] It is sometimes supposed that an adviser's inability to communicate is directly proportional to his education and commitment to his field of specialization. Managers are often reluctant to manifest directly their ignorance of technical intricacies.

[36] See, for example, James W. Souther, "What Management Wants in a Technical Report," *Journal of Engineering Education,* Vol. 52, No. 8 (1962); "How to Communicate Statistical Findings to Management," *Proceedings of the Business and Economic Statistics Section* (Washington, D.C.: American Statistical Association, 1957).

[37] This section draws heavily upon Likert and Lippitt, *op. cit.* Other useful studies include Rensis Likert and Samuel P. Hayes (eds.), *Some Applications of Behavioral Research* (Paris: UNESCO, 1957); Robert K. Merton, "The Role of Applied Social Science in the Formation of Policy: A Research Memorandum," *Philosophy of Science,* Vol. 16, No. 3 (1949); Robert K. Merton, *Social Theory and Social Structure* (Glencoe, Ill.: The Free Press, 1947); M. L. Hurni, "Characteristics of Management Science," *Management Technology,* Vol. 1, No. 2 (1960); M. L. Hurni, "Observations on the Role of Business Research as an Aid to Managers," *Management Technology,* Vol. 1, No. 2 (1960); E. A. Goldenweiser, "Research and Policy," *Journal of the American Statistical Association,* Vol. 39 (1944); E. Jacques (ed.), "Social Therapy: Technocracy or Collaboration," *Journal of Social Issues,* Vol. 3, No. 2 (1947); Robert W. Newman, Edward Tomeski, Arthur Sternhell, and Kirby Warren, "Toward a Communicable Understanding of Planning; Creeds and Objectives," *Management Technology,* Vol. 1, No. 1 (1960); Roger R. Crane, Philip G. Whelan, and T. M. Butler, "Operating Management Speaks," *Management Technology,* Vol. 1, No. 1 (1960); B. E. Wyne, Sr., "A Pattern for Reporting Operations Research to the Business Executive," *Management Technology,* Vol. 1, No. 3 (1961); and David Kreth (ed.), "Action and Research—A Challenge," *Journal of Social Issues,* Vol. 2, No. 4 (1946).

Let us consider three general modes of communication and persuasion which the adviser might utilize.

1. Experimental demonstration.
2. "Selling."
3. Involvement.

Experimental demonstration of the value of one's recommendations is, as has been noted, the most effective method of all. The crucial importance of experiment in management has been examined at length and the difficulties in reaching this point noted. The adviser's problem is more often to bring the manager to agree to do the experiment which will establish the usefulness of the recommendations.

The quotation marks around the word "selling" are intended to indicate that it is to be associated with a particular operational meaning which tends toward what is called high-pressure selling, or the hard sell. The basic premise of this art is to point out to the potential customer, not the qualities of the product but rather what it will do for him. The idea is not to describe the product so that the client can understand it and evaluate it for himself, but to dazzle him with claims about how much better off he will be if he uses it. For management science this means making promises in advance about the results of research, refusing to admit the possibility that there is considerable uncertainty as to how the manager will benefit and suppressing the conclusion that management must be viewed as experimental activity itself. The claims this sort of selling makes must be supported and in the case of advice this is done by ad hominem argument.

The "salesman" of advice dreams of being the doctor, possessed of great and mysterious knowledge, completely trusted by the helpless patient, his bedside manner suggesting infallibility. Those who start down this road soon find it necessary to represent themselves as "experts." The word is used here in the least complimentary sense to describe one who tries to create the impression of omniscience, infallibility, and of being well in possession of solutions to manager's problems. Jargon lends an air of mystery to his knowledge. When his recommendations are forthcoming little room for discussion remains since he has "masterminded" the problem.

"Selling" carries the implication that the findings are presented to management in the form of a final "pitch." There has been little attempt to understand the manager's conception of the decision problem or to permit the findings of the staff to have an evolutionary impact on managerial thinking. The "pitch" runs a great risk of assuming too much or too little knowledge on the part of management, giving little time for absorption of ideas and the resolution of misunderstandings.

The evidence on the general effectiveness of this approach seems clear.

1. It creates far more resistance than acceptance.[38]

2. It means people will not utilize advice that is forced upon them. Management cannot be sold, they must decide to buy.

3. It provokes management efforts to "shoot down" the staff rather than work constructively with it.

4. It is a kind of staff masterminding that reinforces the use of ad hominem criteria for evaluation by managers.

5. It provokes resentments and gives managers the impression that the staff is not only challenging their competence but is ambitious for their power.

6. Its attempts to represent staff members as special experts are largely discounted by managers.[39]

These difficulties suggested by the somewhat overdrawn description of "selling" suggest another approach which is far more demanding upon the manager and the adviser, yet is emerging as far more effective. This approach suggests the manager no longer simply occupy the role of customer or consumer of the research but become involved as far as possible in the actual process of producing the recommendations.

Involvement of the manager ideally begins very early in the emergence of a management science staff group, continues through the selection and definition of the decisions to be studied, and on through the collection and analysis of the data. If the manager can be persuaded to devote sufficient time to become involved in this way, no "selling" is required when the recommendations emerge. Involvement means management understanding and constructive participation on a continuing basis throughout the analysis of the decision situation. It does not mean managers do the hard work of mathematical analysis, data collection, or computer programming. It does not mean they become fluent in the use of the specialized tools of management science. It does mean, however, they take time to impart to the staff their own conception of the decision problem and they provide criticism to the staff as it evolves the management

---

[38] Likert and Lippitt, *op. cit.*
[39] Learned, Ulrich, and Booz, *op. cit.*

problem into the research problem. It means, hopefully, that the manager is aware of the entire process of staff analysis rather than having the end-product recommendations suddenly presented to him.

Many people in an organization must come to support a recommendation before it actually enters the experimental stage. Ideally, as many of these people as possible should become involved with the staff work, up to the point at which things become too cumbersome. If the staff can involve not only the decision makers themselves but also those who must carry out the recommendations, many problems of acceptance and implementation may be suppressed.

Now all this may have the ring of a pious and impractical preachment, for involvement is not easily achieved. Certainly some managers will not, or cannot, use their staffs in this way. They expect other things from staff people. The staff and its output compete with many, many other things for the manager's time and attention. The pressure of ongoing affairs makes the investment of time now to reduce pressures in the future a difficult one. Deadlines force an executive to rely on his intuition rather than on time-consuming conferences with his staff.[40] Nevertheless, attempts to involve managers seem worth some very considerable effort by the staff.

Outlined below are some hypotheses which tend to support this sort of relationship between adviser and manager.

1. The relation of the staff to management is clearly not that of the wise doctor to whom the medically ignorant patient surrenders himself for care. Unless his own reasoning is involved, a manager is not likely to accept advice in areas he considers within his own competence—in technological matters, perhaps, but not in running his business.

2. A prime objective of the staff must be to create, early in a study, realistic expectations on the part of management. Psychological readiness to accept the results must begin even before the staff goes to work on the decision. It must be developed both in terms of the general competence of management science and in terms of the possibilities it holds for the problem at hand. During the early stages of the study, the staff is wise to give the decision maker quite moderate expectations, regarding possible accomplishments conservatively. He may then discover for himself the full possibilities of what can be accomplished.

3. Staff work, if the hypotheses about the decision process are reasonably descriptive, must mesh with the manager's own thinking. His model of the

---

[40] March and Simon, *op. cit.*, p. 15.

decision process must be understood, and he in turn must understand something of the process whereby his model is redefined into a problem with which management science can work. Hopefully, this will help him to undertake the ultimate task of transforming the recommendations which emerge from the research problem into policy for his real problems.

4. If the nature of management and of management science is as suggested in Part II, then the problem of stipulation is more complex than a simple "yes" or "no" to a staff recommendation. Some appreciation of the underlying model, the data, and the analysis is required, and above all an awareness of the assumptions which have been made. The staff must make the manager aware of the indeterminacy, the residue of uncertainty, which surrounds the results, encouraging so far as possible an experimental attitude. The notion of management as experiment is much to be cultivated.

5. In the long run, the staff aims at sensitizing management to problems, bringing about gradual improvements, and transforming experience into experiment. It may well be that the most effective role of staff management scientists is as educators rather than problem solvers. Involvement may be *the* effective means of doing this.

6. Involvement seeks to make available to the staff not only the manager's view of his decision problem but also his vast, intimate knowledge accumulated over long experience. Nothing is more wasteful than an attempt to mastermind a problem, neglecting almost entirely this most important source of useful information. To tap this inside knowledge, the staff may reserve judgment even when it thinks it sees the answer to a manager's problem. Genuine humility in the face of management experience may be a most valuable staff attribute.

7. Clearly, if all this communication is to take place, the staff, although using the formal organizational channels when projects are initiated, will later rely primarily on informal channels.

8. As a study progresses, frequent reports may be used to keep up interest. Nobody should be allowed to feel left out. People change slowly, and time is required for the gradual absorption of the research findings. If the results are quite different from what had been expected, it may be necessary to proceed more slowly than otherwise. If possible, conclusions should be built up gradually by the use of objective data and analysis, letting the manager verbalize them for himself. People change more readily through evolution.

9. In this connection, the staff may well avoid an immediate insistence on its own interpretation of the data or analysis. The manager may be given time to turn the result over in his own mind, exploring for himself the possible ramifications and interpretations. He should be involved in interpreting the preliminary results rather than be presented with final conclusions on a take-it-or-leave-it basis.

10. Those who will be influenced by the results of the research should see first some results which show they are doing things well.

11. Involvement requires that to some extent the staff relinquish direct credit for the recommendations. This will permit the manager and others involved to see the work as partly their own creation. This is not a trivial suggestion to make to a staff person and we shall return to it in Chapter 17.

It may not be an overstatement to suggest that the analysis of management science developed in Part II, and of the process of advice giving in Part III, appear to point toward involvement as the most effective method of operation for management scientists. Involvement is the essential consequence of all that has been said. This conclusion is neither novel nor without empirical support. R. L. Ackoff has confirmed it in considerable experience.[41] The elaborate experimental work discussed by Likert is consistent with this idea, if not in obvious confirmation of it.[42] Advisers in other fields than management science have reached similar conclusions on the basis of experience.[43] Churchman and Ratoosh have even been able to support the idea in laboratory simulations of advice giving. They found that advice was largely ignored except by those who understood it. They came to define implementation as the production of knowledge and not merely persuasion.[44]

At this point two very important threads may be tied up. In the discussion of values in Chapter 10, we emerged with the position that the "ought" in a recommendation had a very particular meaning. It carried the assertion that what the decision maker ought to do meant that the action was *consistent* with his own values as best they could be determined. Here is a specific aspect of involvement: the integration of the decision maker's preferences into the study to produce a recommendation which reflects his objectives in a specific way. It raises, of course, a special problem of involvement: that of how these preferences are to be measured. In the chapter which follows, the problem of the decision maker's estimates of the likelihood of future events presents a similar specific aspect of involvement. It also raises an exactly similar problem of how these estimates are to be measured and integrated into the decision model. Again, if this can be done the result will be to produce a recom-

---

[41] R. L. Ackoff, *Scientific Method: Optimizing Applied Research Decisions* (New York: John Wiley & Sons, Inc., 1962), p. 412. See also Dalton, *Men Who Manage, op. cit.*, p. 76; Chris Agyris, "Explorations in Consulting-Client Relationships," *Human Organization*, Vol. 20, No. 3 (1961); Jacques, *op. cit.;* Douglas McGregor, I. Knickerbocker, M. Haire, and A. Bavelas, "The Consultant Role and Organizational Leadership," *Journal of Social Issues*, Vol. 4, No. 3 (1948); and Robert Tannenbaum and F. Massarik, "Participation by Subordinates in the Managerial Decision-Making Process," *Canadian Journal of Economics and Political Science*, Vol. 16 (1950).

[42] This work is brought together in Rensis Likert, *New Patterns of Management* (New York: McGraw-Hill Book Co., Inc., 1961). See especially L. Coch, and J. R. P. French, Jr., "Overcoming Resistance to Change," *Human Relations*, Vol. 1, No. 4 (1948).

[43] See, for example, Agyris, *op. cit.;* Jacques, *op. cit.*

[44] Churchman and Ratoosh, *op. cit.*

mendation consistent with his estimates of the likelihoods of future events. These two aspects of involvement occupy a central position in present-day study of the decision process.

Finally, this discussion of caveats for the staff will be concluded by itemizing a few additional suggestions.

1. Resistance to the work of the staff will come out sooner or later. It may be best to bring it out early and face it frankly.

2. Formal organizational authority of the manager to whom the staff reports will be necessary in setting up a study but should be used very little in subsequent phases of the work.

3. Management science research is not a surveillance activity nor is it in any way an attempt to carry out the supervisory function.

4. For the staff, there is often a conflict between doing a good job and securing public recognition for it.

5. Awareness of the work of the staff at the higher levels of management is a great stimulus to action.

Chapter 16:

PROBABILITY

AND

STATISTICS

"It is remarkable that a science which commenced with consideration of games of chance, should be elevated to the rank of the most important subject of human knowledge."

—Laplace

"To us probability is the very guide of life."

—Bishop Butler

The Chevalier de Méré, a seventeenth-century decision maker of sorts, sought advice from the great mathematician Pascal in connection with certain gambling operations. Pascal, in turn, got together with another great mathematician, Fermat, and the advice they produced became the beginning of the theory of probability.[1] The chevalier may have set a rather bad precedent, for his reaction to this advice from the leading minds of his time took the form of a vicious pronouncement on the utter worthlessness of science and mathematics. Jerome Cardan, who mixed gambling with teaching mathematics and medicine, had written a book of advice for gamblers some 100 years earlier. Following Pascal, the great mathematical minds brought to bear on probability theory included Leibniz, James Bernoulli, DeMoivre, and Euler. By 1795, Laplace was lecturing on the uses of probability in the moral sciences, politics, law, insurance, and in "institutions which depend upon the probability of events." Statistics, sometimes defined as "messing about with scads of numbers," also got well under way in the seventeenth century. John Graunt, in 1662, wrote what he chose to call "Natural and Political Observations Made Upon the Bills of Mortality." Soon after, in 1693, Halley produced the first mortality table. Thus, in the words of G. B. Shaw's essay, two rather different

---

[1] Edward Kasner and James Newman, *Mathematics and the Imagination* (New York: Simon and Schuster, 1943), pp. 239–40; Morris Kline, *Mathematics in Western Culture* (New York: Oxford University Press, 1953); and Pierre Simon Marquis de Laplace, *A Philosophical Essay on Probability* (New York: Dover, 1951).

institutions put this knowledge to work, and it brought reason to "The Vice of Gambling and the Virtue of Insurance."[2]

Businessmen, perhaps too busy to take note of any abstract similarities between these institutions and their own, needed some sort of a demonstration that probability and statistics had some relevance to their affairs. Part of the problem may have been that in deaths and games of chance, unlike business, it was possible to get large amounts of experimental data and one need not worry about drawing inferences from relatively limited samples. A reasoned theory of how to guess things about a population on the basis of a sample developed early in the present century.

Dr. Walter A. Shewhart, working at the Bell Telephone Laboratories, produced in 1924 what may well be the crucial idea in making scientific methods of service to management. Control is a traditional function of management and, beginning with the control of machines, Shewhart applied statistics to making sense of the decisions involved.[3] He saw that managerial control is uncertain, first because it is usually based on only a sample of the performance of the system being controlled, and second, because these systems are so complicated it is uneconomic to attempt a precise regulation of their behavior. Management must often content itself with trying to control the average behavior of the phenomena it manages. Making this uncertainty operational was an accomplishment of the first magnitude, and coupling this with advice on how to cope with it set the stage for much of the progress of the past thirty years.

At the same time, H. F. Dodge and H. G. Romig, also with Bell, developed the application of sampling inspection to management decisions as to whether or not large lots of goods were of acceptable quality. It became not only legitimate but highly reasonable to indulge in the ancient practice of making a decision about the quality of a barrel of ball bearings on the basis of an examination of a few handfuls of them. Evidently managers were reluctant to accept scientific sanction for what they may well have taken to be a highly dubious practice, and sampling inspection spread slowly. In 1937, Professor Freeman of Massachusetts Institute of Technology noted, "A deep seated conviction of American production engineers [is] that their principal function is to so improve technical

---

[2] This is reproduced in James R. Newman (ed.), *The World of Mathematics* (New York: Simon and Schuster, 1956).

[3] Walter A. Shewhart, "Finding Causes of Quality Variations," *Manufacturing Industries*, Vol. XI (1926).

methods that no important quality variations remain, and that, in any case the laws of chance have no proper place among 'scientific' production methods."[4] World War II brought acceptance of these ideas by the federal government and support in their development. By 1962, The American Society for Quality Control had grown to more than 15,000 members.

It has been argued that some understanding of recent contributions of management science follows from the view that uncertainty has been made to some extent operational, and the logic of probability theory has been used to recommend ways of dealing with it. Probability and statistics thus appear in a central role in management science. In a sense, one might say that managerial decision making and probability theory have had their effects each upon the other. Probability theory has often had the effect of purging the decision process of inconsistencies and vaguenesses and making possible the explicit assimilation of greater amounts of evidence. Managerial decision making has, in return, forced a recognition that the usual interpretation of probability theory is a useful, but not nearly perfect, tool for dealing with uncertainty. It unfortunately exhibits difficulties in cases of foremost importance to management.

It is perhaps not an overstatement to say that no branch of mathematics is more useful in decision making than probability theory, yet none seems more subject to confusion and widespread misconception. The difficulty is not by any means on the side of the decision makers alone, for among analysts who study carefully the interpretation of probability alternate viewpoints are strongly argued.

This chapter undertakes to suggest several points.

1. Probability and statistics are subjects of the utmost practical importance in management but are pervaded by confusion and misunderstanding.

2. At least two senses in which science deals with uncertainty are important for understanding the limits of scientific competence and the nature of the resulting advice.

3. Advice may strive to be consistent with the decision maker's beliefs, it may strive to be consistent with some explicit evidence (that is, valid), or it may strive to be consistent with both.

4. This context offers specific examples of how advice might function in the decision process and suggests a specific aspect of the process of involvement. Probability applied to managerial decision making presents one with a

---

[4] Quoted by Acheson J. Duncan, *Quality Control and Industrial Statistics* (rev. ed.; Homewood, Ill.: Richard D. Irwin, Inc., 1959), p. 2.

particularly difficult problem in communication between management scientist and manager—a problem in which the involvement of the manager in the staff analysis requires considerable effort to reach common understanding.

Perhaps an oversimplified picture will dispel some confusion. Consider first "probability theory," by which is meant a particular body of abstract, formal mathematics. One can study probability theory without being concerned with its applications, and without trying to puzzle over the operational meaning of statements such as, "the probability of the event A is P" or "X is a random variable." Probability theory is then concerned with analytic truths only, and like other branches of mathematics does not ask nor answer questions about the empirical confirmation of its conclusions. The theory includes statements such as:

> The probability of either A or B equals the probability of A plus the probability of B.
> The probability of either A or not A is one.
> The probability of both A and B is the probability of A multiplied by the probability of B given A.

To *apply* probability theory is to ask first what operational meaning is to be attached to the term "the probability of the event A."[5] Given an answer, one then attempts to investigate whether the corresponding operational interpretations of the deductive hypotheses are in agreement with observed events. Through toughmindedness, the scientist tries to form synthetic statements which can be verified. The trick is to do this in a way which will be of some use in decision making, capturing and modifying the decision maker's feelings of uncertainty.

Interpretations of probability theory, attempting to make it operational, have always gone rather well, so it would seem, as long as they were addressed to problems involving coins, cards, and dice. In decisions having to do, say, with the merger of two airlines, things do not go so well, if at all. Operationalizing probability is not a problem on which all agree or have a ready answer. In fact, it usually comes as a considerable surprise to the student of the subject to discover how much the question is being discussed in the literature and how active the controversy is. Surely it seems such a fundamental question must long ago have been settled, considering the wide use being made of the subject.

---

[5] Ernest Nagel, "Principles of the Theory of Probability," in *International Encyclopedia of Unified Science* (Chicago: University of Chicago Press, 1955), Vol. 1.

For our purposes it will suffice to consider three rough types of interpretations of the term "probability," although there are more.[6]

1. *Relative frequency.* The probability of an event *A* is the limit of the relative frequency with which *A* is observed when an experiment is repeated an indefinitely large number of times. This is ordinarily what is meant when it is asserted that the probability of heads when a fair coin is flipped is one half. It is an unhandy kind of an operational definition since the notion of a limit is quite imaginary. In practice, however, we are perfectly willing to make an induction from a large number of replications as to what would happen in the limit. The class of all possible experiments or instances is called a reference class, and the occurrences of the event *A* form a subclass of the reference class. Sometimes the reference class is finite (the number of customers now served by the firm) and the probability of an event (sales of $1,000 or more to a customer) can in principle be learned by examining every member of the reference class. The trouble comes, as we shall see, not when we want to make statements about large or infinite reference classes but when decision making requires something be said about very small reference classes containing perhaps one or two members.

2. *Personalistic or subjective.* The probability of the event *A* in this view is a measure of a person's "degree of belief" in the statement, "The outcome of the experiment will be *A*." It measures his confidence in the assertion or his conviction of its truth. This interpretation is itself the subject of considerable confusion. We will shortly explore more carefully its meaning and the ways in which it may be made operational. Personalistic or subjective probabilities are not, in spite of their name, products of unbounded flights of whim and fancy. The interpretation is appealing because of the possibility of dealing with a manager's confidence in assertions like, "Our chief competitor is coming out with a new model this year." Managers have feelings of certainty or uncertainty about such assertions, and these feelings can in no useful way be dealt with by means of the relative frequency interpretation.

3. *Everyday language.* This is not really an interpretation of probability, but a category into which are placed all the known and unknown, vague and precise, consistent or inconsistent, meanings which attach to the term "probability" in ordinary conversation. What do managers mean when they talk about probability in discussing their decisions? What is a businessman's notion of "running a calculated risk"? Do these meanings have any useful relationship to the interpretations already mentioned?

There is ample evidence that many of the difficulties which arise between adviser and manager are in some way related to a divergence between meanings assigned to words in everyday language and the operational interpretations made of them by manage-

──────────
    [6] *Ibid.;* L. J. Savage, *The Foundation of Statistics* (New York: John Wiley & Sons, Inc., 1954), pp. 56–57; R. Duncan Luce and Howard Raiffa, *Games and Decisions* (New York: John Wiley & Sons, Inc., 1957); Robert Schlaifer, *Probability and Statistics for Business Decisions* (New York: McGraw-Hill Book Co., Inc., 1959); and Harry V. Roberts, "The New Business Statistics," *Journal of Business,* Jan. 1960.

ment science. While this evidence is hardly well documented, there is an abundant but scattered body of anecdotes which suggests hypotheses. We will begin by examining the meanings which "probability" and "statistics" acquire in the language of those who have not studied these ideas carefully.

Earlier it was argued that a basic difficulty involved in making risk and uncertainty explicit stemmed from the lack of a suitable language and thus the lack of conceptualization. Now perhaps this point may be made a little more precisely. The language of probability and statistics finds its way into conversation about risk and uncertainty in decision making, but the way in which this happens is not very helpful to those who use it. Indeed, the words, if examined for meaning, become the source of a fair amount of misunderstanding.

Conversations about management decisions often contain expressions such as "most probable," "in all probability," "taking a calculated risk," "according to the law of averages," "the chances are," or "it is most likely." Many of these expressions have a rather precise meaning in probability theory and its interpretations. They appear, however, to be the subject of all manner of curious conventions and contradictions in common usage. It is interesting to probe for the meaning of the following remarks made by prominent managers: "The board does not try to pin down the future to certainties. We work out our decisions in terms of probabilities—then we adjust to the details as they develop."[7] "Very few things are black and white; mostly they are gray. I don't consider decisions certainties ever. But certainly I consider them good probabilities."

Often when managers discuss uncertainties in decision making they come very close to the relative-frequency interpretation when discussing their past decision-making performance. "I'd say .300 is a good batting average in our business." ". . . The difference between a successful executive and an unsuccessful one is the difference between being right 52 per cent of the time and being right 48 per cent of the time." Clear as this usage is in the role of ex post facto rationalization, the question is whether or not it can be turned into an active decision-making tool to deal with future uncertainties.

A proprietor of the famous casino at Monte Carlo, a businessman whose operations are directly connected with probability, gave

---

[7] The quotations are taken from *The Executive Life* by the editors of *Fortune* (Garden City, N.Y.: Doubleday & Co., Inc., 1956), pp. 177–78.

the following report in answer to the usual question about breaking the bank. "It was out of season. Few people were playing. But among them were three heavy gamblers. If a lot of people are playing, the table gets covered and the percentages will work in our favor. But out of season, these gamblers' bets put the table out of balance. They would bet when they were having a run of good luck and they would stop just as soon as their luck turned bad. We, of course, had to keep the game going, good luck or bad. It was very unfair. We changed croupiers and so on—all the usual things to change luck. But nothing helped us. So, after sustaining heavy losses, we decided to close down the table for three days. That would and did give our luck a chance to change."[8]

Here, all at once, are a considerable variety of misunderstandings about what the "laws of probability" promise. The more common of these difficulties include the following.

1. "The probability of this coin coming up heads *on its next flip* is one half." Here is a problem which troubles not only the manager but the analyst as well. A businessman faces the same predicament when he tries to relate the evidence, "One half of all new business enterprises fail during their first two years" to a decision about investing in one particular new enterprise.

In the case of the coin, it is clear the next flip will come up either heads or tails. The number "one half" has no direct meaning in description of what will happen on a particular flip. We do not know what the coin will do, except to say it will land on one side or the other. The relative-frequency interpretation may hold that one half is the number approached by the long-run ratio of heads to flips, if the experiment is repeated an indefinitely large number of times. The personalistic interpretation may suggest that one half is a number which somehow measures a person's degree of belief in the truth of the statement, "The next flip of this coin will result in heads." These ideas may turn out to be useful in decision making, but not because of anything they assert about what will actually happen on a given flip. More of this later.

2. Mistaken beliefs based on "the law of averages" are popular. What does this law promise about things that will happen in the long run? "If a coin has come up heads ten times in a row, it is almost sure to come up tails on the eleventh flip." Flips of a coin are independent events, with each outcome quite unrelated to what has happened in the past. The coin, after all, cannot remember. To some extent this may parallel the thought behind such remarks as, "The law of averages requires that this decision be right because the last two (or ten, or twenty) have been wrong."[9]

The law of averages is not at all the kind of imperative seemingly assumed by such statements. Poisson called it a "law," and thus led many astray. Its originator, Bernoulli, was careful to call it a "theorem." It promises nothing in

---

[8] *New York Times*, Sept. 3, 1961. See also, as another example of confusion, "The Myth of Magic Numbers," *Dun's Review and Modern Industry*, March, 1961.

[9] Robert M. Coates, "The Law," in *The World of Mathematics, op. cit.*, Vol. 4.

the short run, and not what is commonly supposed in the long run. One version of it roughly stated says, "As the number of flips grows larger, the *probability* that the observed relative frequency of heads will differ from one half by more than a specified amount, grows smaller. As the number of flips approaches infinity, this probability approaches zero."[10]

3. The common decision maker's remark, "We took a calculated risk," is seemingly meant most often as an ex post facto rationalization of a decision rather than as a description of what was done. In the majority of cases nothing resembling the calculating of a risk was carried on. Perhaps at the time the decision was made it was recognized that things might not turn out well. Actually calculating the risk is, as has been noted, the chief contribution of management science.

How little use is made of any of the statistical evidence which is widely available and potentially relevant to decisions. Vast amounts of data exist which decision makers might translate into probabilities, both in their business and personal choices, but they are little used, at least in any explicit fashion. It may even be argued that the probabilities thus derived are not relevant—say, for example, the use of a mortality table by a man buying insurance—but the reasons that support such an argument are not well known.

4. Continued interest and belief in the possibility of gambling systems suggest further this irrationality and inability to calculate the risk in reasonable ways. Hunches, which experiments in extrasensory perception suggest are not to be sneered at, are one thing, but a system which will improve one's chances in a straight gambling game is not to be found. Most are based on false impressions of the nature of independent events and the law of averages. Gamblers may feel they are challenging fate in order to conquer it, or that fate will somehow be especially kind to them, but if this happens it is not a result of their own calculations.[11]

5. Sampling, the process of drawing inferences about a population on the basis of evidence from a sample, is a particularly difficult concept for many to accept. The *theory* of sampling is, of course, a deductive result of the theory of probability. It may be that management's difficulties with sampling are natural ones for those who often deal only with the end products of the process.[12] It may be that the self-confidence of experienced executives manifests itself in a contempt for statistics, especially when the results disagree with their own views.[13]

Everywhere they find ill-considered support for this attitude. There are books called "How to Lie with Statistics"[14] and remarks about "lies, damned

[10] For an exact statement see William Feller, *An Introduction to Probability Theory and Its Applications* (2nd ed.; New York: John Wiley & Sons, Inc., 1957), Vol. 1, p. 228.

[11] *Ibid.*, pp. 185–87; Richard Lewinsohn, *Science, Prophecy, and Prediction* (Greenwich, Conn.: Fawcett Publications, Inc., 1962).

[12] For example, just how a confidence interval estimate is to be used by a decision maker is not clear.

[13] M. J. Moroney, *Facts from Figures* (Baltimore: Penguin Books, 1951), Chapter 1.

[14] Darrell Huff, *How to Lie with Statistics* (New York: W. W. Norton & Co., 1954). See also "The Disparagement of Statistical Evidence," *Science*, Vol. 132 (1960), p. 1859; and "One in Eighteen Thousand," *Science*, Vol. 133 (1961), p. 2037. Ludwig

lies, and statistics." The world of advertising spawns many hopefully misleading uses of statistics, which brings little but contempt upon it: "Nine out of ten doctors recommend the ingredients in _____."

Statements appear in the public press which say, "The relation between smoking and lung cancer is only statistical." Conclusions are disparaged because they are based only on random samples, as if randomness were somehow a guarantee of weakness approaching nonsense. The catastrophe of the famous *Literary Digest* poll which incorrectly predicted the outcome of the 1936 presidential election is still remembered.[15] It is even reinforced by the joy of seeing Univac make "mistakes" before the television cameras during present-day elections. The prevalence of index numbers, from the stock market to the cost of living, adds to the mystery, for few know how these numbers are computed and what, if any, use can be made of them.[16]

The generally uneasy position of sampling extends even to the law. The attitude of the courts toward sampling is interestingly discussed by Kecker, who presents evidence to support the following generalizations:[17]

1. Courts are more likely to admit sample evidence as to objective facts than they are to admit sample evidence as to group or public opinion.
2. Courts are more inclined to admit sample results if they see no alternative method of proof.
3. Courts are more inclined to admit sample results which coincide with their subjective analysis of the true state of affairs.
4. Courts are prone to admit sample evidence only on the showing of precedent for such evidence in the particular field in question.

Typical, perhaps, of this difficulty in management science is the experience of Churchman in connection with what appeared a very economical plan for settling freight revenue accounts between railroads. The plan, most carefully prepared and tested, encountered considerable skepticism among railroad managers. Churchman's explanation included the following insight, "But above all, I think, is the fact that railroad middle management did not trust sampling,

---

von Mises states, "The textbooks of the calculus of probability gratuitously propagandize for the gambling casinos precisely because they are sealed books to the layman." *Human Action* (New Haven: Yale University Press, 1949).

[15] The poll predicted 40.9 per cent of the vote for Roosevelt. He actually received 60.7 per cent. The later Gallup poll had great difficulty convincing newspaper editors that predictions could be made from small samples. Lewinsohn, *op. cit.*, p. 166.

[16] See, for example, Donald I. Rogers, "Why Figures Do Lie on the Financial Page," *Saturday Review*, Oct. 22, 1961; and a letter from Paul Samuelson in *New York Times*, Nov. 12, 1961. "These days there has begun a campaign of vilification of our unemployment statistics. . . . While scholars recognize the problems involved in this matter, they know most of the popular criticisms to be simply misinformed if not malicious and captious."

[17] Fred M. Kecker, "The Admissibility in Courts of Law of Economic Data Based on Samples," *Journal of Business*, Vol. 28, No. 2 (1955).

no matter how many times a check was run."[18] Other applications of sampling even the well-established tools of statistical quality control, have encountered similar objections.

Related to these difficulties are those people have in translating their experience into probabilities. People's reactions to situations in which relative-frequency probabilities are defined are apparently strange. For example, people may tend to overestimate the probability of desirable events and underestimate the probability of undesirable events.[19]

The single case tends to be reflected in people's behavior sometimes far out of proportion to its relative-frequency probability. Elaborate policies and mechanisms are sometimes established to cope with events which have happened once but are of very low relative-frequency probability. Coincidences become distorted in people's reflections on their experience. Edgar Allan Poe remarked, "Coincidences, in general, are great stumbling blocks in the way of that class of thinkers who have been educated to know nothing of the theory of probabilities: that theory to which the most glorious objects of human research are indebted for the most glorious of illustrations."[20]

The capacity problem, by which is meant the general class of problems surrounding the matching of available resources to the demands for them, illustrates some of the difficulties in making public and explicit recognition of risk and uncertainty. Let us suppose that the demand on an inventory, load on a plant, or work-load in a shop, had been expressed, after a study of the data, as a probability distribution. Policy statements based on certainty perceptions are in a somewhat difficult position not only because they cannot be applied to this risk perception but also because of the real or imagined possibilities for misinterpretation of policy statements

---

[18] C. West Churchman, "Sampling and Persuasion," *Operations Research*, Vol. 8, No. 2 (1960).

[19] A very interesting comparison of the predictions made by clinical psychologists compares them with the results obtained by statistical methods. "Of these 27 studies, 17 show a definite superiority for the statistical method; 10 show the methods to be of about equal efficiency; none of them show the clinician predicting better." Paul Meehl, "When Shall We Use Our Heads Instead of the Formula?" in H. Feigl, M. Scriven and G. Maxwell (eds.), *Minnesota Studies in the Philosophy of Science* (Minneapolis: University of Minnesota Press, 1958), Vol. II. Laboratory studies of people's probabilities have been extensive. For a useful summary article see Ward Edwards, "Utility, Subjective Probability, Their Interaction, and Variance Preferences," *Conflict Resolution*, Vol. VI, No. 1 (1962).

[20] *The Murders in the Rue Morgue.*

which recognize risk and the greatly increased difficulties associated with management control.

Consider these policy statements: "We must maintain a sufficient inventory so that we *never* cut an order." "The plant must be built with *the right* capacity to accomplish the work coming into it." "We must embark on an aggressive program to *eliminate* idleness in the shop."

It seems reasonable to suppose that a manager who speaks in these terms does not generally expect these policies will be fully realized. Rather, he may well feel that if he appears verbally to require a completely adequate inventory, then in the first place he may decide for himself what constitutes satisfactory or unsatisfactory performance in this regard. If one announces that *sometimes* it is permissible to run out of stock the operating people might be expected to interpret this as license for general sloppiness in regard to inventory management, and the situation may degenerate in an uncontrollable fashion. The manager is uncertain about the possibility of communication and control based upon the word "sometimes." One might hypothesize, then, that policies couched in terms of certainty perceptions are issued often for their effect rather than as reflections of how the situation is actually perceived.

The management scientist proposes the word "sometimes" be made more precise in the hope it can become an operationally meaningful basis for communication and control. To do this, he suggests the word be interpreted as a probability statement, and the policy, based now upon a risk perception, comes out in the form, "We will tolerate stockouts no more often than one day in two hundred." For this to make sense in terms of the meaning of a probabilistic interpretation of the data, one must, unfortunately, add the word "average." Thus the policy becomes, "Stockouts should not occur more frequently than one day in two hundred on the average." This results in the interjection of uncertainty from a new source, namely the sampling error arising when one attempts to infer a process average from a sample of process performance. Now this problem can be treated, as it is in statistical quality control for example, but it raises further possibilities for difficulties in communication and control.[21]

---

[21] ". . . Many managers are unfamiliar with the concept of error as a useful informational device. A scientist does not take it to be a confession of failure to assert that there is a positive, probable error in his measurements. . . . But accountants and managers want their cost data "exact." . . . The effort to be precise discourages a manager from living with discrepancies. Thus, he tries to resolve different estimates

The relative-frequency interpretation of probability has been traditional in science and engineering. Although there has long been concern with its shortcomings, recent discussions seem closely related to the turning of scientific attention to the explicit study of the decision process. Its virtues seem basic, simple, and, at first glance, hardly in need of defense. It associates probabilities with the relative frequencies of outcomes in physical experiments. It attempts to meet the usual scientific standards of toughmindedness. It handles the problem of experiments which, even when carefully controlled, seldom if ever yield the same results on successive replications. When used in statements which make predictions, it indicates the kind of regularities to be anticipated in further replications of an experiment. Its strongest form insists probabilities can arise from no source other than these observations of experiments or events. This rather strict kind of toughmindedness is thoroughly ingrained in most analysts.

Relative-frequency probability is thus sometimes called "objective probability" to contrast it with the subjective or personalistic interpretation. "Objective" here may give the impression of a method of making probability operational which does not depend *in any way* on a person's state of mind but reflects some fact to which all must agree. Carefully examined, "objective probability" is not so objective as all that, since in practice it requires a number of judgments which different people may well make in different ways.[22]

Suppose, for example, a manager asks, "What is the probability of a fire in a plant like ours in a year's time?" We might take this to mean, "What is the relative frequency with which a randomly selected plant from a population of plants like this one will have a fire?" Suppose the plant has three characteristics such as:

a) It manufactures a certain chemical.
b) It is of a certain type of construction.
c) Its electrical wiring meets a certain standard.

If we consider the plant a member of the population of all plants having characteristic *a*, the probability is *X*. If we consider it a member of population *b*, the probability is *Y*, and if *c*, the proba-

---

of depreciation because he feels that there should be one figure, not a range. He might be persuaded to accept a range if he could see how he could learn thereby." C. West Churchman, *Prediction and Optimal Decision* (Englewood Cliffs, N.J.: Prentice-Hall, Inc., 1961), p. 335.

[22] *Ibid.*, Chapter 6.

bility is Z. In general, X, Y, and Z are not equal. What probability should we use? Perhaps, it will be suggested, the plant should be considered a member of the population of plants having all three characteristics. If the data are available, this provides yet another possible answer. But why stop with only three characteristics of the plant? Soon the population will be found to contain no other plant than the one under study, thus destroying the relative-frequency interpretation.[23]

The data used to obtain probabilities represent nearly always a sample of the population to which the probabilities are intended to refer. Thus, probabilities are usually based upon inferences. As has been seen, judgment is involved in making such inductions. Perhaps all that can ultimately be said about objective probabilities is that the data upon which they are based and the judgments involved in their production are (or can be) made explicit for all to see and question. This is not the case with personalistic or subjective probabilities.

The more troublesome shortcoming of this interpretation is that it provides no way of dealing with one-time events or situations which are repeated only a small number of times. Unfortunately, it is the case that many business decisions, especially those of great consequence, are not what can be usefully or reasonably viewed as repeatable situations. A "repeatable" event means that it can be classed with other events into a reference class in a way which is informative and of some use for decision-making purposes. Thus a strict relative-frequency interpretation leaves one without guidance except in the long run. It makes no logical sense to talk about the probabilities of outcomes in a one-time decision.[24]

This, however, has not prevented people from doing so. Probabilities are used widely in decisions without regard to the number of times the decision is to be repeated. Various arguments have been used to justify this, although in actual practice the necessity for justification is hardly ever appreciated.

1. Although the decision situation is not, in the view of the decision maker, to be repeated, he stipulates an imaginary problem in which it is to be

---

[23] Recall the discussion of repeatability in Chapter 7. This is analogous to the difference in viewpoints of, say, the sales manager and the salesman. The manager, perhaps with the aid of an analyst, deals with customers in statistical fashion while the salesman sees them as individuals. Some salesmen have reacted to histograms of sales volume by an attempt to name the customers represented by various points on the chart.

[24] Churchman, *op. cit.*, p. 41.

repeated many times. He then uses the probabilities which would be useful guides to action for the imaginary problem in exactly the same way for the real problem. This is supposed to "explain" the use of probabilities in the one-time case.

2. The decision maker stipulates that what he is doing is illogical but goes ahead anyway on the premise that being a little bit illogical does only a little bit of harm.[25]

3. The probabilities are redefined so as to be regarded as measures of "degree of belief" in truth of propositions and are thus somehow relevant without regard to the repeatability of the situation. More of this shortly.

4. The decision maker proposes to use probabilities in all decisions, thus taking advantage of long-run effects in the reference class of all decisions rather than in a more restricted reference class.

5. A further consequence of this view, already noted, is that the law of averages or the law of large numbers has no meaning except in the long run. If one does take the long view, then there is much to be said for acting so as to maximize the average or expected return.[26] In Chapter 10, however, is an explanation of the axiom system of von Neumann and Morgenstern which makes average or expected utility always the logically consistent criterion to maximize. If outcomes had been evaluated according to the particular method of scaling they suggested, the consistent decision maker would always, even for unique decisions, wish to choose so as to obtain the largest expected utility.[27]

Insistence on the relative-frequency view means further that evidence which is not of a relative-frequency nature cannot become a part of the explicit decision model unless it is stipulated by the decision maker. That is, the evidence must arise in what has been called a statistical situation. This means one stipulates a probability law relating the relative frequency with which the observations would occur to the condition that a particular statement about the future is true. If one has observed x, and is interested in the occurrence of a future event E, he must be able to exhibit $P(x/E)$, the probability of x under the assumption that E will happen. The cases in which this can be done are the cases in which classical inferential statistics can be applied.

Suppose, however, the evidence is in the form of a rumor that a competitor is about to launch a new product. It will be difficult to say what the relation is explicitly between that hearing of such rumors and the launching of new products. The decision maker, however, may act as though the rumor were true, as though it were

---

[25] Hans Reichenbach, *The Rise of Scientific Philosophy* (Berkeley: University of California Press, 1959), Chapter 14.

[26] William T. Morris, *Engineering Economy* (Homewood, Ill.: Richard D. Irwin, Inc., 1960), p. 212.

[27] Laplace called expectation "mathematical hope."

false, or even as though he attached some intermediate degree of belief to it.

In two general situations the relative-frequency position may lead to a model which does not reflect all the evidence available to and used by a manager. Ordinarily an experienced manager will have a large amount of accumulated information or background data which is not duplicated by the explicit evidence obtained by the staff. In a simple case, suppose a sample of a lot of a product is inspected and the resulting inference is that the lot is of acceptable quality. Suppose, however, that a manager has some information to the effect that the supplier was having a good deal of trouble with his process at the time the lot was produced. He might decide, and wisely so, to hold off on acceptance of the lot until a much larger sample can be inspected. In a more complex situation, consider the manager who is furnished with a sales forecast based on the usual relative-frequency data. He may have a rich background of knowledge and experience, a feel for the market, which he may use to modify this forecast. This is usually referred to as making managerial judgments, but it can equally well be regarded as modification of the decision model on the basis of evidence not assimilable in the relative-frequency theory.

The second case is that in which no relative-frequency data at all are available, and the evidence is solely that which the decision maker himself stipulates. Suppose a new and radically different product is to be launched and no test marketing is to be made. Clearly, the decision must be based on experience which cannot be made explicit in the staff analysis. If the staff operates without any stipulation from the manager it can only view the volume of sales for the new product as a matter of uncertainty. The manager himself may be quite unwilling to take this view, and thus he calls up from this memory all the experience he feels is relevant.

The net effect of a strict relative-frequency interpretation is to restrict staff work to those situations in which relative-frequency evidence is available, or to exclude from explicit consideration by the staff any evidence not of a statistical nature. This is regarded by many as perfectly reasonable since relative-frequency evidence is the source of validity in scientifically based advice. This is the traditional view in engineering. It makes allowances by agreeing that of course the decision maker may, after the staff has done its work, make judgments which do not limit him to the relative-frequency evidence. This is an accepted kind of division of labor between staff and management.

These difficulties, which are of major importance, have been partly responsible for the interest in subjective probability in recent years. It tends to overcome some of these objections, but extracts a price as it does so. Before examining this interpretation, let us take up a difficulty in decision making which cannot be removed by any interpretation.

Suppose we know a certain coin is biased in favor of heads, and we are offered a finite number of even-money bets on the outcome of flips. Suppose further, we accept one or more of the common arguments as to the reasonableness of betting on heads. It may well turn out that at the end of the series of flips we are in a losing position. No interpretation of probability offers a promise this will not happen. Was the decision to bet on heads wrong or unreasonable? Was the advice, upon which it was based, bad advice? If the situation comes up again would we bet differently? Here we encounter a difficulty which seems to arise often in the ex post facto examinations of decisions. It is necessary to understand that no interpretation of probability makes a guarantee of results in finite sequences of decisions, but in spite of this it is not less reasonable to use these interpretations as a basis for choice.[28] Herodotus made the point clearly. "There is nothing more profitable for a man than to take good counsel with himself; for even if the event turns out contrary to one's hopes, still one's decision was right even though fortune made it of no effect; whereas if a man acts contrary to good counsel, although, being lucky he gets what he had no right to expect, his decision was not any the less falacious."

It is clear that, in many important decisions, relative-frequency evidence alone will not seem to the manager a sufficient basis for choice. He will indeed add to and modify this evidence, a process loosely called judgment. To what extent should one try to reflect these judgments or applications of experience explicitly in the analysis of a decision? To put it another way, if one is really serious about the involvement of the manager in the staff analysis, why not reflect the executive's rich background and experience, together with his ability to guess at the future, directly in the model of the

---

[28] Keynes remarked, "The proposition that a course of action guided by the most probable considerations will generally lead to success, is not certainly true and has nothing to recommend it but its probability." Quoted in *The World of Mathematics op. cit.*, Vol. 2, p. 1373.

decision? This problem and its possibilities parallel closely the case of values studied in Chapter 10.

There is a considerable mystique associated with managerial judgment. It is a kind of executive genius which marks out the really successful man of business. His intuition is his sole guide and he makes brilliant guesses as to the future course of affairs without having to fall back on relative-frequency data. As Churchman noted, it is a difficult mystique to test, for the laws of chance suggest that if many businessmen have the courage to guess and act some will appear successful whether or not they have any special abilities as predictors.[29] Walter Bagehot saw this also.[30] "Men of business have a solid judgment, a wonderful guessing power of what is going to happen, each in his own trade, but they have never practiced themselves in reasoning out their judgments and in supporting their reasoning by argument; probably if they did so some of the finer and correcter parts of their anticipations would vanish. . . ."

To transform a manager's beliefs into personalistic probabilities and to integrate them with other evidence in the analysis would doubtless be a considerable task. What would be the advantages of doing this? It would provide one way of explicitly involving the decision maker in the work of the staff. It would help the manager impart to the staff in a careful manner some aspects of his own estimates of the decision situation. It would show the manager that his own thinking was expressly included in the model. Thus the resulting recommendations would be consistent with his beliefs, and indeed partly of his own creation. It would provide a possible means of taking advantage of both the manager's rich background of experience and the data obtained by the staff.[31] If the practice became well developed and generally accepted, it might offer the staff a wider field of operation, including decision problems on which relative-frequency evidence was not available. It might exploit the usefulness of the staff in connection with decisions at higher management levels. It would permit the adviser to extend in a consistent fashion the choice processes of the manager. It is assumed that decision makers can assign probabilities to the simple events well within their experience. The work of the adviser is to

---

[29] Churchman, *op. cit.*, p. 149.

[30] Walter Bagehot, *Works*, F. Morgan (ed.) (Hartford: The Travelers Insurance Co., 1889), p. 245.

[31] In many cases, consistency is not what managers think they are getting from their advisers.

derive from these simple probabilities the probabilities of more complex events which are directly involved in the decision process but with which his experience is lacking. The theory of probability is the criterion for consistency here. The result, combined with that of Chapter 10, assumes that an objective of management science is to identify a course of action which is logically consistent with the decision maker's own preferences, as expressed by numerical utilities and with the weights he attaches to possible future events, as expressed by numerical probabilities. If this is so, then the program of measuring subjective probabilities should increase the chances that a staff recommendation would be accepted by the manager.

Not the least benefit of this program would be to make these probabilities explicit so they could be checked for consistency, criticized by others, and revised as new experience is obtained. But this program raises problems which today are still under active investigation. How are personalistic probabilities to be obtained? How are they to be measured? How are they to be used when relative-frequency evidence is also available? What about the objections of those who regard personalistic probabilities as an abandonment of the sacred standards of toughmindedness?

Consider first how they would be used, if one could measure them. Imagine a decision in which the staff has obtained some data, represented by the symbol x, and stipulates a relation between the probability of observing x and the occurrence of a possible future event, E_j. Thus, here is a statistical situation in which this conditional probability is stipulated. It will be represented by the symbol, $P(x/E_j)$.

Suppose further that one is able to measure or elicit from the manager his degree of belief in the statement, "The event E_j will occur." Some care is taken to express this probability on a scale from 0 to 1 and to see that it meets some criteria for consistency from probability theory. Let the symbol p_j stand for the result. Now the crucial question. If the manager starts out with a personalistic probability p_j as the result of his experience, and the staff confronts him with the data it has obtained, what should happen to his beliefs? Let $P(E_j/x)$ stand for his personalistic probability after having learned of the staff's results. How does p_j (called his a priori probability) become transformed into $P(E_j/x)$ (called his a posteriori probability)? A recommendation as to how this should happen springs from a very important theorem of Thomas Bayes. It suggests

$$P(E_j/x) = \frac{P(x/E_j)p_j}{\sum_j P(x/E_i)p_i}$$

This then blends the results of the staff's statistical analysis with the manager's experience to produce a modification of his experience upon which he may base his choice. If the staff should produce more evidence, the current a posteriori probabilities may simply be regarded as the a priori probabilities for a new cycle. The cycles may continue, of course, until the a posteriori probabilities are such that stipulation occurs. Given the cost of collecting data and the values of the outcomes in a decision one may even recommend the optimal point at which to stipulate.[32]

The way in which this could happen is roughly as follows. The decision maker, at any stage, is assumed to have a priori probabilities with respect to the possible futures. He further stipulates the probability distributions of the data which might be observed, assuming each of the possible futures to be true. With this, he can compute the probability that various observations will actually result from a data-collection program. If data are obtained, Bayes' theorem is assumed as a model of how a priori probabilities are transformed. At any stage in the decision process, the choice between two alternatives may be made.

1. Stipulate and make the best choice given the present conception of the decision.

2. Obtain one more increment of information and then consider the same two alternatives.

It turns out that one can, in such a statistical situation, compare these two actions, if the cost of collecting data and the payoffs in the original decision are estimated. At any stage the expected payoff from the best current choice is compared with the expected payoff from continuing and deciding between alternatives one and two optimally at each future stage.

The sequence

a priori probabilities
data collection
a posteriori probabilities
recommendation

provides an idealized example of how the conceptualization of the decision maker might be enriched and developed toward a recommendation by the staff. The situation here directly parallels that

---

[32] For detailed examples of this process, see Morris, *op. cit.*, pp. 371–98.

encountered in the case of values. Neat as this may be, the problems of meeting the objections raised against subjective probabilities and finding methods of measuring them still exist.

The case in favor of subjective probabilities may include arguments such as the following:

1. All probabilities are to some extent subjective, and thus nothing new in principle is being proposed.

2. Different people, in situations where relative-frequency evidence may eventually be obtained, may have quite different subjective probabilities, but these get modified through further experience. With the aid of the staff, this modification may take place in accordance with Bayes' theorem. If this happens, then in the long run all the different subjective probabilities will converge to the relative-frequency probabilities. The effects of the initial a priori probabilities are soon washed away by the accumulation of evidence.

3. It is foolish to waste the experience of decision makers, especially when little other evidence is available. Here is a way to use and to extend it by deducing useful consequences from it.

4. It is assumed, by those who favor this approach, that reasonable men having similar experience will not differ greatly in their personalistic probabilities. This assumption may indeed be true.

5. If a manager's experience is not considered most extensive and most relevant on a particular question, then an expert may be brought in. The expert is someone believed to have considerable knowledge and experience on the matter in question. He is then integrated into the decision process by obtaining from him his subjective probabilities. This is a particularly interesting idea because it suggests a specific way in which the knowledge of subject matter or "predictive" experts may be utilized. It is an idea carefully developed by Helmer and Rescher.[33] They suggest a predictive expert, who might be used as a source of probabilities, must meet certain qualifications which are far from subjective themselves. He must:

a) Have personalistic probabilities which are reasonably stable over time, providing he receives no new evidence.

b) Have probabilities which are affected in the right direction by new evidence.

c) Be selected for his past predictive performance, his demonstrated record of success and accuracy.

Thus, a good deal of what is most subjective about subjective probabilities would be removed in the case of the expert. He is in fact treated as a kind of powerful computer in the decision process. He digests rich and complex past experience and produces the probabilities as his output.

The problem of measuring a manager's subjective probabilities is much like that of measuring his values which was considered in Chapter 10. It is not supposed that these probabilities will spring

---

[33] Olaf Helmar and Nicholas Rescher, "On the Epistemology of the Inexact Sciences," *Management Science*, Vol. 6, No. 1 (1959).

forth from the mind of the executive or even that they occupy a place in his conscious thought. It is supposed, however, that if it were possible to study in detail his past decisions one could infer from his choices a set of numbers which would be called person-alistic probabilities. Then, always assuming other things were known about the way he conceptualized decisions, one could say his behavior was explainable in terms of these probabilities, or was consistent with them. The results could then be used to *predict* how he might choose in other situations. A recommendation based on such a prediction would carry the same strength as one based on his inferred values. It would be a recommendation he would natu-rally wish to accept for it would be a consistent conclusion from his own model of the situation.

What is actually proposed as a method of measurement is neither simply asking the manager directly how he feels nor at-tempting a detailed and perhaps impossible study of his past actions. Instead, it is assumed that a manager can be asked how he would choose in such-and-such a hypothetical decision situation.[34] He is supposed to respond to these questions according to his best intuitive judgment. By processing the answer one may infer the desired probabilities. It is assumed that a man can think about and reason out his feelings of uncertainty so that his responses are some-how meaningful, and that he will resolve any logical inconsisten-cies which are pointed out to him. Again, the mathematical theory of probability provides the standard of consistency.

Let us examine how such a scheme for inferring his probabili-ties from his answers might work.[35] Imagine a hypothetical decision problem involving a choice between two actions, a_1 and a_2. Three possible future events are considered in the model of this problem, E_1, E_2, and E_3. The events are ones of which we wish to know the probabilities and about which we assume the decision maker to have some experience. The actions are assumed to be meaningful choices to him as well.

One first confronts him with the following choice:

	E_1	E_2	E_3
a_1	0	0	$100
a_2	x	x	x

---

[34] The difficulties of doing this are discussed in Luce and Raiffa, *op. cit.,* pp. 36–37.

[35] For an alternate method, see Schlaifer, *op. cit.,* p. 12.

He is then asked what the value of x would have to be before he would be indifferent between the two actions. Assume he chooses so as to maximize the expected dollar return, and this is a crucial assumption. Suppose he answers that for $x = \$20$ he would be indifferent. Based on this assumption one can say that $20 = 100 \, p_3$, and thus the subjective probability of E_3 is $p_3 = .20$.

By similar questioning p_1 and p_2 could be inferred and then checked to see if the sum of the three probabilities was indeed 1. If this is not so, then this inconsistency must be pointed out to the manager and it is hoped he will adjust his choices. No concept of objective probability enters the scheme at any point.

Without doubt this is a difficult sort of thing to bring off in actuality. There is every possibility that inconsistencies will arise, that the results will be unreliable, and that the whole thing will appear quite "fuzzy" to the manager. So far as the current work of management science is concerned all this is somewhat in the future. Whether managers will indeed be able to answer this sort of question, whether they will accept the resulting recommendation, and whether the resulting decisions will be better or worse than those arising from undisturbed intuition are questions in the early stages of investigation.

Probability, this chapter has tried to say, is basic in the efforts of management science to deal with decisions under risk and uncertainty, and it is basic in the inference making of all science. Unfortunately, the notion of probability presents particular difficulties as adviser and manager communicate and as the adviser seeks to involve the manager in the analysis of the decision. These difficulties follow both from the common misunderstandings which surround probability and from the alternate formal interpretations of it. What, a manager wonders, can he expect from a probabilistic recommendation? Does it promise anything useful about the future course of his affairs? Is the staff telling him something which should supersede his intuitions, which should be rejected if it fails to agree with his intuitions, or with which he must somehow blend his own experience and judgment?

Chapter 17:

FRUSTRATIONS

OF ADVICE

"Almost anything is possible as long as nobody cares who gets the credit for it."

GIVING

It may be true that the business of philosophers is to make ideas available, not to force them on anyone. This, however, is a position which gives small consolation to the hired philosopher. Advisers tend to find their rewards not alone in the production of advice but also in seeing it acted upon. Indeed, their job satisfaction, the justification for their own existence, and the possibilities for advancement depend largely on the extent to which their ideas and studies are used by management. Here these problems and the role of the adviser in organizational life will be examined, attempting as before to suggest interesting hypotheses.

On the one hand there is every reason to assume that scientists and engineers in general, as well as management scientists in particular, should find great prestige and satisfaction in their work. There is great demand for their services and their successes are widely recognized, both professionally and by the general public.[1] Indeed, it is certainly true that the great majority must find satisfaction in their positions and their accomplishments. There is, however, some evidence that this happy situation is not universal, and it is to that evidence attention now turns. Any attempt to focus on the difficulties advisers experience in organizational life seems bound to give a negative impression and appear unduly critical of the advisers themselves and of the managers with whom they work. While this

---

[1] For but a few examples, see Merrill M. Flood, "New Operations Research Potentials," *Operations Research*, Vol. 10, No. 4 (1962); "Will Computers Run Wars of the Future?" *U.S. News and World Report*, April 23, 1962; "Operations Research," special section published by the *Washington Daily News*, May 1962; and P. J. Davis, "The Criterion Makers: Mathematics and Social Policy," *American Scientist*, Vol. 50, No. 3 (1962).

impression cannot be avoided it must be said that the mounting demonstration of success management science is providing, the increasing number of educational programs moving to support it, the number of firms of all kinds using it, and the number of highly qualified persons entering the profession must be taken as considerably outweighing, in any balance, the problems next examined.

Specialists who have taken positions as advisers in action-oriented organizations seem always to have complained of being inadequately appreciated.[2] Managers who have engaged them as advisers have likewise had complaints. The expert in government has been pictured as having a limited viewpoint, lacking common sense, and overcomplicating simple situations. Staff advisers in industry are sometimes regarded as "costing more than they're worth." ("They stir up too much trouble and they are too theoretical.") This kind of evaluation can be obviated through increased understanding by both advisers and managers of the competence of scientific advice on management decisions and the organizational context within which it is produced and consumed. Some of the ways in which dissatisfactions arise for advisers and some of their responses will be outlined now.

A kind of chronic dissatisfaction among natural scientists and engineers in industry was revealed by the University of Chicago Industrial Relations Center.[3] This study, like the others which are available, is not specifically a study of management scientists, operations researchers, or industrial engineers, and thus must be regarded as source of hypotheses rather than conclusions. The attitudes of 399 engineers and 188 natural scientists in some nineteen different work groups show them to be less satisfied with their work situation than skilled workers, foremen, salesmen, and managers. They were generally more satisfied than production workers, and

---

[2] See Harold J. Laski, *The Limitations of the Expert* (Fabian Tract No. 235) (London: The Fabian Society, 1931); Jaleel Ahmad, *The Expert and the Administrator* (Pittsburgh: University of Pittsburgh Press, 1959); Melville Dalton, *Men Who Manage* (New York: John Wiley & Sons, Inc., 1959); Alfred North Whitehead, *Science and the Modern World* (New York: Mentor Books, 1948), p. 196; Thurman Arnold, *The Folklore of Capitalism* (New Haven: Yale University Press, 1937); A. A. Berle, Jr., "Case for the Professor in Washington," *New York Times*, Feb. 5, 1961; James Reston, "On Kennedy's Disenchanted Intellectuals," *New York Times*, Oct. 8, 1961; E. A. Shils, "Social Science and Social Policy," *Philosophy of Science*, Vol. 16, No. 3 (1949); Robert K. Merton, "The Role of Applied Social Science in the Formation of Policy: A Research Memorandum," *Philosophy of Science*, Vol. 16, No. 3 (1949); and E. P. Learned, D. N. Ulrich, and D. R. Booz, *Executive Action* (Boston: Harvard University Graduate School of Business Administration, 1951).

[3] David G. Moore and Richard Renck, "The Professional Employee in Industry," *Journal of Business*, Vol. 28 (1955).

had attitudes interpreted as similar in satisfaction to those of routine office employees. Especially interesting was the tendency among engineers to have a low regard for management. Managers, to them, appeared confused, disorganized, and ill-advised. They apparently felt their communication with managers was poor and they had little confidence in them.

The interpreters of this evidence regard these attitudes as partly the valid criticisms of trained analysts and partly the expression of a chronic frustration. The general conclusion they drew was that whenever the expectations and self-images of professional employees are not matched by their opportunities for achievement on the job, morale will be low.

Three work groups included in this study stood out, two because of exceptionally high morale, and one with very low morale. The two high-morale groups were successful in the sense that they had developed promising new products for their companies. The low-morale group, on the other hand, considered itself a failure and was so regarded by others because its recommendations had not been adopted by management. This tends to confirm, admittedly in a very limited fashion, the hypothesis that morale is related to productivity among professional employees. Here one would think of productivity as "having the group's recommendations adopted by management." Turnover is a measure which also can be taken as roughly related to job satisfaction. Dalton found evidence of dissatisfaction among the staff in his plant which was confirmed by the rates of turnover. The percentage turnover among staff people was roughly three times that among line managers.[4]

The argument which follows is of the nature of a series of hypotheses, not wholly without empirical confirmation but hardly confirmed with respect to staff advisers working in management science. Attention is again directed toward staff people who are "in house" or on the company payroll, rather than members of an outside group who work with the company for a relatively limited period of time. The present discussion takes the following form:

---

[4] Dalton, *op. cit.,* p. 96. The figures for the four years studied are:

Per Cent Turnover

Year	Line	Staff
1	24.2%	78.9%
2	28.2	88.0
3	31.7	88.0
4	31.5	81.5

1. The adviser has certain expectations and needs for such things as monetary rewards, prestige, recognition, advancement, and security.

2. The degree to which these expectations are realized depends on his ability to demonstrate achievement with respect to more or less operational performance criteria. The central criterion of success is having recommendations implemented by management.

3. The organizational context in which the adviser works, together with the very nature of his skills, operate in various ways to frustrate his attempts to realize his expectations.[5] These difficulties have been classified as:

   a) Problems of the selection and definition of the decision situations to be studied.

   b) Problems surrounding the actual production of recommendations.

   c) Problems of demonstrating achievement.

4. The degree of divergence between expectations and accomplishments is directly related to job satisfaction. This, in turn, is related to the way in which the adviser responds to the situation. If he is sufficiently dissatisfied he may quit his job or perhaps look for chances to move into line management.

It is hypothesized that it is not uncommon for a staff adviser to begin his career with the notion that his skills and recommendations will be sought and welcomed by management, and that he will find early recognition and promotion. While admitting that he has much to learn about the functioning of a particular company, he relies on his methodological training in science and his array of hypotheses to make it possible for him to analyze all sorts of decision situations effectively. As Dalton discovered in his intensive study of three industrial firms, such a person may well be in for some initial disappointments.[6] He may find his freedom to function and the acceptance of his recommendations are snarled in the complexities of the informal relationships among the members of the organization. The naive presumption that the staff produces advice and the line acts on it turns out to be something less than the true picture. He may find his academic training is not as immediately relevant as he had been led to suppose. This happens in two general ways. First, the problems with which he must work may not lend themselves to the kind of elaborate or sophisticated techniques which represent to him a high level of professional performance. Indeed, the problems may yield best to relatively simple analysis and a rather tedious amount of hard work. He hardly feels his full capacities are called for. Second, he may find either that the central

---

[5] A particularly good summary is given by Douglas P. McGregor and Thomas L. Whisler (eds.), *Management Organization and the Computer* (Glencoe, Ill.: The Free Press, 1960).

[6] Dalton, *op. cit.*, p. 95.

issues in a decision problem fall within some other professional field such as electrical engineering or mechanical engineering, or that those whose training is in other fields are doing the work he had supposed himself uniquely qualified to perform. Finally, the uses which management makes of advice and the criteria with which they evaluate advice may not be those which he had supposed. It may indeed develop that the way to get recommendations implemented is to find out what ideas are acceptable to management and to learn the special kinds of tactics which are effective in getting them accepted. These kinds of discoveries are widely regarded as the benefits of "getting some real experience in industry." The kind of adjustment the adviser makes to this experience is the problem here.

There is some specific evidence on the expectations and needs of professional people in industry which may be used as a basis for hypotheses about management scientists. In a study of 250 research engineers in twenty-one industrial research laboratories, it was found that the engineers themselves ranked their wants in the following way:[7]

1. Higher salaries.
2. Increased general competence.
3. More challenging technical problems.
4. More consultation on major decisions.
5. Increased competence in a specialty.
6. More freedom to determine their own work.
7. More power in the organization.
8. More people to supervise.
9. More opportunity for professional recognition.

It is not particularly necessary for this discussion to insist on evidence as to the priority of these goals, but only to identify some which can reasonably be assumed generally important. In newly formed industrial engineering or management science groups, the problem of survival for the staff group and job security for the individual is a central one. Management seemingly tends to regard the group as very much on trial and to view its existence as an experiment. The failure to produce demonstrable results in a reasonably short time raises the very real possibility of discontinuation. Survival becomes an issue again when business conditions take a turn

---

[7] Hollis W. Peter, "Human Factors in Research Administration," in Rensis Likert and Samuel P. Hayes, Jr., *Some Applications of Behavioral Research* (Paris: UNESCO, 1957).

for the worse. Managers have in some cases stated frankly that when cuts become necessary, the staff groups will be among the first to go.[8] However shortsighted this view may appear, it is perhaps another manifestation of the fact that staff advice is not regarded by management as an essential element of the conduct of affairs.

With some assurance of survival as a staff group and job security for individuals, other expectations come to the fore. For example, among management scientists one would hypothesize the need for financial rewards, recognition, prestige, mobility (advancement), and professional development and achievement.

March and Simon regard dissatisfaction with a job as arising in part out of differences between the characteristics of the job and the self-image of the job holder. They suggest two general hypotheses which have application in this context.

1. The greater the rewards, say in the form of money and prestige, the less the conflict between job and self-image. This is obvious enough and widely accepted, but leads to some interesting and highly tentative corollary hypotheses.[9]

a) There may well be a trade-off between the needs and expectations which constitute the adviser's self-image. Given enough status and prestige, he may be willing to forgo some of his desires for money. Given sufficient monetary rewards, he may be willing to forgo his ambitions to develop professional competence and attain professional recognition. Later, some of the ways will be suggested in which the opportunities open to advisers force them to make account of such trade-offs.

b) Tendencies toward highly routinized wage-payment systems of the civil service type, and efforts toward collective bargaining which bring greater uniformity of financial rewards and status, will be resisted by staff advisers. They tend to feel they will gain more when evaluated and rewarded individually.

2. At a given job level, dissatisfaction will tend to be greater among those who have had more education.[10] Clearly, holders of the doctoral degree find satisfaction in a relatively small number of jobs, usually in large organizations. On the other end of the scale, some staff jobs such as taking time studies or routine computations have been filled with persons having no college degree since graduate engineers were highly dissatisfied in these positions even for a short period of time.

To go on to more specific hypotheses, it is useful to consider some of the orientations the adviser may have toward his job.

---

[8] McGregor, *op. cit.;* and Dalton, *op. cit.*, p. 97. Note, however, that this is not confirmed by the facts on staff expansion and growth presented in Chapter 3.

[9] James G. March and Herbert A. Simon, *Organizations* (New York: John Wiley & Sons, Inc., 1958), p. 95.

[10] *Ibid.*, p. 96.

1. The adviser may regard his staff job as a step toward line management. It is well known that many persons trained in management science view it, at least early in their careers, as an opening which will provide eventual opportunities to move into management.[11] In these jobs, their dissatisfaction is not high as long as the possibilities for movement into management appear good and as long as they do not remain there too long. While it is true that very few of the top managers whose careers were studied by Newcomer rose by this means, it need not always be so.[12] Persons with this orientation, one would hypothesize, would be less interested in the development of professional competence and in attaining professional status than in getting specific knowledge of the persons and procedures of the firm together with recognition within the firm.

2. Alternatively, the adviser may regard his staff job as a career. This would suggest that he would be interested in gaining professional competence and professional recognition, and in doing well at the job. The data cited by Peter show that research people in industry tend to regard staff jobs as careers in a way which increases with their level of education.[13] The higher their last degree, the less interest they exhibit in being promoted out of staff work and into management. Simon and March also suggest the following useful series of hypotheses[14] interpreted here in terms of staff advisers. Consider a given staff position. A person holding this position will tend to be relatively satisfied if he holds it early in his career when the possibilities for mobility and the realization of his expectations still appear good. If he holds the job later in his career, his satisfaction will be reasonably high because his expectations for mobility will have been replaced by identification with the job and the desire to do well at it as a career. During the period between these two conditions, when his desires for moving up and out have been frustrated but have not been replaced with the career identification, his dissatisfaction will be highest.

3. One might distinguish a third job orientation also, that of the individual who regards the staff job as a step toward staff supervisory positions, such as chief engineer, group leader, director of research, and so on. The number of these jobs in most organizations appears to be small, but they may nevertheless represent an appealing compromise for persons who seek more money and prestige while at the same time maintain some limited identification with their professional field.

What trade-offs are staff advisers forced to make in evaluating the opportunities open to them? Everyone tends to find his opportunities permit something less than the simultaneous realization of all his expectations, but perhaps the kind of conflicts professional staff persons face may be especially difficult to resolve. For example,

---

[11] Dalton, *op. cit.*, p. 98; The editors of *Fortune, The Executive Life* (Garden City, N.Y.: Dolphin Books, 1956), p. 89; and March and Simon, *op. cit.*, p. 97.

[12] Mabel Newcomer, *The Big Business Executive: The Factors That Made Him, 1900–1950* (New York: Columbia University Press, 1955). Recently there have been indications of a reversal. Atwood quotes data which show engineers and scientists leading all other professionals among the presidents of 200 large companies. See J. L. Atwood, "The Challenges We Face," *News in Engineering*, Vol. 34, No. 3 (1962).

[13] Peter, *op. cit.*

[14] Simon and March, *op. cit.*, p. 97.

it is often true that a substantial increase in salary can only be realized at the expense of nearly all opportunities for professional development and recognition. This is particularly true for the staff person with advanced degrees, who discovers that the real money is in management and he must make a rather severe choice between his professional interests and his financial stature.[15] The same is true of other rewards, such as status and recognition within the firm, which are more abundantly bestowed on managers than upon staff people. Opportunities for mobility are usually more limited in staff departments than in management. The hierarchy of staff jobs contains perhaps three or four levels while there can be many more in the management ladder.

The trade-off between professional achievement and company achievement goes right down to the level of a particular staff study. Often, the sophisticated and detailed development of the management decision problem which would be professionally rewarding fails to meet the needs of management. In choosing the kind of research strategies likely to be rewarding in the company, the staff man may view what he is able to do as "quick and dirty" and of little note professionally. In the extreme, it may well be that the problems managers would really like to have "solved" and would be most willing to reward the staff for, do not fall substantially within the competence and interest of the staff advisers.

Central to the remainder of this argument is the importance of having staff results implemented. Data already mentioned from the University of Chicago Industrial Relations Center suggest that morale is directly related to having results used by management. Several mechanisms for this might be suggested. It is not unreasonable to suppose that the rewards the company has to offer the staff man will show an important relationship to the degree to which management acts upon his recommendations. Survival and job security in the first instance, as well as pay, promotion, recognition, and status, would appear to increase more or less directly as a function of implementation. Results based upon implementation are defensible and understandable among managers, on whom the staff man depends to a major extent for the realization of his expectations.

In management science especially, there is an important element of professional accomplishment and recognition which is a direct

---

[15] Victor A. Thompson, "Hierarchy, Specialization, and Organizational Conflict," *Administrative Science Quarterly*, Vol. 5 (1960).

function of the extent to which results are implemented by management. In the first instance, of course, implementation provides the opportunities for validation which add greatly to the stature of any analysis of a decision situation. Secondly, many management scientists are far more willing to recognize professional accomplishment in a study which was implemented than one which was not. There are those in the field who would rather do a relatively simple, perhaps technically unsophisticated piece of work which actually leads to action, than one which manifests great technical virtuosity but does not become a basis for action. This attitude seems more a part of professional recognition in management science than in most other scientific fields. This, after all, is the central purpose of management science.

As Ann Roe has pointed out, scientists tend to develop a strong personal commitment to particular hypotheses, methods, and techniques.[16] These considerations have played an important role in the history of relations among scientists. Clearly, the same personal involvement may well surround the advice produced by a management scientist and the tools he uses in its production. Whether or not his results form a basis for managerial action is thus likely to be a matter of intense personal concern. From the moment the adviser becomes a part of an organization he is confronted with the fact that in questions of managerial decision making it is not ideas which win in the end, but people.[17]

The process of advice giving raises obstacles which make it difficult for the adviser to realize his objectives. These obstacles seem to force him into conflicts between his own professional goals and the goals of his management and his company. He may find his relations with management troubled by frictions, and progress toward the implementation of his advice may falter. Here, problems which are roughly connected with the selection and definition of the decision problems to be studied will be considered first, subsequently, problems related to producing advice and demonstrating staff accomplishment will be examined.

It would seem that the extent to which the staff itself participates in choosing decisions to study and in working out definitions of the scope and content of its work could emerge as a crucial vari-

---

[16] A summary of her extensive work is given in: Ann Roe, "The Psychology of the Scientist," *Science,* Vol. 134 (1961), pp. 456–59.

[17] Lyman Bryson's remark is, "In practical affairs the question always gets settled but it is a man and not an opinion that wins." "Notes on a Theory of Advice," *Political Science Quarterly,* Vol. 66 (1951).

able for the explanation of job satisfaction and productivity.[18] The whole philosophy of participative management developing out of the experimental work of Likert and others indicates this.[19] Pelz has demonstrated that research productivity increases directly as the freedom to select problems is increased.[20] Autonomy, freedom, and participation in problem selection are generally regarded as desirable by staff people themselves. Certainly, for the basic technical problem of selecting a decision for which the state of the art of management science promises some useful results, and clearly the staff must be the judge of this.

Obviously, the problems to be studied cannot be selected without careful regard for management objectives as well. Management retains formally the ultimate veto on what the staff does and whether or not it exists. However, the wise management gives the staff considerable freedom, and the wise staff makes sure management prerogatives are not challenged, its needs are attended to, and that involvement rather than independence is sought. Clearly, the problems of implementation shrink when the decision studied is under active consideration by management and staff advice is strongly sought.

The pressure of justification raises from time to time the problem of choosing the proper mix of problems. Some projects are needed which will yield immediate results and some projects of a long-term nature should be considered as well. Freedom confronts the adviser with the need to balance the manager's immediate interests, today's "fires," and the decisions which lie beyond daily concern, further into the future. Should the staff attempt "good, clean solutions" to minor problems or somewhat cruder solutions to major ones? How should the quick, small, payoff studies be blended with the long, time-consuming, but hopefully big, payoff studies?

How best to reckon with the complex web of social relationships within the firm which are influenced by staff activities and, in turn, influence the effectiveness of staff results? These must be guessed at when problems are selected. A manager involved in the study with the staff, who knows the in's and out's of "office politics," can be of considerable help in this connection.

---

[18] March and Simon, op. cit., p. 96.

[19] Rensis Likert, New Patterns of Management (New York: McGraw-Hill Book Co., 1961).

[20] D. C. Pelz, "Some Social Factors Related to Performance in a Research Organization," Administrative Science Quarterly, Vol. 1, No. 3 (1956).

The management scientist himself may well feel the best way to work is on problems of his own choice in which he is intensely interested at the moment, on which he feels ready to move ahead with a good idea immediately, and from which he is free to turn in order to follow up whatever good leads emerge as the work goes on. It would perhaps be a rather rare accident if these conditions were also met by a problem of immediate concern to management. Almost inevitably, compromises are required between the free-wheeling, stimulating, creative ideal and the hard work of a difficult job to be done.

Other problems connected with problem selection include the following:[21]

1. Are the problems assigned to the staff by management spelled out in a sufficiently specific fashion so it is clear what is wanted? How well does the staff succeed in grasping the manager's own conception of the situation? Does management take the time to communicate its problems, to check on the staff's explicit rendering of its idea, and to participate in the evolution of the problem definition?

2. Is the problem undertaken by the staff at a stage in the decision process sufficiently early to permit effective recommendations? Have commitments already been made by management? Is there too little time to do useful staff work? Is the staff effectively called upon to find ways of justifying and executing decisions which have already been made?[22]

3. A management decision problem is always more or less gradually reformulated by the staff into a research problem in order to bring the problem within the bounds of scientific competence and to get at issues more fundamental than those perceived by management. How far can this necessary process be carried without producing a recommendation on a problem which management hardly recognizes as its own?

Involvement perhaps holds some solutions to these problems, but involvement is a strategy with its own difficulties and sacrifices for the staff.

The hard work of actually producing the recommendations, the research itself, likewise confronts the adviser with a series of stumbling blocks. He must win the cooperation and the confidence of the organization from which he is to get his data and which may eventually be influenced by his results. By reporting to top management, he would like to clothe his work with authority and support, thus forcing cooperation. This authority, unless used with great subtlety, tends to have quite opposite effects. Useful cooperation can-

---

[21] Learned, Ulrich, and Booz, *op. cit.*
[22] Merton, *op. cit.*

not be forced nor will help which is impressed on the operating organizations be utilized.

Consider also these points.[23]

1. Operating people tend to regard staff work as the source of changes which are inherently threats, interferences, and burdens. Furthermore, these changes may be forced on them if they do not do something to impede the research at an early stage.

2. Operating people see the staff people as narrow, long-haired, impractical men who have never really "done anything." They react negatively to differences in age, education, and experience.

3. Operating people view the staff as policemen, reporting operating policy violations, shortcomings, cherished bad practices, and inefficiencies to top management. The role of the helper is inconsistent with that of policeman.

For such reasons, it may seem like a very good idea to operating management to make it as difficult as possible for the staff to do its work. Dalton found and documented what many regard as common.[24] Operating groups cooperate to make it difficult for the staff to find out what is going on and to get data. If this resistance to staff activity fails in the working stage of the research, operating management always has another chance to sabotage the recommendations when they are put into practice and thus frustrate staff achievement.

The pressure of time coupled with limitations of manpower and funds may well force the staff adviser to terminate his research and stipulate prematurely, in his view. He may be able, in the time at his disposal, to do a "quick and dirty" study, perhaps confirming only what management had already thought obvious. He may be forced to use what he regards as simple and routine methods rather than acquiring or developing more refined and powerful research techniques. He may, in short, find it difficult to satisfy his own criteria for competent and rewarding work. He may be frustrated in his attempts to pursue the theoretical development of the problem, get adequate data, do a suitable literature search, follow up various tangential questions, clean up the study by investigating some of the assumptions, emphasize aspects of particular professional interest, communicate with other workers in the field, or clearly demonstrate his skill and originality.

Management may find it difficult to appreciate the need for some of these things. Are they really important for practical solu-

---

[23] Dalton, *op. cit.*
[24] *Ibid.*, pp. 80–87.

tions? The staff may be regarded as carrying both theoretical development and data collection beyond the needs of the real problem. It is frustrating for management, skilled at simplifying its complex affairs and cutting through masses of detail, to work with staff advisers who seem to be complicating the situation beyond reason. The manager, after all, is the master of decisions based on flimsy evidence while the scientist is the opposite.

Certainly the most trying of the adviser's frustrations must be those that arise in the attempt to demonstrate evidence of his own accomplishments. Chapter 14 has suggested some of the unintended uses to which staff recommendations are put, and Chapter 15 hypothesized some criteria used by managers to evaluate advice. These considerations are part and parcel of the difficulties the adviser experiences in attempting to make his recommendations the basis for action. The uses, other than implementation, and the evaluations made by managers may very well seem not only irrelevant but even deliberately perverse to the staff man.

Justifying the existence of a staff is complicated by still other considerations.

1. Staff scientists tend to be impatient with the difficulties of communicating with management, persuading, and overcoming resistance. They regard the efficacy of their recommendations as established on objective rather than subjective grounds.

2. Even if recommendations are consistent with management action it is usually difficult, as has been said, to establish that the action is a direct consequence of the efforts of the staff.

3. The tendency of managers to see the staff as the first to go in time of trouble, and to require periodic dollars-and-cents justifications, leads to sometimes futile attempts to isolate specific savings due to staff recommendations.[25]

4. If one argues that the staff must content itself with the knowledge that because of its efforts things will go better in the long run, then the staff is cut off from any operational criteria for its own effectiveness.[26] It is universal that the more operational the criteria for success and the more distinguishable the output of a group the greater the job satisfaction. Further, without operational standards of achievement, such as implementation, it is difficult for the staff to learn. If there is no way to tell whether things are better or worse as the result of staff activity, if it cannot be shown where mistakes were made, then there is little possibility for the staff to increase its effectiveness.

5. The position of staff adviser in the formal organizational structure is inherently difficult for purposes of seeking implementation. If the staff takes its position as one of literally making advice available and does not concern itself

---

[25] McGregor, *op. cit.*

[26] Harold L. Wilensky, *Intellectuals in Labor Unions* (Glencoe, Ill.: The Free Press, 1961).

with implementation, management will often take the easy route of simply ignoring staff results. If, on the other hand, the staff man becomes impatient for achievement and tries to force acceptance of his ideas, this may give the already suspicious managers the impression that he is reaching for more power. This power is formally theirs, and they guard it well. The frequent comment that emerges from studies of informal organization structure to the effect that the "staff advises, but management decides" formality is not observed in practice, may be an indication of the unworkability of the "organization-chart" position of the staff. In time, the successful staff may be able to evolve informal modifications of this structure which permit it to function more effectively, or at least to satisfy its own ambitions.[27]

6. Even if management agrees staff recommendations should be implemented, it often falls to the staff to carry them into practice. This confronts the staff with all the problems and difficulties of dealing with the operating organization, which have been mentioned elsewhere. The point here is that the staff may well feel that the skills required and the time spent in such efforts are not consistent with their professional roles as scientifically trained advisers.

7. One aspect of getting recommendations into practice is especially difficult for the staff to accept. This book has argued strongly for management participation in the process of producing staff recommendations. Carried to an extreme, this leads to the time-honored method of getting a manager to accept a staff recommendation. *Make the manager think of the idea as his own.* This is an effective way of gaining acceptance without doubt, but of course it means that the staff pays for acceptance by relinquishing all claims for whatever success may result. To suggest this to a staff man is not only to expect him to be exceedingly skillful in manipulating managerial thinking but also to invite him to give up his authorship and opportunity for establishing staff accomplishment.

8. This same idea has been pressed further in the case of putting ideas into practice at the operational level by extensive and very convincing experiments in industry. These have resulted in a loosely formulated collection of managerial methods called "participative management."[28] To oversimplify, inevitably, one might say that highly favorable results have been achieved by having all members of an organization participate in formulating goals and developing methods for achieving them. The necessary information is made available throughout the organization so that wide participation in organizational decision making may be realized. This organizational participation has been

---

[27] Many other questions relating to the organization and administration of the staff group have been omitted from consideration. How big should it be? What professions should be represented? How should it be supervised and organized internally? What policies are effective with respect to travel, publication, salary, promotion, and education? See Ahmad, *op. cit.;* John R. Platt, "On Thinking as a Chain Reaction," *Saturday Review,* Nov. 17, 1959; Pelz, *op. cit.;* Paul R. Lawrence and others. *Organizational Behavior and Administration* (Homewood, Ill.: Richard D. Irwin, Inc., 1962), pp. 210–12; Herbert A. Shephard, "Nine Dilemmas in Industrial Research," *Administrative Science Quarterly,* Vol. 1 (1956); David B. Hertz, *The Theory and Practice of Industrial Research* (New York: McGraw-Hill Book Co., 1950); Stanley H. Milberg and Robert T. Livingston, *Human Relations in Industrial Research Management* (New York: Columbia University Press, 1957).

[28] Likert, *op. cit.*

shown to lead to greater productivity and success than more conventional and authoritarian forms of management.

For the adviser, the emergence of participative management may mean that, in at least some problems, the tradition of giving advice to a decision maker may become much more complicated. The usual stereotype of the staff specialist who presents his recommendations to top management and then goes out with its authority putting these into practice may not be even approximately the case in certain problems. Indeed, for some operating problems participative management might place upon the staff the burden of organizing programs which lead the operating people to work out solutions of their own. This would be involvement on a more considerable scale. The staff might function as organizers of these efforts; it might obtain and make available relevant data and stand ready to provide the specialized tools of analysis where possible. The staff would be consultants in the design of experiments to test the solutions produced by the participating line people and keep them aware of progress. Most experimental study of this sort of thing, which goes back at least to Alan Mogensen's work-simplification programs, has been at the shop level. Many management scientists have, however, seen its possibilities at higher levels and have done effective work in providing managers with the tools to work out their own problems.

Clearly, the emergence of participative management, with its impressively documented promises of higher productivity, may require quite a different order of human relations skills on the part of the staff. It will also present them with greater and perhaps subtler difficulties of demonstrating staff accomplishments.

9. As has been noted, it happens that the results produced by the efforts of management scientists simply confirm the predispositions and current policies of management. Discovering this may make the adviser wish he had chosen a different problem, but the result itself does not reflect on the quality of the scientific work involved. How is the importance of such a contribution to be demonstrated to management?

10. In a sense, the whole theme of this study is that managers hold variously unrealistic expectations about management science and that a prominent difficulty which plagues management scientists is the evaluation of their output against these expectations. The time and effort to produce scientifically based advice, the results which can be expected from making such an investment, and how it is to be utilized are little understood by anyone, but the aim of Part II has been to dispel some of the more obvious myths.

11. Finally, the pressures to go beyond the bounds of professional competence in order to demonstrate results might be mentioned. The pressures to provide promises rather than predictions, to give speculative answers to difficult questions, and to take responsibility for untested assumptions, all push the management scientist (albeit quite unwillingly) beyond the conservative bounds of his discipline.

But of course, all is not frustration and failure in management science.[29] Its success is great and growing. Staff advisers seem to

---

[29] Dalton, *op. cit.*, pp. 98, 108.

work out various responses to the divergence they find between their expectations and their achievements. One might try to suggest the general nature of these responses.[30]

1. In the majority of cases, staff and management gradually learn what to expect of each other and discover what accommodations are necessary for an effective working relationship.

2. Sometimes a management scientist will move to a new firm in the hope of greater opportunity and more favorable conditions.[31] In management science the brisk demand for people gives one the perception that movement is easy, and casual observation suggests that turnover may be considerable.

3. Advisers may compensate for limited achievement within the firm through increased professional identification and activity. They may seek publication in professional journals and offices in the professional societies.

4. Advisers may seek to transfer to line management positions where the pay, opportunities to rise, and prestige appear greater. They do this at a cost of much of their professional activity and development.

---

[30] For a useful presentation of the relevant theory and evidence see March and Simon, *op. cit.*, pp. 83–111.

[31] For additional general references, see Don K. Price, "The Scientific Establishment," *Science*, Vol. 136 (1962), pp. 1099–1106; W. V. Owen, "Scientists and Industrial Production," *Advanced Management*, Vol. 26, No. 12 (1961); Harriet O. Ronken and Paul R. Lawrence, *Administering Changes* (Boston: Harvard University Graduate School of Business Administration, 1952); and Chris Agyris, "Human Problems with Budgets," *Harvard Business Review*, January–February, 1953.

Chapter 18:

POSTSCRIPT

"Never try to exhaust a subject, for you cannot; but you will certainly succeed in exhausting the reader."

Many people, including both those with staff and with management outlooks, are enthusiastic about management science. Its momentum is considerable and its record is promising. This study has tried to turn management science upon itself, looking at the problem of its relation to management decisions. If this is a problem, it has been argued, it might be solved through two kinds of understanding: understanding by managers of how science works and what it can do, and understanding by advisers of the organizational complexities within which they work.

Scientists, it has been said here, bring a toughminded attitude to the study of management, aiming to make their statements about it clear and unequivocal. They represent the affairs of the firm with models, systematizing ideas in such a way as to make possible prediction of the consequences of policy. Generally confirmed predictions, or laws, are difficult at present to achieve in the world of management, and thus hypotheses must serve to organize observation and experience. Management science thus views management as an adaptive, self-correcting, experimental process. A business ought to be run so as to produce not only goods and services for its market but also information on how to do this more effectively. The role of the staff is to raise the hypotheses and design the experiments with which useful knowledge is efficiently squeezed out of experience.

Managers, so went the hypotheses, share the common need for assurances about the future. In seeking them, they may choose from among several strategies, one of which is to call for the assistance of the staff. The advice the staff develops, however, does not always hit its mark, both because the manager finds a variety of uses for it and because he finds its worth difficult to judge. It is not always clear to him how the staff's results are to become a part of his own conception of his firm's affairs. One way, it was suggested, of promoting this process of assimilation was to involve the manager in the ongoing work of the staff. The research would then perhaps have an evolutionary impact on management thinking, rather than a climactic one. The staff would thus produce understanding, rather than masterminded recipes for action.

If, for the moment at least, one accepts all this, what next? Taking some of these ideas as hypotheses, management scientists might move ahead with the work of transforming their own professional experience into experiment. Hypotheses about their relations with management might be tested in the real-world context, with results which could be written down and discussed. For those doing scientific work in industry, this is to invite a deliberate consideration of their own methods, on top of their already difficult tasks. Yet some are doing it already and others, agreeing to the need for it, will perhaps find time eventually. This, it seems, is the only way to end the distinctions between "theory" and "practice."

Index

INDEX

303

*This book has been set on the Linotype in
9 point and 11 point Caledonia, leaded 2 points.
Part numbers and chapter numbers and titles
are in 18 point Corvinus Medium; part titles are
in 24 point Corvinus Medium. The size of the
type page is 27 by 46½ picas.*